Lecture Notes in Computer Science   5741

Commenced Publication in 1973
Founding and Former Series Editors:
Gerhard Goos, Juris Hartmanis, and Jan van Leeuwen

Payam Barnaghi   Klaus Moessner
Mirko Presser   Stefan Meissner (Eds.)

Smart Sensing
and Context

4th European Conference, EuroSSC 2009
Guildford, UK, September 16-18, 2009
Proceedings

 Springer

Volume Editors

Payam Barnaghi
Klaus Moessner
Mirko Presser
Stefan Meissner

Centre for Communication Systems Research
Faculty of Engineering and Physical Sciences
University of Surrey
Guildford, Surrey, GU2 7XH, UK

E-mail:
{p.barnaghi, k.moessner, m.presser, s.meissner}@surrey.ac.uk

Library of Congress Control Number: 2009934115

CR Subject Classification (1998): I.2.9, C.2.1, C.2.4, D.4.2, D.4.7, H.3.4

LNCS Sublibrary: SL 5 – Computer Communication Networks
and Telecommunications

ISSN   0302-9743
ISBN-10   3-642-04470-0 Springer Berlin Heidelberg New York
ISBN-13   978-3-642-04470-0 Springer Berlin Heidelberg New York

springer.com

© Springer-Verlag Berlin Heidelberg 2009
Printed in Germany

Typesetting: Camera-ready by author, data conversion by Scientific Publishing Services, Chennai, India
Printed on acid-free paper   SPIN: 12752102   06/3180   5 4 3 2 1 0

Preface

Welcome to the proceedings of the 4th European Conference on Smart Sensing and Context hosted by the Centre for Communication Systems Research, University of Surrey, in Guildford, UK.

Smart sensing and context are the key enablers for effective autonomous systems, providing transparent technologies to realize the vision of ubiquitous computing, intelligent services and networking. (Wireless) Sensor and actuator networks, tightly integrated into the structure of the Internet provide the underlying manifestation of the physical world into the Internet of Things. Networked sensors can infer context from raw data and capture user and application needs to provide smart adaptive services. Higher-level context can be deducted locally or remotely by combining and abstracting information from smart sensors. The 4th European Conference on Smart Sensing and Context explored new techniques, algorithms and architectures on utilizing context and context-aware services and their applications. The conference builds on the success of the past editions held in Zürich, Switzerland in 2008, in Kendal, UK in 2007 and in Enschede, The Netherlands in 2006. EuroSSC is a forum to exchange ideas and to discuss the most recent developments in smart sensing and context field. It explores the latest findings and state-of-the-art developments in technology, covering human and user aspects. The main topics discussed this year focused on embedded applications, context-aware platforms, context processing, semantic technologies, mobile platforms and real-world deployment and exploitation scenarios. The development of integrating sensor and actuator networks and context-platforms in a wider scale setting has added a new dimension to global networks and has enabled users and applications to interact with the physical world more efficiently. The vision of integrating millions of interconnected resources which are accessible through different services to intermediate interaction between the physical world and the digital world will form the structure of the future Internet and services and will create a platform for networked knowledge. At the conference and also during the poster and demo session research outcomes were presented with this vision in mind. We hope the presented work and demonstrated systems will help researchers and developers in this field to discuss and exchange innovative ideas and plans. A total of 16 full papers were accepted to the conference. Each paper received at least three peer reviews. The Program Co-chairs selected the accepted papers based on their technical merit and the review reports. The conference and proceedings were structured into six main tracks which discussed the key themes addressed by EuroSSC 2009: activity recognition, information aspects of context-aware sensor and actuator systems, context-aware service platforms, Context processing, reasoning and fusion, real-world experiences with deployed systems, and context-aware frameworks in mobile environments.

Amit Sheth from Kno.e.sis Center, Wright State University, and Marimuthu Palaniswami from ARC Research Network on Intelligent Sensors, Sensor Networks and Information Processing (ISSNIP), the University of Melbourne, were invited to give keynote speeches. Amit Sheth's keynote was entitled "Computing for Human Experience: Semantics-Empowered Sensors, Services and Social Computing on Ubiquitous Web." He discussed how sensing, semantics, and social computing work in concert to enrich the Web-based interactions; multisensory devices, computing and ubiquitous connectivity involving multimodal information engage transparency in human activities to enrich them in ways not possible before. Marimuthu Palaniswami's talk focused on "Large-Scale Sensor Network Deployment: Research Challenges and Opportunities." Marimuthu Palaniswami presented different issues regarding deployment of large scale sensor networks—making the transition from the lab to the real world—through case studies in environmental monitoring and healthcare.

EuroSSC 2009 was sponsored by the EU FP-7 project SENSEI and also had technical co-sponsorship by the IEEE United Kingdom and Ireland section. We are thankful to the Centre for Communication Systems Research (CCSR) at the University of Surrey, the Springer LNCS staff, the University of Surrey Conference Office and the Wearable Computing Lab at ETH Zürich for their help in organizing this conference.

We owe special thanks to the 90 contributing authors and to the Technical Program Committee members and reviewers of the papers. We would also like to thank Safa Sway, who helped with the local arrangements and who worked hard to make everything run smoothly and pleasantly. Our gratitude also extends to numerous volunteers who helped us during the organization and running of this conference.

September 2009   Payam Barnaghi
                                                          Klaus Moessner
                                                          Mirko Presser
                                                          Stefan Meissner

Organization

EuroSSC 2009 was organized by Centre for Communication Systems Research (CCSR), University of Surrey.

Organizing Committee

General Chair

Payam Barnaghi	CCSR, University of Surrey, UK

Program Co-chairs

Klaus Moessner	CCSR, University of Surrey, UK
Mirko Presser	CCSR, University of Surrey, UK
Stefan Meissner	CCSR, University of Surrey, UK
Daniel Roggen	ETH Zürich, Switzerland
Clemens Lombriser	ETH Zürich, Switzerland
Paul Havinga	University of Twente, The Netherlands
Gerd Kortuem	Lancaster University, UK

Poster and Demo Chair

Clemens Lombriser	ETH Zürich, Switzerland

Local Co-organizers

Safa Sway	CCSR, University of Surrey, UK
Stefan Meissner	CCSR, University of Surrey, UK
Tarek Elsaleh	CCSR, University of Surrey, UK

Technical Program Committee

Heikki Ailisto	VTT, Finland
Marwan Al-Akaidi	De Montfort University, UK
Nigel Baker	University of the West of England, UK
Martin Bauer	NEC, Germany
Luca Benini	Università di Bologna, Italy
Jesus Bernat Vercher	Telefonica, Spain
Francois Carrez	University of Surrey, UK
Jessie Dedecker	Sirris, Belgium
Simon Dobson	University College Dublin, Ireland
Henk Eertink	Telematica Instituut, The Netherlands
Martin Elixmann	Philips Research, Germany
Elisabetta Farella	Università di Bologna, Italy

Dieter Fensel	DERI, Austria
Daniel Fitton	Lancaster University, UK
Elgar Fleisch	ETH Zürich, Switzerland
Patrik Florèen	Helsinki Institute for Information Technology, Finland
Kaori Fujinami	Tokyo University of Agriculture and Technology, Japan
Elena Gaura	Coventry University, UK
Alexander Gluhak	University of Surrey, UK
Sandeep Gupta	Arizona State University, USA
Manfred Hauswirth	National University of Ireland, Ireland
Alban Hessler	NEC, Germany
Theo Kanter	Ericsson, Sweden
Julia Kantorovitch	VTT, Finland
Ralf Kernchen	University of Surrey, UK
Marc Langheinrich	ETH Zürich, Switzerland
Rodger Lea	University of British Columbia, USA
Peter Leijdekkers	University of Technology Sydney, Australia
Maria Lijding	University of Twente, The Netherlands
Feng Ling	Tsinghua University, China
Paul Lukowicz	University of Passau, Germany
Nirvana Meratnia	University of Twente, The Netherlands
Florian Michahelles	ETH Zürich, Switzerland
Kevin Mills	NIST, USA
Tatsuo Nakajima	Waseda University, Japan
Santosh Pandey	CISCO Systems, USA
Christian Prehofer	Nokia Research Center, Finland
Kay Römer	ETH Zürich, Switzerland
Kurt Rothermel	University of Stuttgart, Germany
Kamran Sayrafian	NIST, USA
Albrecht Schmidt	University of Duisburg-Essen, Germany
Wolfgang Schott	IBM Research Zürich, Switzerland
Mihail Sichitiu	North Carolina State Univiversity, USA
Frank Siegemund	European Microsoft Innovation Center, Germany
Tod Sizer	Bell Labs, USA
Vera Stavroulaki	University of Piraeus, Greece
Kristof van Laerhoven	Darmstadt University of Technology, Germany
Roberto Verdone	University of Bologna, Italy
Matthias Wagner	DoCoMo Euro-Labs, Germany
Adrian Waller	Thales Research and Technology, UK
Chen Xiang	Agency for Science, Technology and Research, Singapore
Anna Zhdanova	FTW, Austria
Michele Zorzi	University of Padova, Italy

Additional Reviewers

Majid Ghader	University of Surrey, UK
Wei Wang	University of Nottingham (Malaysia Campus), Malaysia

Sponsoring Institutions

The EU FP-7 project SENSEI (http://www.sensei-project.eu/).
The IEEE United Kingdom and Ireland section co-technical sponsorship.

Table of Contents

Context Processing, Reasoning and Fusion

Real-World Experiences with Deployed Systems

Context-Aware Frameworks in Mobile Environments

Episode Segmentation Using Recursive Multiple Eigenspaces

Aziah Ali[1], Surapa Thiemjarus[2], and Guang-Zhong Yang[1]

[1] Department of Computing, Imperial College London, UK
[2] School of Information, Computer and Communication Technology,
Sirindhorn International Institute of Technology, Thailand
aali@doc.ic.ac.uk

Abstract. Activity recognition is an important application of body sensor networks. To this end, accurate segmentation of different episodes in the data stream is a pre-requisite of subsequent pattern classification. Current techniques for this purpose tend to require specific supervised learning, thus limiting their general application to pervasive sensing applications. This paper presents an improved multiple eigenspace segmentation algorithm that addresses the common problem of under-segmentation in episode detection. Results show that the proposed algorithm significantly increases the segmentation accuracy when compared to existing methods.

Keywords: Episode segmentation, multiple eigenspaces.

1 Introduction

In recent years, Body Sensor Networks (BSNs) have made a marked impact on a variety of applications, ranging from healthcare to sports and well-being monitoring [1]. One important aspect of BSN is context-aware sensing, which requires human activity recognition based on the BSN data.

For most activity recognition systems, correctly labeled sequence of activities (episodes of activities) are required before subsequent recognition algorithm can proceed. Accurate determination of activity boundaries, however, is challenging due to a number of inter-related factors [2]. Firstly, the activity boundaries are highly subjective and can vary in different trials of the same subject. Typically, a set of manually annotated markers are used to segment different episodes of activities, but this can be labor intensive, especially when large datasets are involved [6]. Furthermore, manual segmentation involves significant intra- and inter-observer variabilities [7]. To circumvent these problems, a number of studies have been proposed for episode segmentation. Kang and Ikeuchi [3] used temporal segmentation of grasping task sequences based on hand motion using fingertip polygon area, a sensing glove and 3D tracking. While the study shows good results, it requires rather complex sensing devices. The activities segmented were also limited. Hierarchical activity segmentation was proposed in a study to segment dance sequence videos, however, it requires training models from human observers and the method only predicts how each observer would segment the video sequence [2]. Two studies have proposed the use of Hidden

P. Barnaghi et al. (Eds.): EuroSSC 2009, LNCS 5741, pp. 1–10, 2009.

Markov Models (HMMs) for episode segmentation, where Feng and Mohamed [4] applied threshold-based HMMs to segment video sequences of four activities, but the activity models needed to be pre-trained to determine the thresholds. In the other study by Hudntofte et al [5], activities were segmented and modeled as gestemes, which are defined as small segments of a certain task. These gestemes were then used to build a task vocabulary that can later be used for task recognition.

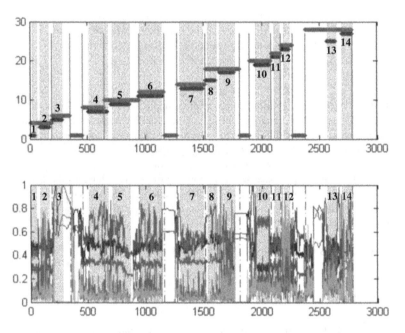

Fig. 1. Top: Example of under-segmentation problems with MES applied to a data of activities of daily living (Blue horizontal lines-Ground Truth, Red horizontal lines-MES segments).
Bottom: Raw data (5 accelerometer signals) with manual markers for activity 1 to 14 where 1) entering room and going out of the room, 2) sitting on chair and getting up, 3) slicing bread, 4) preparing tea, 5) eating, 6) getting dressed, 7) talking on the phone, 8) reading, 9) lying on bed and getting up, 10) lying down, 11) walking, 12) running, 13) walking with sway, and 14) falling down). Blue-shaded regions indicates segments with activities.

An automatic method for the discovery of structures in activity data was reported in [6], which applied a statistical-based method, namely Multiple Eigenspaces (MES) originally proposed by Leonardis et al [8]. It used features from acceleration data to segment and classify walking and ball-juggling activities. In [7], MES has been used for laparoscopic task segmentation combined with HMM recognition.

An example of segmentation results obtained from applying MES on daily activities dataset is shown in Fig. 1. The bottom figure illustrates the segmentation results with blue lines representing the ground truth, i.e., manually annotated markers for the activities (14 in this example where activity 1 to 14 were marked with odd numbers from 1 to 29 respectively), and red lines representing the segments discovered by MES algorithm. It can be seen that the algorithm inadvertently grouped more than one activity into a single segment, as in the first two activities for example. This occurred in a number of occasions which could be due to the presence of significantly higher number of activity types in longer duration. This problem of under-segmentation could adversely affect the subsequent step of activity recognition. To address this issue, an improved MES episode segmentation method is proposed in this paper. The method incorporates a recursive process to further divide a segment into multiple episodes. We will first introduce the method - MES and recursive MES, followed by the experimental setup for daily activities dataset, results and finally discussion and conclusions.

2 Method

2.1 Data Preprocessing

Before analyzing the data, three preprocessing steps were applied to the data, namely feature extraction, filtering and normalization. Long datasets can significantly increase computational time and cost, thus in this study features were extracted using sliding window of varying sizes from a lab collected activities dataset which typically involve 150000 samples each. Two types of simple features were extracted: the mean and standard deviation of the 3-axis acceleration data over window sizes of 64, 128 and 512 samples. A fixed window shift of 64 samples was used for all feature extraction window sizes to preserve uniform data length when different feature windows are used. Median filtering was applied on the features to remove noisy spikes. All the extracted features were then normalized before being sent to the MES algorithm for segmentation.

2.2 Multiple Eigenspaces

An eigenspace is defined as the set of all principal components or eigenvectors from a data vector that shares a same eigenvalue. In many sensor datasets, the variability of activities or episodes recorded could lead to multiple variations in one continuous data. In these cases, a single eigenspace may not be sufficient to represent the inherent structure of the data. It would be more appropriate to divide the data into smaller data vectors and then calculate the eigenspaces for sufficiently correlated data vectors.

Consider a continuous data stream divided into a set of data vectors $G = \{x_1, x_2, ..., x_m\}$. MES solves the problem of finding sets $G_j \in G$, eigenspaces $E_j(G_j)$ and data dimensions p_j so that each data vector $x_i \in G_j$ can be approximated by its projection

$$x_i = e_{0j} + \sum_{k=1}^{p_j} y_{kj} e_{kj} \tag{1}$$

where e_{0j} is defined as the mean of all $x_i \in G_j$ and $e_{1j}, e_{2j}, ..., e_{pj}$ as the eigenvectors corresponding to the p largest eigenvalues of the covariance matrix of the vectors in

G_j. The final output of the algorithm is a set of significantly correlated subsets, which are represented by the corresponding eigenspaces.

In the first step of MES algorithm, called eigenspace initialization, the data is divided into same-sized data vectors, referred to as segments in this paper. Small subsets of these segments are then chosen to become the 'seeds' for the next step - eigenspace growing. The seeds can be selected using clustering algorithms. In the worst case scenario, all the segments can be selected as seeds. The eigenspace for each subset is then calculated and its dimension p_j is set to zero, *i.e.*, the eigenspace equals the mean of the segment.

In the eigenspace growing step, each subset is grown by adding other subsets from the data vectors that share the same eigenspace as the initial seed subset. This growing process is determined by three threshold values, δ_t, ρ_{t1} and ρ_{t2} where δ_t relates to the reconstruction error of a single segment when projected onto an eigenspace while ρ_{t1} relates to sum of reconstruction errors of all segments in an eigenspace before dimension increase and ρ_{t2} relates to sum of reconstruction errors of all segments in an eigenspace after dimension increase [8].

Once each of the initial seeds is fully grown, *i.e.*, there are no more subsets that could be added to it, the final step called eigenspace selection is performed. In this step, an eigenspace that best represents each highly correlated subset is chosen. This is necessary since the eigenspace growing process can result in overlapping and redundant sets of eigenspaces. An optimization procedure, for example Minimum Description Length (MDL) algorithm [8], can then be applied to find the subset of eigenspaces that best represents the data while minimizing redundancy. A more detailed description of MES algorithm can be found in [8].

2.3 Recursive MES

In order to solve the problem of under-segmentation for MES, a recursive MES is proposed. In the original version of MES given in [8], the threshold parameters for eigenspace growing step were set to different multiples of per-pixel standard deviation of images, as shown in in [8]. In the proposed algorithm, the three thresholds, denoted by δ_t, ρ_{t1} and ρ_{t2} are set to averaged standard deviation of segments, denoted by ∂_t. This eliminates the need to empirically determine the values of three different multipliers for eigenspace growing thresholds.

In the new algorithm, the lengths of every resulting segment are checked against a threshold length, denoted by SL_t after performing the first stage of MES on the dataset. The threshold (SL_t) is determined empirically and is selected as the average length of the different episodes in the recorded data. MES is performed again on every segment with length greater than SL_t; this time, with the size of the segments in the MES initialization step and the threshold involved in eigenspace growing phase, ∂_t halved. With a smaller segment size, more detailed description of the data

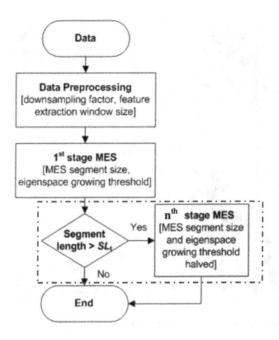

Fig. 2. Flowchart illustrating the proposed recursive MES algorithm, with additional steps highlighted in dashed box

could be captured, thus improving segmentation. Figure 2 illustrates the key steps involved in the proposed algorithm.

3   Experimental Setup

To validate the proposed method of two-stage MES, an experiment involving six subjects in a laboratory setting was carried out for the assessment of activities of daily living. An e-AR sensor (ear-worn Activity Recognition sensor [9]) was used for this purpose. It collects data at 50Hz and then transmits it over wirelessly to a receiving workstation for further analysis. The e-AR sensor contains a BSN node [9], consisting of microcontroller, radio communication chip, flash memory, antennae and a 3-axis accelerometer.

Datasets of the six subjects performing 14 different activities were collected in a laboratory simulating a home environment. The 14 activities chosen were mostly daily activities a person would normally perform in his/her home. Subjects were required to wear the e-AR sensor while performing these activities in similar sequence: 1) entering room and going out of the room (3 times), 2) sitting on chair and getting up (5 times), 3) slicing bread, 4) preparing tea, 5) eating, 6) getting dressed (shirt provided to be worn and taken off 5 times), 7) talking on the phone (3 minutes), 8) reading (1 minute), 9) lying on bed and getting up (5 times), 10) lying down, 11)

Fig. 3. Experimental setup a) e-AR sensor worn by a subject, b) a subject lying on bed, c) reading and d) eating

walking (2 minutes), 12) running (2 minutes), 13) walking with sway (2 minutes), and 14) falling down (3 times). A set of corresponding markers were manually annotated during data collection to be used as the ground truth. Figure 3 shows the experimental setting for some of the activities recorded. The data collected from six subjects was then used for feature extraction. Features were then filtered using median filter and then normalised, as described earlier. For feature extraction, no overlapping was applied between moving windows through the time-series data. The datasets will be referred to as DS64, DS128 and DS256 for feature window of 64, 128 and 256 samples respectively for the rest of the paper.

4   Results and Discussion

To compare the relative performance of the original MES and the proposed algorithm, both methods were tested on the all three datasets. The segments detected by MES are labeled according to the ground truth label with the most overlap. MES segments that fall entirely in between activities are assigned the label zero. Since both high precision and recall are desirable in segmentation, the average of precision and recall rate is used as segmentation evaluation metric to compare the performance of both algorithms, which can be formulated as follows:

$$Accuracy = \frac{(\frac{tp}{tp+fp}) + (\frac{tp}{tp+fn})}{2}\% \tag{2}$$

where tp is defined as true positives, *i.e.*, number of MES segments with non-zero labels that overlap with the ground truth segments. In Eq. (2), fp represents false positives, *i.e.*, number of segments that are detected in MES segments (non-zero labels) but not in ground truth (zero labels) and finally fn as false negatives, *i.e.*, the number of ground truth segments (non-zero labels) that are not detected by MES segments (zero labels).

In Figure 4, an example segmentation result using both the one-stage and recursive MES on the DS64 dataset is illustrated. The blue lines in the graphs represent the activity markers which were manually annotated, whereas the red lines represent the segments resulting from MES. From this figure, it can be seen that the results for the original MES algorithm consist of several long segments with under-segmented episodes (*e.g.* the first three activities highlighted in the figure). For the new algorithm, however, they were accurately divided into individual segments. The segmentation accuracy as defined in Equation 2 was calculated for all datasets and illustrated in Figure 5.

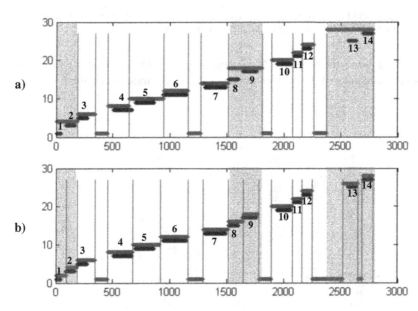

Fig. 4. a) Sample segmentation results for 1-stage MES and b) recursive MES on same data (Blue-Ground Truth, Red-MES segments). Blue-shaded regions highlight the improvement in segmentation with recursive MES.

It is evident that recursive MES performed better than the 1-stage MES in all cases. Highest accuracy is 86.38%, achieved by performing recursive MES on DS64, almost 10% higher than the result for 1-stage MES. High accuracy is achieved with dataset using smallest feature extraction window, i.e. DS64, for both 1-stage and recursive MES. This is due to the higher number of feature samples in each individual MES segments with smaller feature window size, thus providing more information for the same length of data in DS128 and DS256. For example, 640 raw data samples will give 10 feature samples for DS64, 4 feature samples for DS128 and only 2 feature samples for DS256.

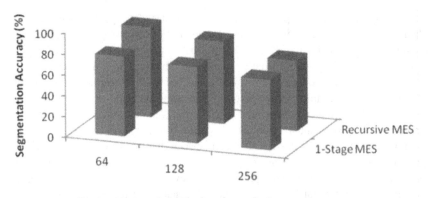

Fig. 5. Segmentation accuracy for one-stage MES and recursive MES for data with feature window of 64 (DS64), 128 (DS128) and 256 (DS256), respectively

A similar trend for recursive MES against 1-stage MES can also be observed in per-subject accuracy of the segmentation output, as illustrated in Figure 6.

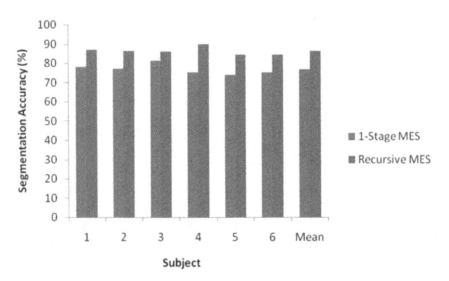

Fig. 6. Per-subject segmentation accuracy for one-stage MES and recursive MES for data with feature window of 64 (DS64)

As described earlier, in the initialization phase of the MES algorithm, data was divided into small same-sized segments, referred to as MES segment size in Figure 2. To examine the effect of the size of these segments on segmentation results, different MES segment sizes were used on DS64. In all previous analysis, the number of MES segments is fixed to 100, thus the MES segment size is determined by dividing the feature samples with 100. By varying the fixed number of MES segments, the segment size was correspondingly varied. Results of performing recursive MES on DS64 with MES segment number of 50, 100 and 150 segments are presented in Table 1.

By comparing the results for segmentation with different number of MES segments, *i.e.*, 50, 100 and 150, recursive MES performed slightly better when MES segment number is higher. However, the computational time increased significantly when the number of segment is higher, where only 181 seconds were taken to perform MES with 50 segments, but by increasing it to 150 segments the time taken was increased to 1190 seconds. This suggests that using smaller number of MES segments, while only slightly decreasing the overall segmentation accuracy, does significantly decrease computational time and cost, provided the number of MES segments used are sufficiently large.

Table 1. Segmentation accuracy for different number of MES segments (%)

MES segment number	Segmentation Accuracy (%)	Computational Time (seconds)
50	86.10	181
100	86.38	577
150	88.16	1190

5 Conclusions

In this paper, an improved MES segmentation algorithm is proposed. The results show that by recursively performing MES, the problem of under-segmentation can be significantly reduced. This is important when data are segmented prior to recognition, ensuring reliable overall recognition system. This work also demonstrates that in general, different numbers of MES segments tend not significantly affect the segmentation accuracy, but computational time is significantly increased when the number of MES segments is increased. The proposed recursive MES can generally be used in detecting boundaries in time-series data, but in this paper the objective was to detect activity boundaries in data collected from body sensor networks. The output of segmentation algorithm will then be used for activity recognition, for example in daily activity monitoring system or surgical workflow analysis.

In future work, the effect of simultaneously varying threshold parameters on segmentation accuracy will be analyzed for datasets involving a variety of activities. In addition, combining segmentation with recognition would lead to a better understanding of individual activities as well as the analysis of inter-activity transitions.

References

1. Yang, G.Z.: Body Sensor Networks. Springer, London (2006)
2. Kahol, K., Tripathi, P., Panchanathan, S.: Gesture Segmentation in Complex Motion Sequences. In: Proceedings IEEE International Conference on Image Processing 2003, pp. 105–108 (2003)

3. Kang, S.B., Ikeuchi, K.: Toward Automatic Robot Instruction from Perception- Temporal Segmentation of task from Human Hand Motion. IEEE Transactions on Robotics and Automation 11(5), 670–681 (1995)
4. Feng, N., Mohamed, A.: HMM-Based Segmentation and Recognition of Human Activities from Video Sequences. In: Proceedings of IEEE International Conference on Multimedia and Expo, pp. 804–807 (2005)
5. Hundtofte, C.S., Hager, G.D., Okamura, A.M.: Building a Task Language for Segmentation and Recognition of User Input to Cooperative Manipulation Systems. In: Proceedings of the 10th IEEE Virtual Reality Conference, pp. 225–230 (2002)
6. Huynh, T., Schiele, B.: Unsupervised Discovery of Structure in Activity Data using Multiple Eigenspaces. LNCS, pp. 151–167 (2006)
7. Ali, A., King, R.C., Yang, G.Z.: Semi-supervised Segmentation for Activity Recognition with Multiple Eigenspaces. In: Proceedings of 5th IEEE Body Sensor Networks Conference, pp. 314–317 (2008)
8. Leonardis, A., Bischof, H., Maver, J.: Multiple Eigenspaces. Pattern Recognition 35, 2613–2627 (2002)
9. Lo, B., Thiemjarus, S., King, R.C., Yang, G.Z.: Body Sensor Network – A Wireless Sensor Platform for Pervasive healthcare Monitoring. In: Proceedings of 3rd International Conference On Pervasive Sensing, pp. 77–80 (2005)

Keep on Moving! Activity Monitoring and Stimulation Using Wireless Sensor Networks

Stephan Bosch[1], Mihai Marin-Perianu[1], Raluca Marin-Perianu[2],
Paul Havinga[1], and Hermie Hermens[3]

[1] University of Twente, The Netherlands
{s.bosch,m.marinperianu,p.j.m.havinga}@utwente.nl
[2] Inertia Technology, The Netherlands
raluca@inertia-technology.com
[3] Roessingh Research and Development, The Netherlands
h.hermens@rrd.nl

Abstract. Because health condition and quality of life are directly influenced by the amount and intensity of daily physical activity, monitoring the level of activity has gained interest in recent years for various medical and wellbeing applications. In this paper we describe our experience with implementing and evaluating physical activity monitoring and stimulation using wireless sensor networks and motion sensors. Our prototype provides feedback on the activity level of users using a simple colored light. We conduct experiments on multiple test subjects, performing multiple normal daily activities. The results from our experiments represent the motivation for and a first step towards robust complex physical activity monitoring with multiple sensors distributed over a person's body. The results show that using a single sensor on the body is inadequate in certain situations. Results also indicate that feedback provided on a person's activity level can stimulate the person to do more exercise. Using multiple sensor nodes and sensor modalities per subject would improve the activity estimation performance, provided that the sensor nodes are small and inconspicuous.

1 Introduction

In recent years, monitoring the level of daily human activity has gained interest for various medical and wellbeing applications. It has been shown that health condition and quality of life are directly influenced by the amount and intensity of daily physical activity [1]. This is particularly relevant to persons with chronic conditions, such as Chronic Obstructive Pulmonary Disease (COPD), asthma and diabetes. The reason is that persons suffering from chronic conditions enter a vicious circle, in which being active causes discomfort, making them progressively more sedentary, and deteriorating their health. Monitoring the daily activity can stimulate people to perform exercises and to be more active in general by providing feedback and assistance to better manage the physical condition. Apart from medical applications, daily activity monitoring can also

P. Barnaghi et al. (Eds.): EuroSSC 2009, LNCS 5741, pp. 11–23, 2009.
© Springer-Verlag Berlin Heidelberg 2009

be useful for healthy users that want to assess and improve their overall fitness level. Activity monitoring systems can remind, stimulate and motivate people to be more active, especially when used within groups with a competitive nature.

The activity level of a person is best assessed in terms of energy expenditure [2]. This is a relatively complex and intrusive process, because the rate of human metabolism needs to be measured. As an alternative, we can estimate the energy expenditure rather than measuring it explicitly. Estimation can provide an unobtrusive alternative, which assesses the level of activity without affecting the subject's wellbeing and freedom of movement. The energy expenditure is commonly estimated by measuring the amount of motion a person performs during daily life. A proven method [2] is to use an accelerometer to record the bodily motion, which can provide a measure that usually correlates well with the actual energy expenditure. This solution is limited to a single acceleration sensor mounted near the center of mass of the subject, e.g. worn at the waist of the person.

However, the quality of this accelerometer-based activity measurement method is not always optimal. People are engaged in many more activities than those usually considered in current activity monitoring and recognition research. In this paper we show that some activities, such as skiing, do not cause much net acceleration, although the amount of effort involved in these activities can be significant. This causes a discrepancy between the estimation and the actual energy expenditure. Using more than a single sensor node for the estimation could improve the quality of the estimation. However, there exists a trade-off between the number of sensors spread across the user's body and the system's unobtrusiveness. Therefore, activity monitoring applications are usually limited to only one sensor. The experiments outlined in this paper represent the motivation for and a first step towards robust complex activity monitoring with multiple sensors distributed in a wireless sensor network.

Concretely, the contributions of this paper are as follows:

- We show that it is feasible to implement activity monitoring on resource-constrained wireless sensor nodes, which provides the basis for having activity monitoring on distributed nodes, making the system better suited for a large diversity of activities.
- Using practical experiments, we show that the estimation of energy expenditure using only one sensor node with an accelerometer is not always adequate and is sensitive to context dependencies.
- We investigate the feasibility of simple and intuitive feedback devices, such as ambient light, in order to make the system accessible to non-technical users.
- We conduct a usability study to evaluate whether:
  1. Users are more willing to be active when they get feedback on their activity level and when they compete with other people wearing sensors.
  2. Users are willing to wear multiple sensor nodes to monitor their activity levels.
  3. Users are prepared to share activity data with others or have privacy concerns.

2   Related Work

The state-of-the-art electronic method to assess physical activity is to use an integral of three-dimensional acceleration measurements. For instance, Bouten [2] provides a solution for activity monitoring called the Tremor, describing a method that uses a three-dimensional accelerometer to estimate metabolic energy expenditure. It uses the integral of the modulus of bodily acceleration, referred to as the IMA value, as measure for physical activity. Bouten provides validation for this method by establishing the correlation between the true metabolic energy expenditure and the IMA result using two laboratory experiments and one field experiment. In a later publication [3], Bouten et al. explore the effects of orientation and placement of the sensor on the resulting IMA value. This yields the conclusion that the sensor is best placed near the waist at the lower back. Bouten also recognizes that static exercise can cause discrepancies between the IMA value and the actual energy expenditure. Later work by Steele et al. [4] and Fujiki [5] et al. use a different integration algorithm than IMA, but in essence the methods are similar. Fujiki [5] et al. also provide further insight in the effect of sensor placement on the activity estimation.

Alternatively, pedometers can be used to estimate physical energy expenditure. However, pedometers are only capable of detecting step counts and not the true intensity of the activity. This is particularly a problem for slow-walking patients. According to Pitta et al. [1], multiaxial accelerometers can provide more detailed information on activity patterns, time and intensity of activities. In comparison to pedometers, accelerometers have good sensitivity to low-intensity activities and the small activity variations seen in relatively inactive, i.e. sedentary, populations.

Also, subjective methods like questionnaires can be used to quantify physical activity. The work by Pitta et al. [1] provides a survey and a comparison of the subjective methods and the methods involving motion sensors. It concludes that subjective methods do not provide an accurate means to assess physical activity quatitatively, showing large variation among different subjects.

Recently, physical activity monitoring has gained interest also for the consumer market. FitBit [6] is a commercial product to monitor and review one's fitness and quality of sleep. Data is collected continuously and uploaded to a website to provide feedback. ActiSmile [7] is another commercial wearable device to estimate the physical activity level. It first classifies the type of activity among sitting/lying, walking and running, then it uses this result to assess the level of activity and it provides feedback on the display using a smiley face.

With respect to the related work, we focus in this paper on three important aspects. First, we claim that users are involved in more types of physical activities than typically considered and that one sensor node may not be enough to assess energy expenditure in all situations. Second, we implement and test the IMA algorithm on resource-constrained wireless sensor nodes, which creates the basis for having activity monitoring on distributed nodes, and thus being better suited for a large diversity of activities. Third, we implement and evaluate the usability of light-based feedback, taking therefore the computer out of the loop and making the system accessible to also non-technical users.

3   System Description

In this section we provide an overview of all system components, describing how our system operates, the hardware involved, the user interface and the algorithms we use to assess energy expenditure.

3.1   System Overview

The core of our system is represented by wireless sensors nodes that monitor the users' daily activities. The nodes include an accelerometer and are capable of processing the accelerometer samples into a measure of activity. This activity level is stored internally and can be communicated to a local user interface when the user wants to review his or her current daily or hourly activity. For the evaluation presented in this paper, the sensors also log the last day of activity measurements with a granularity of one hour. This enables us to compare the daily activities reported by our test subjects to the logged activity levels.

The subjects wear the sensors on their pant belt. Earlier research [3] has shown that the center of mass, i.e. the waist, is a sensible position for wearing such a sensor, being less prone to bias towards particular activities. For example, when the sensor were located on an arm it would show high levels of activity when the person is sitting somewhere and waving his arms, which does not correspond well with the amount of activity actually involved.

The user interface of our system is a spherical LED lamp, also referred to as Orb, that lights up in different colors. Using a color in between red and green, the user can get a rough idea of the level of activity in the last 60 minutes and

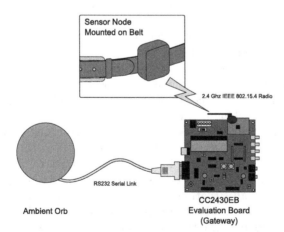

Fig. 1. An overview of the activity monitoring prototype

Fig. 2. ProMove inertial sensor board

the last 24 hours. The user can send commands to the user interface by tapping the sensor node.

Figure 1 shows an overview of the system. The sensor node is worn on the user's belt. When it is tapped by the user, it sends a message to the gateway containing the daily and hourly activity statistics. The gateway interprets the data and controls the orb to change its color accordingly.

3.2 Hardware

We use the ProMove [8] wireless inertial sensor nodes for our activity monitoring application. The ProMove board shown in Figure 2 features a three-axial accelerometer, a two-axial gyroscope and a three-axial digital compass. For this application, we only use data from the accelerometer sampled at a frequency of 100Hz. These inertial sensors are sampled through a low-power MSP430 microcontroller [9], which communicates the data wirelessly through the CC2430 radio [10]. The radio is IEEE 802.15.4-compatible and transmits at 2.4 GHz. A useful feature of the CC2430 is that it combines an 8051 CPU with a radio pheripheral. This allows us to implement our system in a two-tiered fashion: performing data processing on the MSP430 and wireless networking on the CC2430.

As shown in Figure 1, we use a CC2430EB evaluation board from Texas Instruments [10] as gateway for our nodes. These boards only have the CC2430 radio processor and are equipped with an RS232 serial interface, that we use to connect to the orb (see Figure 1).

3.3 Assessing Energy Expenditure

We use the accelerometer of the ProMove sensor nodes to assess a person's energy expenditure. We implement the IMA algorithm described by Bouten [2] on the ProMove nodes. The accelerometer signal is first high-pass filtered to remove the gravity component of the accelerometer signal. The resulting acceleration signal is then integrated according to Equation 1 to obtain the IMA value. The integral produces a value that correlates with the signal energy over the three axes, which is a good measure for the intensity of the measured motion. The integration time T is set to one minute. To calculate the IMA value for one hour or one day, the IMA minute values are averaged over the period involved.

$$IMA = \int_{t=t_0}^{t_0+T} |a_x(t)|\ dt + \int_{t=t_0}^{t_0+T} |a_y(t)|\ dt + \int_{t=t_0}^{t_0+T} |a_z(t)|\ dt \qquad (1)$$

3.4   User Interface

We use the Ambient Orb [11] as our user interface. This is a LED-based light housed in a diffuse glass orb. It contains the necessary control electronics to make the orb light up in many different colors. The device has a serial RS232 interface through which it accepts simple commands to change the color of the light. The color can either be selected from a table of pre-defined colors or custom colors can be composed by specifying the required RGB color channel values.

As shown in Figure 1, we connect the Orb to one of our CC2430 evaluation boards using its serial interface. This evaluation board acts as an IEEE 802.15.4 coordinator and listens for incoming commands from the user nodes. Currently, two commands are distinguished: display the activity level of the last 24 hours and display the activity level of the last 60 minutes. The user can issue these commands by tapping the sensor node, by tapping it twice or three times respectively. When the hourly activity level is requested, the orb first becomes white and then glows towards the activity level represented as a color between red and green. To distinguish the daily activity level display, it is indicated by a bright blue initial color instead of white.

Multiple users can interact with the orb simultaneously. Each sensor node has an internally stored identifier code that is displayed as a two-color sequence on the orb when a user first interacts with it. Each time a different user interacts with the node, his identifier is shown on the node first, followed by the activity level display after a short pause.

The tap commands are picked up by the accelerometer of the sensor node. A tap causes high-frequency vibration, which is picked up as a high frequency acceleration pulse by the accelerometer. The actual tap instances are detected by high-pass filtering the signal with a cut-off frequency of 35 Hz, then rectifying the signal and finally low-pass filtering the result to obtain a signal that correlates with the amount of high-frequency vibration. The actual tap detection uses thresholds to mark the onset and end of a tap. The main advantage of this technique is that the sensor nodes do not need additional hardware to receive user commands.

3.5   Energy Saving

The sensor nodes that are attached to the users need to monitor activity for several days. Energy conservation is therefore an important aspect. The main power drain on the sensor nodes is the activity of the radio. The sampling process on the MSP430 draws about ten times less current, thus it is imperative to turn off the radio when it is not needed. Since our sensor nodes do not need to communicate unless the user tries to interact with the orb, the radio is turned on only when the user taps the sensor. If the user does not issue any commands for 30 seconds, the radio is turned off by putting the CC2430 chip in deep sleep mode. In this situation the whole ProMove board consumes only 7.2 mW, mainly for sampling the accelerometer.

4   Experiments

4.1   Method

The normal mode of operation of the system is to report the activity level in the last 24 hours or the last 60 minutes to the person wearing the hardware. However, for our experiments the system needs to log the activity during a longer period of time at multiple instances. To achieve this, the software is amended with a storage subsystem that logs the hourly activity levels into the controller's flash memory. It can store the activity of the last 36 hours. The radio protocol is adjusted as well, making it send the full data log each time the user issues one of the tap commands. A separate CC2430EB evaluation board listens for the transmitted data and forwards it to a computer through its serial link.

The hourly recording yields a relatively low data granularity. Consequently, the boundaries between successive activities can fall in the middle of a recorded hour, which makes it difficult to infer to what extent the recorded activity value corresponds to which of the two activities. To mitigate this problem, our current approach is to only consider those hourly data points that pertain to only a single activity.

4.2   Tests

To obtain a view on how well the IMA value maps to the energy expenditure of a particular person, we conduct tests with multiple subjects performing various activities of interest. The tests are performed in the course of several experiments.

Office. The main and longest experiment is performed by nine members of our department. This includes the daily office and home activities. The sensors are worn the whole day, except during sleep. The experiment lasts three days.

As the nodes can only record 36 hours, the logs are collected each day during a collective meeting in the afternoon. The subjects keep a coarse log of what they have been doing all day. These logs are evaluated during the meeting and compared to the logged hourly activity levels.

The recorded activities include the normal office activities, home activities and transportation.

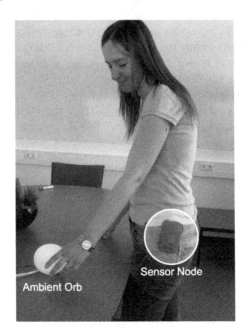

Fig. 3. Subject wearing the ProMove node and receiving feedback on the Orb

Ski. Two sensor nodes are taken on a skiing holiday in the mountains. The two subjects keep a coarse log of their daily activities, including skiing, resting and driving the car.

Sports. Four separate experiments are performed in which the subjects are engaged in sports: tennis, badminton, volleyball and cycling. Tennis is performed by two persons, volleyball is performed by four persons and cycling is performed by three persons at the same time. The badminton experiment is spread over multiple parallel matches involving four subjects. Each experiment lasts more than an hour to record only the activity of interest.

5 Results

Table 1 shows the average IMA value for various activities. Because the sensor nodes log the activity level on a per-hour basis, the presented values are the hourly averages of the same activity performed by multiple persons at multiple time instances. The table also shows how many hours of data are involved in computing the average and how many subjects were involved in a particular activity. Since activities do not necessarily change on the hour boundaries, the IMA averages are solely based on those hours during which only one activity was performed with certainty.

The recorded activities are as follows:

- *Not worn*: the sensor node is not worn by anyone and just lies stationary somewhere.

Table 1. Activity recording results

Activity	Recorded Hours	Persons Involved	IMA
Not Worn	129	9	373
Home Activities	33	6	1581
Office Activities	58	9	1144
Sitting	25	6	1120
Walking	4	2	7767
Cycling	3	3	6466
Tennis	2	2	11411
Badminton	6	4	10874
Volleyball	4	4	9464
Skiing	40	2	1496
Driving a Car	31	2	827
Presenting	1	1	2655

- *Home activities*: the subject is engaged in the typical home activities, such as cooking, washing, childcare etc.
- *Office activities*: the subject is engaged in the typical office activities, which mainly consist of sitting, but also intermittent walks between offices and fetching coffee.
- *Sitting, walking*: the subject is continuously sitting or walking respectively.
- *Tennis, Badminton, Volleyball, Cycling*: the subject is playing tennis, playing badminton, playing volleyball or riding a bicycle respectively.
- *Skiing*: the subject is skiing downhill.
- *Driving in a car*: the subject is driving in a car.
- *Presenting*: the subject is giving a presentation during a meeting.

Figure 4 graphically illustrates the difference between the activities in terms of the measured IMA value. We notice that the results show that the IMA value always greater than zero, even when the sensor is not worn, due to the integration of accelerometer noise.

The results show that home activities produce higher activity values than office activities. The reason is that in the office people barely leave their desk for hours. At home, activities such as doing laundry, cleaning etc. contribute to a higher activity level. It is interesting to see that what people describe as sitting matches well with the office activities.

The activity value for cycling is the average of the IMA value from three persons making a bicycle trip. For this test the activity results vary wildly, with values ranging from 5635 to 7542. These differences are probably caused by differences in the bicycles, the exact path taken on the road and the way the subjects ride their bicycle.

The results for tennis and badminton are very similar, since these two sports and the movements involved therein are very similar as well. Volleyball produces lower activity values. This is due to two main reasons: more people are involved in the ball game, spreading the activity over more persons, and the game is interrupted for longer periods of time.

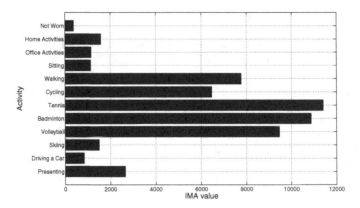

Fig. 4. IMA values for various activities

The most interesting data results from the skiing activity. Although skiing is certainly not an activity with a low energy expenditure, the sensors show a low activity value. This value is lower than walking, even though skiing is much more exhausting. The reason is that during skiing the amount of variation in the acceleration of the person is relatively limited in comparison to walking. The regular motion of the gait of walking is not present when sliding down a hill on skis. The energy expenditure from skiing is more the result of the act of leaning in the bends and keeping ones legs steady.

According to the results displayed in Figure 4, walking is more active than riding a bicycle, but the spread in the activity values is relatively large. This is unexpected, since the walking experiments were conducted with a normal walking pace, whereas the cycling experiments were performed at speed. Therefore, we would expect to see a higher activity result for the cycling experiments. We attribute this discrepancy to the same effect as for the skiing experiments.

The ski experiment also shows that the orientation and the way sensor is mounted influences the result. After in the middle of the experiment, the pouches in which the sensors are worn were exchanged between the subjects. The persons kept their own sensor. During the week, the recorded activity values were similar, with the trend that one was reported to be more active than the other most of the time. After the exchange of the pouches, this trend inverted. The main observable difference between these pouches is the fact that one is worn vertically and the other horizontally.

Figure 5 shows an example of an activity log for two subjects. For most of the day, these subjects were together and engaged in the same activities. The graph shows a clear correlation between the two subjects. At 19:00 they played a tennis match for one hour, which is much more active than anything else recorded during the experiment. Between 23:00 and 7:00 the sensors were not worn. As shown, the IMA values are constant in stationary conditions.

Results indicate that the use of a single accelerometer is not always adequate to accurately and consistently estimate the level of physical activity. Also, the orientation and way the sensor is mounted on the subjects have an influence on

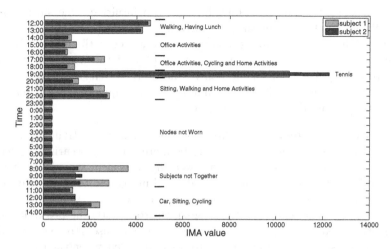

Fig. 5. Example activity values recorded during 27 hours from two subjects

the measurements. However, the activity measurements do correlate well between subjects that are engaged in identical activities.

5.1 Usability

To evaluate usability aspects of the system, the nine test subjects filled in a questionnaire. The questions target the wearability and unobtrusiveness of the system, the feedback quality of the user interface, the effectiveness of the activity stimulation that the users perceive, and the privacy concerns users may have.

Wearability and Unobtrusiveness. The first question pertains to how subjects feel while wearing the sensor node. Most subjects (78 %) are not constantly aware that they are wearing a sensor node or they are not bothered by its presence. One subject indicates that it is unpleasant to wear, mainly due to its size but also due to its looks. Another subject notices that a relatively large belt-mounted device can be annoying when sitting in a chair, lying somewhere or when doing sports. All subjects agree that the sensor node should be smaller than it is now.

We also ask how many sensor nodes subjects are prepared to wear. Most subjects (67 %) answered that they would accept wearing two or three sensors. Two subjects are prepared to wear more than three sensors and one user accepts only one sensor. However, the subjects indicate that the limit on the number of nodes is inversely proportional to its size. The intended mounting positions and the type of sensors have an influence on the acceptable number of sensors, such that the integration of very small sensors into clothing would be preferred.

Feedback Quality. To assess the feedback quality of our visual user interface, the users are asked about their opinion on the Orb light interface. Most subjects

(67 %) find the interface appealling, but not too intuitive. One subject likes it unconditionally. Two other subjects have a very hard time interpreting the colors, especially when multiple subjects are interacting with the Orb. In fact, most subjects are initially confused by the display of the user identifier and struggle to distinguish between the hourly and daily activity display. It should be clear without much explanation what the color sequences mean, but that turns out to be more difficult than expected.

Activity Encouragement. The first question regarding activity encouragement is whether subjects feel motivated to be more active by wearing the sensor node. Most subjects (67 %) indicate that wearing the sensor stimulates them to be more active. Three subjects did not really feel motivated to do more exercise and regarded the sensor to be just a monitoring device.

The second question extended this assessment to include the possibility that the competitive nature of a group could further stimulate users to be more active. We ask whether subjects feel motivated to be more active when their results are compared to others. Most subjects (67 %) do feel that this competitive property of the system further stimulates their activity. The same three subjects that were not motivated as much by the sensor alone were also not impressed by the competitive stimulation.

Privacy Concerns. We ask whether subjects would be prepared to share their activity results with others, e.g. on a website. Most subjects (67 %) would be prepared to do so to some extent, but only with friends. Three subjects see no merit in doing so and wonder who would be interested in this information.

Conclusion. Even though our prototype sensor node is not very small (see Figure 3), most subjects are not bothered much by its presence. However, there is the consensus that it needs to be smaller and this is one of our goals for future work. Depending on the form factor, most subjects would be willing to wear more sensors spread across the body.

The light interface needs improvement. The distinction between the hourly and daily display is not intuitively clear and the display of a user's personal color sequence is sometimes confusing.

The opinion about whether the system encourages activity varies among the subjects of the questionnaire. Most subjects are encouraged to be more active, but others only recognize the system as an activity monitor. This is also true for the envisioned competitive encouragement.

6   Conclusions

We described in this paper our experience with implementing and evaluating activity monitoring in wireless sensor networks. The results from our experiments represent the motivation for and a first step towards robust complex activity monitoring with multiple sensors distributed in a wireless sensor network. Wireless sensor networks create a promising basis for achieving distributed activity recognition and monitoring for a large diversity of physical activities.

In our experiments, multiple subjects were monitored during their daily activities (both at home and at the office) and additionally while performing sports such as badminton, tennis, volleyball, cycling and skiing. The results show that the recorded values correspond to the expected intensity for some of the performed activities, but certain activities, such as skiing and cycling, produce lower activity measurements than expected. Using multiple sensor nodes and sensor modalities per subject would improve the activity estimation performance, provided that the sensor nodes are small and inconspicuous, as indicated by the results of our usability study.

The usability study indicates two other directions of future work. First, simple feedback with an ambient light is appreciated by the users, but it is not considered to be intuitive enough. The capabilities of the feedback device should allow for faster user identification and provide more granular information on the activity level. Second, the competitive nature of group interaction should be better exploited to motivate and stimulate users to increase their level of daily physical activity.

References

1. Pitta, F., Troosters, T., Probst, V., Spruit, M., Decramer, M., Gosselink, R.: Quantifying physical activity in daily life with questionnaires and motion sensors in COPD. European Respiratory Journal 27(5), 1040–1055 (2006)
2. Bouten, C.: Assessment of daily physical activity by registration of body movement, p. 145. Eindhoven Univ. Technol., Eindhoven (1995)
3. Bouten, C., Sauren, A., Verduin, M., Janssen, J.: Effects of placement and orientation of body-fixed accelerometers on the assessment of energy expenditure during walking. Medical and Biological Engineering and Computing 35, 50–56 (1997)
4. Steele, B., Holt, L., Belza, B., Ferris, S., Lakshminaryan, S., Buchner, D.: Quantitating Physical Activity in COPD Using a Triaxial Accelerometer* (2000)
5. Fujiki, Y., Tsiamyrtzis, P., Pavlidis, I.: Making sense of accelerometer measurements in pervasive physical activity applications. In: CHI EA 2009: Proceedings of the 27th international conference extended abstracts on Human factors in computing systems, pp. 3425–3430. ACM, New York (2009)
6. Fitbit, Inc., http://www.fitbit.com/
7. Krauss, J., Solà, J., Renevey, P., Maeder, U., Buchholz, H.: ActiSmile: A Portable Biofeedback Device on Physical Activity. In: Proceedings of the Sixth IASTED International Conference on Biomedical Engineering, International Association of Science and Technology for Development,# 80, 4500- 16 Ave NW, Calgary, Alberta, T 3 B 0 M 6, Canada (2008)
8. Inertia Technology: ProMove wireless inertial sensor node, http://www.inertia-technology.com
9. Texas Instruments: MSP430 family of ultra-low-power microcontrollers, http://focus.ti.com/docs/prod/folders/print/msp430f1611.html
10. Texas Instruments: CC2430 System-on-Chip Solution for 2.4 GHz IEEE 802.15.4 / ZigBee, http://focus.ti.com/docs/prod/folders/print/cc2430.html
11. Ambient Devices: Ambient Orb, http://www.ambientdevices.com/cat/orb/orborder.html

Time-Lag as Limiting Factor
for Indoor Walking Navigation

Andreas Riener, Markus Straub, and Alois Ferscha

Johannes Kepler University Linz, Institute for Pervasive Computing,
Altenberger Str. 69, A-4040 Linz, Austria
Tel. +43/732/2468–1432, Fax. +43/732/2468–8426
{lastname}@pervasive.jku.at

Abstract. Several navigation situations can be imagined where visual cueing is not practical or unfeasible, and where the hands are required exclusively for a certain task. The utilization of the sense of touch, as relatively new notification modality, should provide sufficient possibilites to cope with this issue.

The focus in this research work is on two questions (*i*) how the distance encoding schemas affects the overall navigation speed (or in more detail to what level the time lag contributes to the navigation precision) and (*ii*) if, beside the vibro-tactile stimulation, the transmission of the noise generated by the individual vibration elements influences the speed and/or precision of route guiding. To deal with these questions we have defined and conducted three waypoint following experiments with two different tactor activation methods, one without and the other two with the distance encoded in the vibration patterns. Additionally, we did studies where we masked the noise of the vibration elements and compared the results against the general setting where masking was not applied.

Our results shows that notification latency led to an increasing number of walking anomalies and consequently affects the walking precision and time to a high degree. Furthermore, we could not find evidence that multimodal stimulation with both vibration force and vibration "noise" tends to result in an increased system performance compared to the system with unimodal feedback using vibrations only.

Keywords: Time-lag, Indoor Navigation, Human Perception, Vibro-tactile Notification, Space Awareness, Stimulation Patterns, Vibration Noise, Reaction Latency.

1 Introduction and Motivation

The sensory modalities *seeing* and *hearing* utilized in traditional human-computer interaction have limited information capacity [1], [2], [3, p. 44], [4, p. 242], [5] so that visually or auditory delivered navigation information (or more precarious alerts) tend to fail to raise the required user attention. The sense of touch which is a "private" medium and operates hands, eyes and ears-free is attributed to offer potential to assist the highly charged eyes and/or ears in information transmission.

P. Barnaghi et al. (Eds.): EuroSSC 2009, LNCS 5741, pp. 24–37, 2009.

In special situations the visual and auditory channels are actually unfeasible to be used for notifications – mention for instance a fire figther in action, escaping from a loud, smoky factory building. A second issue which probably could be resolved by utilizing vibro-tactile feedback systems (or more general the sense of touch) is the difficulty of navigation for disabled (blind) people, particularly in unfamiliar places like public authority offices, on the university campus or on airports – they cannot just unfold the map of the region and orientate themselves.

1.1 Research Hypotheses

Under consideration of the above discussed visual and auditory limitations the following hypotheses have guided our work in order to improve vibro-tactile directed navigation.

(i) Encoding of distance information into vibro-tactile messages will allow persons to find waypoints faster. However, latency in the notification loop affects the speed of waypoint finding: a larger time lag results in a longer timespan to find a certain destination point. This is due to the drift between a person's actual position and the original position the notification is based on.

(ii) A navigation performance degradation is expected when removing the auditory sensory channel as information carrier (blanking the noise caused by the vibration elements). This is motivated from earlier work, e. g. [6, p. 225], where it has been found that the noise generated by vibration elements provided an additional information source.

2 Related Work

In recent years, researchers have investigated the potential of vibro-tactile displays in human-machine interfaces. Through the skin vibrations can be felt on the whole body, however, the focus in this work is on two-dimensional navigation in indoor walking scenarios, thus the center of interest is related work from experiments with tactile waistbelt or torso displays[1].

2.1 Vibro-Tactile Information Presentation

In order to enhance navigation in 2D spaces with vibro-tactile assistance systems it would be a good choice to place the system around the waist so to get a direct orientation mapping.

Jones *et al.* [8] tested a wirelessly controlled tactile display (built up from a 4 by 4 array of vibrating motors, and mounted on the lower back) for assisting navigational tasks. The evaluation of the vibro-tactile display regarding outdoor navigation confirmed, that the interpretation of presented vibration patterns for directional or instructional cues performs almost perfect. A further experiment

---

[1] A tactile torso display conveys information by presenting localized vibrations to the torso [7].

showed that the ability to recognize vibro-tactile stimulation on the back was superior as compared to the forearm.

Lindeman *et al.* [9] used a vibro-tactile system built up from a matrix of 3 by 3 tactor elements mounted on the back to investigate visual and vibro-tactile stimulations. They reported that the performance increase was most significantly enhanced by visual cueing, however, haptic cues alone (unimodal feedback) provided a lower significant performance increase as well. Under consideration of these results, they suggested to use vibro-tactile cues in situations when visual cueing is not practical. Jan van Erp [10] investigated the direction in the horizontal plane using a linear tactor display with fifteen vibro-tactile elements (oscillating frequency fixed to 250Hz) placed on the torso of test persons. Results confirm that people have the ability to indicate a direction that matches a vibro-tactile point stimulus on the torso. Van Veen *et al.* [7] have investigated whether a tactile torso display can help to compensate for degraded visual information. A tactile display consisting of up to 128 vibrating elements (arranged in twelve columns and five rows) attached to a vest was developed. Their results showed an observable performance increase for tactile display variants compared to operation without tactile displays. Lindeman *et al.* have developed a body-worn garment to deliver haptic cues to the whole body. First evaluations regarding vibro-tactile navigation for collision avoidance or obstacle detection in real or virtual worlds have been presented, e.g. in [11] or [12], however, no qualitative statements about the usability and accuracy of the system, compared to "traditional navigation" approaches, have been given so far.

2.2 Hands- and Eyes-Free Walking Navigation

The guidance system proposed within this work is designed with the aim to relieve cognitive load from the eyes and ears, so it would be unfeasible to charge them with vibro-tactile information.

Elliott *et al.* [13] investigated tactile waistbelts for the transmission of navigational information in order to leave eyes and hands free for other tasks. The utilized tactile display was expected to reduce the high visual and cognitive workload of persons by reason of Wicken's Multiple Resource Theory (MRT) [14]. The results of their experiments showed that tactile navigation achieved best accuracy, followed by navigation with a GPS device, and by navigation with an ordinary compass. Duistermaat *et al.* [15] evaluated the performance of navigation and target detection tasks in night operation with a vibro-tactile waistbelt compared to a GPS device and a head-up navigation device. They found that the tactile system was rated higher than the GPS system in all test cases, and higher or as high as the head-up navigation system in many or most cases. Tsukada and Yasumara [16] developed a wearable tactile display called "ActiveBelt" for the transmission of directional cues and found that it is more desirable to activate the vibration elements only when users get lost in their navigation task rather than activating them constantly, and that the disposition of four tactors would be enough for accurate "walking navigation". Erp *et al.* [17] investigated the feasibility of navigation information presented on a tactile display instead of using a common visual display. Results of their studies using a vibro-tactile waistbelt indicated that both the vibro-tactile and the visual display perform with a similar reaction time.

2.3   A Basic Waistbelt Display

Ferscha *et al.* [18] presented a belt-like vibro-tactile notification system for assistance in raising users' attention, however they used simple activation patterns and the developed system featured a high latency between position detection and the corresponding notification. Riener and Ferscha described in [19] the results of a distance estimation experiment with different parameters of vibro-tactile stimulation.

2.4   Summary

Research on vibro-tactile stimulation, particularly for application in navigational scenarios, has increased considerably in the last years. Most of the reported work deals with outdoor navigation, often in combination with GPS position tracking. The reason for this is that (*i*) outdoor route-guiding operates acceptably accurate even with imprecise (tactile) feedback and (*ii*) a detected time lag has only little influence on the navigation quality and/or positioning precision due to the long distances to walk.

However, with technology advances in both position tracking (e. g. Ubisense 7000 series[2] or Intersense IS-900[3] Wireless Inertial Position and Orientation Tracking System for Real-time Location Sensing) and vibro-tactile feedback systems (for instance EAI C2-tactors[4] as used in this work), directed and accurate indoor route guiding might still come true.

Nevertheless, a number of issues still remain open and have to be considered, e. g. (*i*) the prevention or compensation of latency times or (*ii*) the definition of vibro-tactile notification patterns for precise route-guiding. The results of the authors' earlier work (as for example described in [18] or [19]) have provided a basis for determining an appropriate set of parameters for the investigations conducted in the frame of this work.

Outline

The rest of the paper is organized as follows. Section 3 describes the hardware setting used in the studies including placement and variation parameters of the vibro-tactile elements. Furthermore, definitions as well as a short characterization for the conducted experiments are given. In Section 4 the results

---

[2] Ubisense Platform Homepage, URL: `http://www.ubisense.net/content/8.html`, last retrieved March 20, 2009.

[3] Intersense Inc. IS-900 Systems, URL: `http://www.intersense.com/IS-900_Systems.aspx`, last retrieved March 20, 2009.

[4] Engineering Acoustics Inc., URL:`http://www.eaiinfo.com/TactorProducts.htm`, last retrieved March 21, 2009.

of evaluations regarding latency and stimulation parameters are presented and discussed. Section 5 concludes the work and gives some suggestions for future improvements.

3   Experimental Design

For the studies conducted within this work a vibro-tactile waist belt – built up from eight high-precision C-2 tactor elements creating a strong, punctuated vibration force – has been used (see Fig. 1). Each of the tactor elements has a diameter of $30.48mm$, a height of $7.87mm$, and uses electromechanical voice-coils to generate vibrations with a resonance frequency in the range between 200 and $300Hz$. In order to allow precise delivery of orientation information the vibration elements have to be spaced equally. Considering this quality issue we used two differently sized belts, one with a length of $720mm$ and one with a measure of $850mm$, to be able to process the experiments with test participants with different waist girths (in the range of $75cm$ to $100cm$).

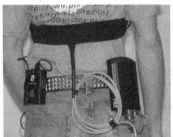

Fig. 1. The waist-belt system consisting of the vibro-tactile belt, the Intersense transceiver, and the belt controller, a detail view of the waist belt, a participant wearing the belt and the headphones in a two-dimensional indoor navigation experiment (from left to right)

3.1   Parameter Definition

Tactor Placement: As described by Cholewiak *et al.* [20] vibro-tactile perception is insusceptible to the vertical alignment of actuators on the body in the region from hip to chest, even if the underlying tissue (Epidermis) touched by a certain tactor varies widely and consists either of tendons, bones, muscles, etc. Instead, perception of vibrations is highly influenced by the position of tactor elements around the waist, for instance higher perception is reported for tactors positioned on the anatomical keypoints navel and spinal column, lower perception for vibration elements placed on the sides.

Position Tracking: For high-precise and accurate indoor position and orientation tracking of "navigating" test persons an Intersense IS-900 6-DOF[5] ultrasonic

---

[5] Degrees of Freedom.

positioning system was used. The wireless tracker, which had to be carried along by the candidates, was mounted on top of closed-back headphones (type AKG K55), worn throughout all experiments and playing "masking music" during the two experiments 1 and 3.

Vibro-Tactile Stimulation: In the different experiments, as described in Section 3.2 below, a combination of frequency and amplitude variation was used to notify test persons about distance and orientation.

(i) *Frequency Range:* We used frequency variation in the range from 200 to $300Hz$, since it is known to be perceived best by the Pacinian Corpuscles (PC) (see for instance Cholewiak *et al.* [20] or Riener [6, p. 115f]). Initial studies conducted on higher and lower frequencies confirmed that using frequencies below approximately $150Hz$ or above $350Hz$ are difficult to perceive and thus should not be used in Tactograms[6]

(ii) *Amplitude/Gain Variation:* For notifications using different vibration intensities the full range offered by the tactor system has been utilized. The overall range encompasses $24dB$, fragmented into 256 intensity levels. The linear mapping between distance and corresponding intensity level results in a logarithmic sensation.

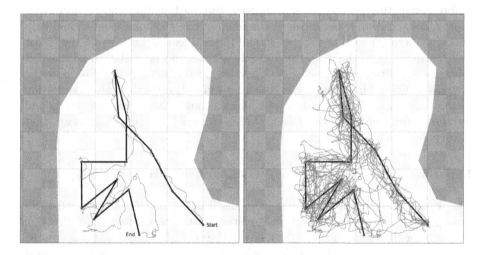

Fig. 2. The left image shows a navigation track (combination of thick, straight lines) with the overlayed trace of one test participant (thin solid line). Overlayed traces of all test persons on the same track indicate a rather good navigation precision, however, with several outliers (right image).

Route Design: For each of the three processed experiments a different course, as exemplarily shown in Fig. 2, was defined. The illustration shows a top view

---

[6] The notion of *Tactograms* for describing vibration patterns has been introduced in [6, p. 123f].

of our laboratory room with a tile size of 60 by 60*cm* and an overall room size of 730 by 745*cm*. The light-shaded area was accessible for test participants (and limited by the coverage area of the Intersense tracking system[7]).

To guarantee comparability between the different courses they have been designed according to the following properties, equal for any experiment.

(i) Entire walking distance: 18.0*m*
(ii) Waypoints: 13
(iii) Distance between waypoints: 1.50*m*
(iv) Track sections:
   (a) A nearly straight part consisting of 3 track sections (defined by 4 points), +15° and −15° angles.
   (b) One 170° U-turn.
   (c) Two consecutive angles of 90° each.
   (d) A zig-zag path, +160° and −160° angles.
   (e) The four remaining angles were 16°, 40°, 117°, and 127°.

3.2   Definition of Experiments

Before conducting the actual experiments, test participants had to perform a short familiarization experiment. It consisted of five waypoints and should help participants to get used to the system and the notification behavior of the tactor belt, particularly to the distance encoding scheme and its variation parameters vibration amplitude and frequency. They got no instructions at all on how the systems works or that distance is coded into vibrations – the only information they got was that (*i*) they had to walk along a route with several waypoints and (*ii*) a simultaneous pulsation of all vibration elements for one second means that a waypoint has been reached.

Experiment 1: Fixed Frequency/Gain with Auditory Masking

The results of this most trivial test case conducted at first for all test attendees were used as "baseline" for further investigations. The distance and direction mapping for this experiment was as follows. The two vibro-tactile elements on the waist belt closest to the destination (waypoint) were activated with the highest possible vibration amplitude and a fixed frequency of 250*Hz*, thus there was no notification about the actual distance to the next waypoint. If a participant was more than 1.9*m* away from the next Point of Interest (POI), the tactor element with shortest distance to this POI was activated in a 180*ms* pulse, 180*ms* pause pattern in order to guide the person to that waypoint. However, since the distance between waypoints was specified to be exactly 1.5*m*, this pattern was only used in very rare occasions, namely when a test person completely got lost.

---

[7] The routes for all the experiments have been defined with respect to fit into the Intersense coverage area.

Reaching a Waypoint: If a POI was reached, all tactor elements were activated in a $100ms$ pulse - $100ms$ pause pattern for 1 second, to clearly notify
the walking person about its arrival at a waypoint. Immediately after this notification pattern the direction to the next waypoint was delivered. The covered
path as well as the time required for approaching each waypoint were recorded
and later used as reference values to evaluate the performance of the other two
experiments featuring frequency and gain variation.

Masking Vibration Noise: For the purpose of auditory masking the noise
generated by vibrating tactors a harmonic title of drone music [21] was played
at such a person dependent volume, that the person could no longer hear the
vibration source.

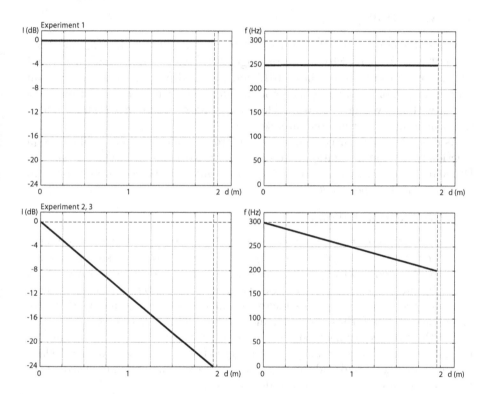

Fig. 3. Encoding schemes for the three experiments. Constant vibration intensity (peak
value, 0dB attenuation) and frequency (250Hz) has been used in experiment 1, for the
experiments 2, 3 a variation of vibration intensity (0dB to -24dB attenuation) and
frequency (300Hz to 200Hz) depending on the distance (0.0m to 1.9m) has been utilized

Experiment 2: Frequency/Gain Variation without Auditory Masking

In this test case the distance of the test person to the next waypoint was encoded
using vibration frequency and amplitude variation as follows. If a participant

enters a freely configurable area around a Point of Interest (in all of the presented and discussed test sets a circle with a radius of $1.9m$ has been utilized) the parameters described in the paragraph "Vibro-tactile Stimulation" above were linearly mapped to the distance by increasing both frequency and amplitude with decreasing distance to the waypoint. Beyond the defined area directional notifications were given as described in the baseline test above.

Experiment 3: Frequency/Gain Variation with Auditory Masking

This experiment was similar to the previous one with the only difference that auditory vibration information was masked with music as described and used in the first experiment.

4   Evaluations

The experiments were conducted with 11 voluntary male test persons, aged between 23 and 32 years with an average age of 25.7 years, sized between 174 and $194cm$ with an average height of $181.7cm$, weighted from 65 to $104kg$ with an average weight of $78.5kg$, and with abdominal girths around the navel from 75 to $100cm$ with an average of $85.6cm$. Three of the participants were staff members, the remaining eight were computer science students.

As it has been evidenced that there is a strong gender dependent difference in reaction speed and navigation precision (e. g. in Kosinkski [22], Dane *et al.* [23], Der and Deary [24], Surnina *et al.* [25]), thus only male persons were allowed to take part in the experiments.

4.1   Notification Latency

The time lag from Intersense, sensing a person's movement, until the vibro-tactile waist belt emitted the corresponding tactile notification consisted of around $10ms$ for the acquisition of position data via the Intersense server (WLAN delay), added by another $180ms$ for sending one command to the tactor controller (more precisely, the tactor controller's microcontroller needs approximately $180ms$ to process a command, thus one command can be sent only once every $180ms$).

For the first experiment only one command was required for changing vibration patterns (Tactograms), the time lag is therefore $10ms+180ms=190ms$. However, for the second and third experiment three commands were needed, the latency calculates to $10ms + 3 \times 180ms = 550ms$.

4.2   Interviews and Observations

In general, the reaction from test attendees on the experiments and the vibro-tactile navigation was quite positive. Even though 73% of the participating persons had no experience with this kind of notification, they stated that (i) the belt-type navigation system was intuitively useable for navigation and (ii) they could imagine being guided by such a system in the real. More specifically, following conclusions can be drawn from observations and interviews following the user tests.

(i) *Latency:* Some of the test candidates quickly learnt how to compensate the indicated time lag. They seldomly turned around their own axis, but tended to step sidewards and backwards. 55% (6) of the test candidates explicitly complained about the latency of the system and that this made it particularly difficult to navigate efficiently when being close to a waypoint.

(ii) *Tactor placement:* Three test participants felt the strongest vibrations on the frontmost tactors, two persons had problems in feeling vibrations on the tactile element placed nearby the navel, one felt that the vibration elements placed left/right on his sides provides best vibration feedback. 45% (5) complained about a generally low vibration intensity on the back. Even if Cholewiak et al. [20] stated that belly and back are two anatomical reference points where vibrations are sensed better than on the sides, this did not hold true in our experimental setup, presumably caused by the fact that the tactor elements on the back were only pressed against the skin with low force.

(iii) *Masking vibration noise:* A piece of music delivered via headphones was used to mask the vibration noise in two of the three experiments. This was regarded as a good option by four participants (36%) – they stated that the masking helped them to focus their attention on the vibro-tactile sensations. One person missed the noise and felt less capable of precise navigation, the other six participants felt indifferent to the music.

(iv) *Vibration amplitude:* 73% (8) test persons noted that in some cases the vibration signal was not strong enough, which was obviously caused by the applied distance coding scheme used in the experiments two and three. 64% (7) participants perceived the changed distance coding scheme between the first and the other two experiments, and furthermore found the distance dependent variation of frequency and gain a useful addition to the first experiment.

4.3   Walking Traces

All participants successfully accomplished the three navigation (or waypoint finding) experiments. The only briefing carried out just before conducting the tests was a a short training with five waypoints, in order to get familiar with the system. In the course of the experimental processing three "walking anomalies" recurred again and again, namely (i) extensive zig-zaging when approaching a waypoint, and then passing by, (ii) revolving around the waypoint, and (iii) make a fast beeline to a waypoint, missing it, and come back again, see Fig. 4 (from left to right).

Both the boxplots in Fig. 5 and Table 1 show that the performances of the second and third experiment were significantly worse compared to that of the first one, thus hypothesis 1 cannot be accepted. This result holds true for the number of occured anomalies as indicated in the righthand plot of Fig. 5. The number of anomalies was significantly lower for the first experiment (e. g. on average 2.18 compared to 4.73 for the second experiment), the result for the third experiment is slightly better than for experiment two.

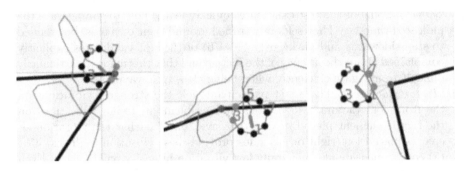

Fig. 4. Walking anomalies (from left to right). Zig-zaging before, revolving around, and passing by a waypoint. The bigger circle represents the vibration belt with eight tactors, the actual destination to be reached is the intersection point of the two straight lines.

Table 1. The walking distance is on average 27.64% (20.23%) higher for the second (third) experiment compared to the first one. This relationship holds true for the walking time and the counted anomalies (p<0.05).

	Walking Time (sec.)			Walking Distance (cm)			Anomalies (quantity)		
Attribute	Exp. 1	Exp. 2	Exp. 3	Exp. 1	Exp. 2	Exp. 3	Exp. 1	Exp. 2	Exp. 3
Min. (x_{min})	7.44	7.91	8.61	217.00	221.61	251.49	0	2	1
Median ($\widetilde{x}$)	8.81	12.31	10.75	264.50	357.56	305.92	2	5	4
Max. (x_{max})	10.31	13.69	13.27	301.81	399.16	410.11	6	7	7
Mean ($\overline{x}$)	9.64	12.43	11.74	285.00	363.77	342.65	2.18	4.73	4.27
SD (σ_x)	1.86	2.12	1.76	41.88	62.20	63.34	1.83	1.74	1.85

One of the main reasons for this performance degradation between the first experiment and experiments 2 and 3 originates from the increased time lag ($550ms$ for the second and third, $190ms$ for the first experiment). However, this seems not to be the only cause as (i) the kind of notification (or vibro-tactile message) changed from experiment 1 to the experiments 2, 3 and (ii) 73% (8) of the test persons noted that the vibration intensity was partly too low for the experiments 2 and 3 (particularly at higher distances).

Hypothesis 2, which states that a test person will perform faster and/or better in experiment 2 than in experiment 3 by reason of multimodal instead of unimodal feedback have to be rejected, the results even show that it is rather the other way round (see Table 1). All individual results, the walked distance, the duration required for completing a trace and the number of anomalies are lower for the third experiment than for the second (however, statistically not significant). This result can be explained by the fact that the multimodal stimulation (vibration noise from a tactor element and the vibration itself) confuses and distracts a test person – 36% of the test participants noted that using a masking music during the experiment helped them to improve their concentration on the

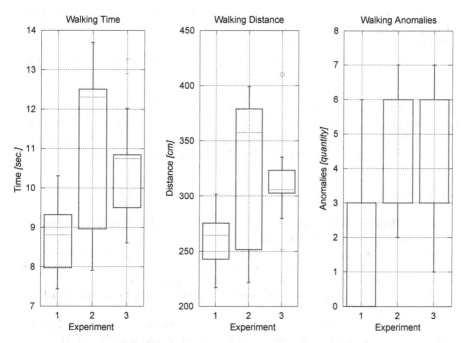

Fig. 5. Boxplots indicating the overall walking time, walking distance, and the number of anomalies (from left to right)

main task. Additionally, a learning effect from experiment 2 to experiment 3, although different route traces have been used, cannot be ruled out definitively.

5   Conclusions and Further Work

In this paper we have described a belt-type body-worn indoor navigation system. Both the findings from the questionnaires and the empirical results confirmed that latency (or time lag) negatively affect precise and fast route guiding.

The proposed distance encoding scheme (varying both vibration frequency and amplitude) missed its expected performance. This result can at least be partly explained by observations from several test participants, who noted that sometimes vibrations were very difficult to sense. From combining these statements with our observations while conducting the experiments it became clear that the occurence of this problem correlates with high waypoint distances – and therefore low vibration amplitudes – during experiment 2 and 3. On the other hand, the positive feedback from other test persons with respect to the distance depending encoding model motivates further research on distance encoding.

The hypothesis on a noticeable performance degradation when blanking the noise generated by the vibration elements, and thus reducing the feedback dimensionality from bimodal to unimodal, has to be rejected. Test persons reported that the masking of vibration sound leads to a higher focus on the vibration force, the empirical results also showed an improvement in navigation speed and/or precision.

Further research questions relate to the interrelationship of performance degradation and (i) notification latency or (ii) distance depending variation of vibration intensity.

Acknowledgements. This work is supported under the FP7 ICT Future Enabling Technologies programme of the European Commission under grant agreement No 231288 (SOCIONICAL) and under grant FACT (Flexible Autonomic Context Technologies) of SIEMENS CT SE-2, Siemens AG, Munich.

References

1. van der Heijden, A.H.C., Bem, S.: Eye movements and attention. Consciousness and Cognition 6(2-3), 437–440 (1997), Article No. CC970308
2. Broadbent, D.E.: Perception and communication. Pergamon, London (1958)
3. Mayer, R.E., Moreno, R.: Nine Ways to Reduce Cognitive Load in Multimedia Learning. Educational Psychologist 38(1), 43–52 (Winter 2003)
4. van der Heijden, A.H.C.: Selective Attention in Vision, illustrated edn. Routledge, New York (1992)
5. Hsia, H.: The information processing capacity of modality and channel performance. Educ. Technology Research and Development 19(1), 51–75 (1971)
6. Riener, A.: Sensor-Actuator Supported Implicit Interaction in Driver Assistance Systems. PhD thesis, Johannes Kepler University, Linz, Austria (January 2009)
7. Veen, H.A.V., Erp, J.B.V.: Providing Directional Information with Tactile Torso Displays. In: Proceedings of EuroHaptics 2003, TNO Human Factors Soesterberg, The Netherlands. LNCS, pp. 471–474. Springer, Heidelberg (2003)
8. Jones, L.A., Lockyer, B., Piateski, E.: Tactile display and vibrotactile pattern recognition on the torso. Advanced Robotics 20(12), 1359–1374 (2006)
9. Lindeman, R.W., Yanagida, Y., Sibert, J.L., Lavine, R.: Effective vibrotactile cueing in a visual search task. In: Rauterberg, M., Menozzi, M., Wesson, J. (eds.) Proceedings of 13th International Human-Computer Interaction (INTERACT 2003), pp. 89–96. IOS Press, Amsterdam (2003)
10. van Erp, J.B.: Presenting directions with a vibrotactile torso display. Ergonomics, Taylor and Francis Ltd. 48(3), 302–313 (2005)
11. Lindeman, R.W., Page, R., Yanagida, Y., Sibert, J.L.: Towards full-body haptic feedback: the design and deployment of a spatialized vibrotactile feedback system. In: VRST 2004: Proceedings of the ACM symposium on Virtual reality software and technology, pp. 146–149. ACM, New York (2004)
12. Lindeman, W., Yanagida, Y., Noma, H., Hosaka, K.: Wearable vibrotactile systems for virtual contact and information display. Virtual Real. 9(2), 203–213 (2006)
13. Elliott, L.R., Redden, E.S., Pettitt, R.A., Carstens, C.B., van Erp, J., Duistermaat, M.: Tactile Guidance for Land Navigation. Technical Report ARL-TR-3814, Army Research Laboratory, Aberdeen Proving Ground, MD 21005-5425 (2006)
14. Wickens, C.D.: Processing resources in attention. In: Parasuraman, R. (ed.) Varieties of Attention, pp. 63–97. Academic Press, New York (1984)
15. Duistermaat, M.: Tactile Land Navigation in Night Operations. Technical report, TNO Defence, Security and Safety Kampweg 5 3769 ZG Soesterberg, The Netherlands, R&D No. 9954-AN-01 (December 2005)

16. Tsukada, K., Yasumura, M.: ActiveBelt: Belt-Type Wearable Tactile Display for Directional Navigation. In: Davies, N., Mynatt, E.D., Siio, I. (eds.) UbiComp 2004. LNCS, vol. 3205, pp. 384–399. Springer, Heidelberg (2004)
17. van Erp, J.B., van Veen, H.A., Jansen, C., Dobbins, T.: Waypoint navigation with a vibrotactile waist belt. ACM Trans. Appl. Percept. 2(2), 106–117 (2005)
18. Ferscha, A., Emsenhuber, B., Riener, A., Holzmann, C., Hechinger, M., Hochreiter, D., Franz, M., Zeidler, A., dos Santos Rocha, M., Klein, C.: Vibro-Tactile Space-Awareness. In: Adjunct Proceedings of the 10th International Conference on Ubiquitous Computing (Ubicomp 2008), Seoul, South Korea, September 2008, pp. 117–120 (2008), Video paper
19. Riener, A., Ferscha, A.: Raising awareness about space via vibro-tactile notifications. In: Roggen, D., Lombriser, C., Tröster, G., Kortuem, G., Havinga, P. (eds.) EuroSSC 2008. LNCS, vol. 5279, pp. 235–245. Springer, Heidelberg (2008)
20. Cholewiak, R.W., Brill, C.J., Schwab, A.: Vibrotactile localization on the abdomen: Effects of place and space. In: Perception and Psychophysics, vol. 66, pp. 970–987 (2004)
21. Krebs, K.M.: Illumination and division (2009), http://www.restingbell.net/releases/rb009-symmetries (last retrieved March 20, 2009)
22. Kosinski, R.J.: A Literature Review on Reaction Time. Clemson University, Department of Biological Sciences (September 2009), http://biology.clemson.edu/bpc/bp/Lab/110/reaction.htm (last retrieved January 15, 2009)
23. Dane, S., Erzurumluoglu, A.: Sex and handedness differences in eye-hand visual reaction times in handball players. International Journal of Neuroscience 113, 923–929 (2003)
24. Der, G., Deary, I.J.: Age and Sex Differences in Reaction Time in Adulthood: Results From the United Kingdom Health and Lifestyle Survey. Psychology and Aging 21(1), 62–73 (2006)
25. Surnina, O.E., Lebedeva, E.V.: Sex- and Age-Related Differences in the Time of Reaction to Moving Object in Children and Adults. Human Physiology 27(4), 436–440 (2001)

A Query Service for Raw Sensor Data*

Dónall McCann and Mark Roantree

Interoperable Systems Group,
Dublin City University,
Dublin, Ireland
{dmccann,mark}@computing.dcu.ie

Abstract. Sensor networks generate a compact form of data in order to efficiently use the available power of the device. Query engines require a richer form of this data in order that users can express meaningful and useful queries. This enrichment of the sensor stream leads to an inevitable increase in the volume of data transported across the network. If this data is enriched and stored in a database on the same server and used only for offline queries, matters such as enrichment time and increased data volumes can usually be managed quite efficiently. However, when there is a requirement to query sensor output in real time, the time required to enrich data and increased data volumes lead to slow query response times. In this research, we present the liveSensor system which offers the benefits of an enriched sensor stream, providing a high level query interface to the user. However, it delays the enrichment of sensor data until after query results have been generated and thus, maintains a high level of performance by processing raw sensor streams.

1 Introduction

Flexible or freeform queries over wired and wireless sensor networks are generally difficult to achieve due to the minimalist nature of sensor data. It generally requires some form of data enrichment (with semantics) to provide the query language with sufficient expression and variables to extract the required result. This assumes that data has been captured, harvested and enriched before storage inside a database management system. Querying live data streams presents a further set of problems due to the dynamic nature of streaming data. The basic characteristic of stream processing is that the data must be processed in a single pass and in the order in which it is received. Values may be temporarily stored in buffers but this becomes increasingly less practical as the size of the data stream increases, particularly due to the fact that the total size of the data stream may exceed the storage capacity of the machine performing the query processing.

The second problem is that sensors will generate data in a proprietary format, requiring constant redevelopment of systems that require new drivers and processors each time a new sensor is deployed. While the eXtensible Markup Language (XML) can provide a basic framework for interoperability and some

---

* Funded by Enterprise Ireland Grant No. CFTD/07/201.

P. Barnaghi et al. (Eds.): EuroSSC 2009, LNCS 5741, pp. 38–50, 2009.

of the additional services can be provided by efforts such as the Open Geospatial Consortium[12], this approach is not without issues, as we shall demonstrate in the following section.

The research carried out in this paper is part of a collaboration between a team of information management specialists and a group of sports scientists monitoring the performance of top class athletes. In a series of sports-based experiments, participants wear heart rate sensors that broadcast heart rates, timing based data and additional contextual data, with the requirement that specialists can monitor and adapt the behaviour of athletes according to the results of queries. Using a team-based system of Polar devices [13] and building a software layer to the base station, we have developed a proof of concept system to demonstrate the usability and range of queries that are possible. This type of sensor network is similar to the system described in [2] where wearable devices are used to stream data to a base station (RFID reader) before being presented, together with other contextual data, to the user or specialist through a dedicated interface. In our system, the contextual data describes both participants and the type of activity in which they are involved.

1.1 Motivation and Contribution

There are many advantages to storing sensor data in an XML format: a canonical model for representing sensor data, interoperability between disparate sensor devices, a combined format for representing both content and structure and the provision of standard querying capabilities. The OGC [12] have expanded on the usage of XML to provide a suite of services and workflow to track and detail sensor interaction and output. However, the XML format is not without its disadvantages. Converting a flat-text sensor stream into an XML format will have a significant impact on network transmission times and the performance of queries.

A good example of this is the system described in [1], where they present a method for enriching *raw* sensor data into an XML format and storing it in an XML database, from which it can be queried using XPath or XQuery. The resulting XML files were larger than the raw sensor files by a factor of six, on average. This increase in file size has significant effects on both storage requirements and query response times, especially as XML has an inherent problem with query performance [8].

Thus, while we favour the approach of XML enrichment in order to provide the user with the required semantics to express powerful queries, it is this enrichment process that will have a negative side effect on query performance. Our contribution in this paper is a system for querying raw sensor data streams using a standard XML query language.

Our solution combines the advantages of the XML format while avoiding the disadvantages of increased data volumes and reduced query performance caused by the enrichment process.

This is achieved by using XML *metadata* to describe the data stream and provide the user with an interface to accept XML queries. Queries are then transformed from XML to lower level primitives that execute on raw sensor streams. Our metadata-based approach ensures that the deployment of new sensors requires no changes to the system programs or processes: merely the addition of a new entry to the Metabase.

This paper is structured as follows: §2 describes the system architecture in terms of processors and the importance of metadata constructs; §3 provides a detailed case study demonstrating the operational workflow of the system; §4 describes the experimental setup used to evaluate our system and provides a discussion of the experimental results; §5 examines other approaches to similar problems and, finally, §6 concludes and describes future research.

2   Query Processing Architecture

In this section, we describe the system architecture necessary to query raw sensor data using an XML language interface. The system is comprised of a series of processors, each responsible for different aspects of query transformation and execution. In addition to the processors, there are a number of metadata constructs that provide extensibility and interoperability, allowing new sensors to be processed by the system.

2.1   Metadata Constructs

There are two categories of metadata constructs: persistent constructs that are stored in the system's Metabase and transient constructs that are created during query processing and deleted after the results are passed to the user. There are four persistent metadata constructs, all of which are XML documents:

1. **Templates.** Templates describe a sensor and provide information on how to parse the output generated by the sensor. Each sensor device type must have a corresponding Template so that the system can process and query its output. In turn, each Template file is associated with a single Schema construct as illustrated in figure 1. A Template contains mappings to the Schema, providing a means of converting raw sensor data and storing data in databases or generating query results. These mappings are implemented in two stages:

   (a) The Template file splits the sensor data stream into one or more *sections*. Each section is associated with a particular node or subtree of a Schema file and thus the sensor data stream can be mapped to a particular subtree of the Schema.

   (b) Within each section, the Template also specifies a number of unique *variables*. Each variable represents an XML element (such as an attribute or node text) that will contain sensor data. Each variable is associated with some information for processing the sensor data stream. This information will be used to build a parser for the sensor data stream and the resulting tokens from this parser are therefore mapped to a specific element within a subtree of the Schema.

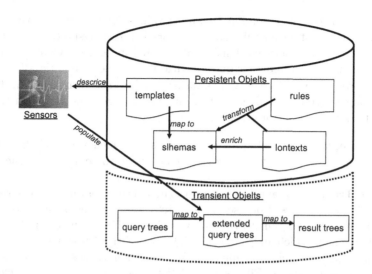

Fig. 1. Metadata Interaction

2. **Schemas.** The Schema construct provides both structure for storing sensor data and an interface for users to interact with and query sensor data.
3. **Contexts.** Sensors are generally deployed in a specific context (health and fitness monitoring, environmental monitoring, etc.) with a specific interaction between objects in the sensor network. Context information is used to provide additional semantics for transforming and querying the sensor data. It is used to enrich Schema objects to provide new knowledge or information that is stored in the sensor database. While the same Heart Rate monitor is interpreted by a single Template, it may be used in a number of different contexts: a laboratory, football or tennis match, training exercise, and may be worn by different genders or age groups. Each Context object is associated with the particular session during which the Heart Rate monitor generated data. For the live query processing described in this paper, the Context

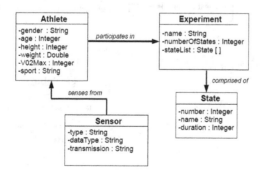

Fig. 2. The Bangsbo Context

can be used to plot or section streaming values. The sporting activity that provided the context for this sensor network is the Bangsbo test [7] with the main objects and their relationships illustrated in figure 2. Contextual data is optional but will allow for queries with much richer semantics.

4. **Rules.** Rules, together with `Contexts` are used to transform the data stream of a specified sensor. This is part of ongoing research and is currently only used to detect outlier or erroneous sensor data,

There are three transient metadata constructs, all of which are closely linked (see the case study in §3). Unlike the previous constructs, these are tree structures.

1. **Query Tree.** The `Query Tree` is used to model the user query. The structure of the `Query Tree` will be used to identify those sections of the sensor data stream that are relevant to the query. This is achieved in conjunction with the `Template`, which maps specific subtrees of the `Schema` (and therefore the user query which is formulated for the `Schema`) to specific sections of the sensor data stream. Filters in the XPath query which require an element to have a specific value, conform to a certain range, etc. are modelled as variables which are stored in the relevant nodes of the `Query Tree`.

2. **Extended Query Tree.** This tree is derived from the `Query Tree`. Two things happen when creating this tree: the first is that any wild cards in the XPath query are resolved and all possible paths are added to the `Extended Query Tree`; the second is that the root node of the result set is identified and all the nodes in its subtree are added to the `Extended Query Tree` from the

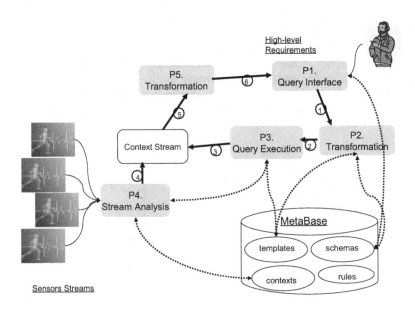

Fig. 3. Metadata Driven System Architecture

Schema. As these nodes are added, any associated mappings (`Template` based) are added as variables, to be populated with data during query execution.

3. **Result Tree.** The `Result Tree` will contain the final result set. As the `Extended Query Tree` is populated with data from the sensor data stream it is checked to see if the data satisfies the query. When a suitable subtree matches the query requirements, it is moved to the `Result Tree`. The final result is transformed (Processor P5) to the XML format expected by the user.

2.2 Query Processors

The system processors are the components that transform queries from the high level XPath language into low level primitives that manipulate the sensor data.

- **P1. Query Interface.** The role of the Query Interface is to retrieve the XML `Schema` from the Metabase and present it to the user. The `Schema` is used to express queries against the sensor data. This is not a major part of this research as it requires some means of transforming the natural language queries of non-IT users into XML languages XPath or XQuery. For the purpose of this paper, we assume that the user can express XML queries.
- **P2. Query Transformation.** The role of the Query Transformation processor is to convert an XML query into a set of Java-based primitives. The output from this processor is the `Query Tree` structure shown in figure 1. An example of a query tree in figure 4 is discussed in detail in the following section.
- **P3. Query Execution**
  The Query Execution Processor takes as input the `Query Tree` structure and creates the `Extended Query Tree`. It then populates this tree with values from the sensor data stream according to the mappings stored in the Template. Data that will not form part of the final result set is removed from the tree structure during query processing. Effectively, this means that there are two cursors operating on the Extended Query Tree: one pointing to the top of the *data stack*, and the second pointing to the top of the *verified data stack*. Depending on the query type or user interaction, the verified data stack is emptied into the `Result Tree` structure and passed to the next processor.
- **P5. Results Transformation.** This processor takes as input, the `Results Tree`, tranforms the data into an XML document that conforms with the Schema representation, and returns the query result to the user.
- **P4. Stream Analysis.** The Stream Analysis processor is optional. Where appropriate, it retrieves a `Context` from the Metabase and uses it to parse and section the sensor stream.

3 Heart Rate Sensor Case Study

In section 4, we will describe the results from a set of queries executed on the sensor streams. Before this, we use this section to describe the operational scenario using one of the queries from this set. In this query, the coach wants to

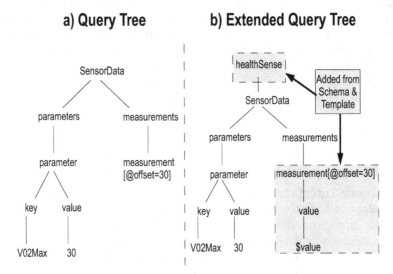

Fig. 4. Query Tree and Extended Query Tree

see if any of his players reaches their maximal heart rate during the opening 10 minutes (600 seconds) of activity. This maximal value is stored as VO2Max in Context data, while the time and heart rate values are part of the continuous data stream.

Example 1. Search for Maximal Heart Rate Figure
```
//sensorData[parameters/parameter[key=VO2max]/value[text()=202]]
/measurements/measurement[@offset=600000]
```

The Query Interface receives a query from the user requesting a subject's heart rate after 600 seconds of activity. The subject must also have a VO2Max value of 202. The XPath expression is shown in Example 1.

Once the query is received by this Transformation processor, it is converted into the Query Tree structure shown in figure 4a.

The Query Execution stage comprises two steps: generating the Extended Query Tree and processing the sensor stream. The Extended Query Tree is built by adding information from the Template and the Schema to the Query Tree. Wildcards are evaluated by analysing the Schema and adding all possible paths that could be used by the query. This can be seen in figure 4b by the addition of the healthSense node to the tree. Any other nodes that will be required to populate the Result Tree are then identified in the Schema and added to the tree. This results in the addition of measurement and value to the tree.

The Template is examined for mappings to any of the nodes in the Extended Query Tree. Mappings for the key, value and offset variables specified in the query are located. In addition, a mapping corresponding to the text of the value node is identified and the appropriate variable ($value) is added to the

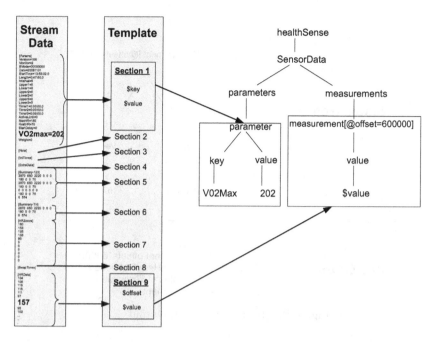

Fig. 5. Template Mapping Between the Data Stream and Extended Query Tree

tree. These mappings are then used to create a parser for the sensor data stream, which is now split into sections, each of which is associated with a specific subtree of the Schema. Figure 5 shows how the Template maps values to specific elements of the Extended Query Tree according to these sections.

For section 1, the corresponding subtree of the Extended Query Tree contains the requirements expressed in the query. The stream is processed until the token VO2Max=202 is evaluated as true against the query. Sections 2-8 are not relevant to this query and are ignored.

Section 9 values are evaluated against the offset query parameter. However, the offset variable is not part of the data stream and must be computed for each value according to the specifications of the Template. Further, section 9 has an uninstantiated variable added from the Template ($value) which represents an element that will be populated with data from the sensor stream.

The data stream continues to be processed until the offset matches the requirements of the query, as illustrated in figure 5. At this point, the $value variable is instantiated to 157 and, as all requirements are satisfied, the relvant nodes are moved to the Result Tree. At some point specified by the user or query, the Result Tree is transformed to XML and returned to the user. The XML output illustrated in figure 6 can be displayed as a table, graph or web interface, depending on the user's requirements. This is one of the major benefits of using a highly interoperable interface format such as XML.

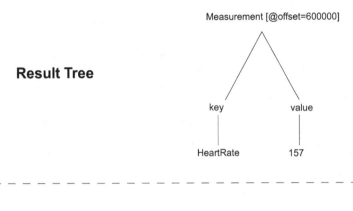

Result Tree

Measurement [@offset=600000]

key   value

HeartRate   157

- -

XML Output

```
<measurement offset="600000">
  <key>HeartRate</key>
  <value>157</value>
</measurement>
```

Fig. 6. Results Tree and XML Output

4 Experimental Evaluation

As part of our research programme, we developed a system using the components described in section 2 which we have called liveSensor as it operates on live streaming data. In order to evaluate the effectiveness of our approach, we compared our system with an existing query engine for XML streaming data. While our system has a working prototype with both XML query interface and a query execution module for the sensor stream, existing systems require sensor data to be converted to XML. Thus, two existing applications were used to build a comparable system. The HealthSense application [1] is used to convert any sensor stream to XML and YFilter [5] is used to run queries. YFilter is one of the leading XPath query engines. It optimises a number of user-specified queries for a specific data stream. It was chosen from the available streaming XPath engines as it provided a working implementation and was shown to have the greatest coverage of query types [11].

4.1 Experimental Setup

All experiments were performed on an Intel(R) Core(TM) 2 Duo CPU E6750 processor at 2.66GHz with 3.4 GB of RAM, running the Java Virtual Machine 1.6.0 on the Ubuntu 8.10 operating system. The sensor network is formed by a group of athletes wearing Polar Heart Rate monitors [13] while all athletes are subject to the Bangsbo test [7], which is described by the appropriate Context in the Metabase. In this test, athletes perform a series of tests without stopping and the test (and sensor network) will terminate when the last athlete drops out.

Our collaborators in Sports Science specified queries 1 to 5 for this experiment while query 6 is a system query to capture all data generated by the sensor network.

1. At what times did the user generate a heart value greater than 150?
   - `/healthSense/sensorData/measurements/measurement[reading/value[.>150]]/reading/value`
2. What was the heart rate value after 15 minutes of activity?
   - `/healthSense/sensorData/measurements/measurement[@offset=900000]/reading/value`
3. What is the subject's resting heart rate value?
   - `/healthSense/sensorData/parameters/parameter[key[text()="restHR"]]/value`
4. What is the heart rate value after 10 minutes for a user with a VO2max value of 202?
   - `/healthSense/sensorData[parameters/parameter[key=VO2max]/value[text()=202]]/measurements/measurement[@offset=600000]/reading/value`
5. Return all heart rate values.
   - `/healthSense/sensorData/measurements/measurement/reading/value`
6. Generate the entire sensor stream as a document.
   - `/healthSense`

4.2 Experimental Results

As can be seen from table 1, the liveSensor query engine outperforms the YFilter query engine in all cases except query 6. Query 4 was not supported by the XPath grammar specified in the YFilter User Manual [14] and the suggested solution (rewriting the query) was not applicable due to the complex nature of the query; therefore, no comparison was possible. Query 1 was similarly unsupported due to the use of the *comparator* operator, so a similar query using a different operator was used for purposes of comparison.

In addition to calculating the YFilter querying times, it was necessary to convert the raw sensor file into an XML format so that it might be queried first.

Table 1. Query Evaluation Results

Query	liveSensor (ms)	YFilter (ms)	YFilter+HealthSense(ms)	Result size
1	287	1474	4996	10.5Kb
2	193	1478	5000	20b
3	154	1417	4939	18b
4	211	N/A	N/A	19b
5	220	1621	5143	10.5Kb
6	7508	1436	4958	169.8Kb

This was performed using the HealthSense application, requiring a processing time of 3.5 seconds and adding considerably to the overall processing time.

In the case of both query engines, it can be seen that query execution time remains reasonably constant for the given queries, regardless of the complexity involved or the size of the returned data set. With the exception of query 6, liveSensor easily out-performed the well-regarded YFilter implementation.

In order to provide a 'worst case' scenario for our system, we devised Query 6 to return all data from the sensor stream. In effect, what this does is to convert the entire sensor stream (using Processor P4) into XML. The reason for the slower performance of liveSensor is that XML transformation was not part of our research focus and the larger the result set, the slower our performance. By examinining the internal times of each of the processors, we know that 7129ms is devoted to converting the result set into an XML format, while only 379ms was required to return the entire data stream. The relationship between the size of the result set and the length of processing appears to be linear: reducing the size of the XML output (by simplifying the schema) will result in a corresponding reduction in the processing time. This transformation algorithm is part of current research as we continue to optimise liveSense.

5   Related Work

An XML-based middleware for processing streaming sensor data is described in [9]. It uses an extended form of XQuery designed specifically for streaming data, known as XQueryStream. It is conceptually similar to liveSensor in that it uses templates for enriching the data stream and allows the user to specify the structure of the schema. However, their approach is closer to XML streaming appraoches such as [1] as queries are executed on XML sensor data. The novelty of liveSensor is that it queries raw sensor data using an XML query language.

The Sensor Web Enablement group is a working group of the Open Geospatial Consortium[12] and is responsible for specifying interoperable interfaces and metadata encodings for the integration of heterogenous sensor data. It has specified a number of standards for dealing with sensors and sensor data with support for new sensors added to OGC standards in a similar way to the liveSensor system - by specifying a number of metadata files. However, our system differs from the OGC approach in that the structure of the output schema in the liveSensor system may be freely specified by the user. The OGC standards were not used in this proof of concept as they have yet to achieve an adequate level of maturity, as noted in [3].

The efficient processing of continuous XML streams is addressed in [6]. This is achieved in part through the use of *punctuation* in the data stream. This punctuation is supplemented by a *tag structure* that is periodically transmitted alongside the sensor data stream. The template-schema mappings employed by the liveSensor system constitute a similar approach. Both systems have knowledge of the stream based on the contents of these files and this knowledge is used for more efficient querying. The difference in the two approaches is that our system stores the metadata in advance and thus avoids the extra overhead of periodically transmitting the tag structure and inserting punctuation into the stream.

In [10], they describe a system to recognise the daily activities of elderly people in their own homes. Similar to liveSensor, they provide a context for each experiment. In their case, they provide an ontology of daily events while we provide a framework and semantics for interpreting our sensor data. Their description of the contextual data is more exhaustive than we provide here and their experiments focus on the accuracy of their detection of specified events. However, they do not focus on the speed at which this information is delivered, nor on the flexibility of the types of queries that can be expressed. In our work, one of the aims is to measure how quickly we can determine results so as to adapt the behaviour of participants.

Another research project to focus on sensor networks in the sporting doamin is presented in [4]. They have a similar contextual platform to their experiment in that they treat a single sporting event as the basis for generating the sensor data. Furthermore, they use an ontology in the same way that we employ our Metabase, to model metadata constructs and store key contextual metadata. The difference in our approach is that we have a range of metadata constructs used not only to describe the context for the sensor network, but also to describe sensor outputs and query interfaces. They also have a similar set of experiments with comparable query response times, although they do not provide explicit information on the size of the output to queries.

6   Conclusions and Future Work

In this paper, we presented the liveSensor system, a prototype for querying sensor streams using a high level, XML-based user interface. The system comprises a set of processors that focus on each aspect of query processing and utilise metadata constructs to provide genericity and interoperability across sensor devices. By adopting a metadata approach to sensor management, we can add new sensors without modification to any of the systems processors. Furthermore, we can provide the user with both high level and standard query interfaces while the data remains in the format generated by the sensor device. This provides the dual benefit of flexible query expressions and a highly optimised query processor. A small set of experiments were used to demonstrate the functionality and effectiveness of liveSensor.

As we record the internal times of each liveSensor processor, we have identified one area for improvement in terms of processing speed. The final transformation processor converts the query results from a raw format to a high level format for user management. When result sizes are large, other research [1] demonstrates that we can obtain faster transfer times. This is one area of current research. Additional current research focuses on the further development of our query interface. The aim is to extend the XQuery language to facilitate the more domain specific queries required by the user groups that build the sensor networks.

References

1. Camous, F., McCann, D., Roantree, M.: Capturing Personal Health Data from Wearable Sensors. In: 2008 International Symposium on Applications and the Internet (SAINT), pp. 153–156. IEEE Computer Society, Los Alamitos (2008)
2. Cheng, J., et al.: A Wearable Conductive Textile Based User Interface for Hospital Ward Rounds Document Access. In: Roggen, D., Lombriser, C., Tröster, G., Kortuem, G., Havinga, P. (eds.) EuroSSC 2008. LNCS, vol. 5279, pp. 182–191. Springer, Heidelberg (2008)
3. Churcher, G., Bilchev, G., Foley, J., Gedge, R., Mizutani, T.: Experiences Applying Sensor Web Enablement to a Practical Telecare Application. In: 3rd International Symposium on Wireless Pervasive Computing (ISWPC), pp. 138–142 (2008)
4. Devlic, A., Koziuk, M., Horsman, W.: Synthesizing Context for a Sports Domain on a Mobile Device. In: Roggen, D., Lombriser, C., Tröster, G., Kortuem, G., Havinga, P. (eds.) EuroSSC 2008. LNCS, vol. 5279, pp. 206–219. Springer, Heidelberg (2008)
5. Diao, Y., Franklin, M.J.: High-Performance XML Filtering: An Overview of YFilter. Bulletin of the IEEE Computer Society Technical Committee on Data Engineering 26(1), 41–48 (2003)
6. Fegaras, L., Levine, D., Bose, S., Chaluvadi, V.: Query Processing of Streamed XML Data. In: 11th International Conference on Information and Knowledge Management (CIKM), pp. 126–133. ACM, New York (2002)
7. Impellizzeri, F.M., Marcora, S.M., Castagna, C., Reilly, T., Sassi, A., Iaia, F.M., Rampinini, E.: Physiological and Performance Effects of Generic Versus Specific Aerobic Training in Soccer Players. Int. J. Sports Medicine 27(6), 483–492 (2006)
8. Koch, C., Scherzinger, S.: Attribute Grammars for Scalable Query Processing on XML Streams. The VLDB Journal 16(3), 317–342 (2007)
9. Lee, H.S., Jin, S.I.: An Effective XML-Based Sensor Data Stream Processing Middleware for Ubiquitous Service. In: Gervasi, O., Gavrilova, M.L. (eds.) ICCSA 2007, Part III. LNCS, vol. 4707, pp. 844–857. Springer, Heidelberg (2007)
10. Naeem, U., Bigham, J., Wang, J.: Recognising Activities of Daily Life Using Hierarchical Plans. In: Kortuem, G., Finney, J., Lea, R., Sundramoorthy, V. (eds.) EuroSSC 2007. LNCS, vol. 4793, pp. 175–189. Springer, Heidelberg (2007)
11. O'Connor, M.F., Conroy, K., Roantree, M., Smeaton, A.F., Moyna, N.M.: Querying XML Data Streams from Wireless Sensor Networks: An Evaluation of Query Engines. In: Research Challenges in Information Science (RCIS 2009). IEEE, Los Alamitos (2009)
12. Open Geospatial Consortium (accessed May 2009),
http://www.opengeospatial.org/
13. Polar Electro (accessed May 2009),
http://www.polar.fi/
14. YFilter User Manual (accessed July 2009),
http://yfilter.cs.umass.edu/html/manual/YFilter_User_Manual.html

A Context Lifecycle for Web-Based Context Management Services

Gearoid Hynes, Vinny Reynolds, and Manfred Hauswirth

Digital Enterprise Research Institute,
National University of Ireland, Galway
firstname.lastname@deri.org

Abstract. During the development of context aware applications a context management component must traditionally be created. This task requires specialist context lifecycle management expertise and hence can be a significant deterrent to application development. It also removes the developers focus from differentiation of their application to an oft repeated development task. This issue can be addressed by encapsulating the context management lifecycle within a web-service, thus providing applications with a low-overhead alternative to managing their context data. The adoption of a web-based approach maximizes the potential number of interacting applications, including smart spaces, web and mobile applications, due to ease of access and widespread support of web technologies. The contribution of this paper is the development of a lifecycle, based on existing work on enterprise data and context aware lifecycles, which is optimized for web-based context management services (WCXMS) and the provision of a web-service implementation of the lifecycle.

Keywords: context data, lifecycle, webtechnologies, context management.

1 Introduction

Development of context-aware applications is no longer limited to the domain of ubiquitous computing, mobile and web-based context-aware applications are also being developed. Recently several location broker applications, including FireEagle by Yahoo![3] and Google Latitude [1], have been launched and their growing popularity illustrates the demand for real world location data within the virtual world. However, location alone is only a small portion of a user's context, the remainder of which has thus far been ignored. In order to provide truly context-aware applications we must move beyond serving location data alone by providing a service capable of managing multiple types of context in a time-sensitive manner. By providing *context as a service* (CXaaS) we can provide application developers with a foundation upon which they can build their context-aware applications. This enables developers to focus on their application functionality rather than the development of context management components.

The use of a web-based approach facilitates interaction with many different types of applications, including traditional context consumers such as smart-spaces

P. Barnaghi et al. (Eds.): EuroSSC 2009, LNCS 5741, pp. 51–65, 2009.

and the more recent consumers of context data such as web-applications and mobile applications. Additionally, the use of a centralized approach facilitates the sharing of context data between applications. This means applications can access context data from sources which they would not ordinarily have access to.

The realization of CXaaS requires as much of the context lifecycle as possible to be encapsulated within the web-service. In order for this to occur a formal model for the lifecycle of context data within a WCXMS must be developed. Current web-based location management services do not provide a reference lifecycle which can be extended to include other types of context data, therefore the lifecycle presented in this paper is based upon related lifecycle work from other domains, in particular enterprise data lifecycles and ubiquitous system context lifecycles. In this paper we will present a lifecycle for web-based context management services, we begin with the requirements on the lifecycle, followed by development of the lifecycle itself and how it was influenced by existing lifecycles. The paper continues by introducing ConServ, which is an implementation of the lifecycle, and then describing two applications which have been developed using ConServ. The paper finishes with some related work and conclusions.

2   Lifecycle Requirements

In order to provide CXaaS there are several requirements which the lifecycle must fulfill in addition to the *standard lifecycle requirements such as acquiring, storing and delivering the context data*. As outlined in the introduction, CxaaS has two primary goals, firstly *to enable the rapid development of context aware applications* and secondly *to facilitate the sharing of context data in a controlled manner between context applications*. Stemming from these two key requirements are some additional criteria without which the service would not succeed, of which the main ones are described below.

The development of a generic context lifecycle which would be applicable to all types of context data is not feasible, therefore, the lifecycle should be optimized for personal context data as it is the most common category of context data used by existing context aware applications. When dealing with personal context data privacy is crucial. Users must have complete control over who has access to what parts of their context data and at what level of granularity, at what time, from what location etc. Therefore, *expressive privacy policies are necessary to ensure the safety of users' context data.*

Context data can come from a variety of sources such as GPS sensors, accelerometers, calendars and online profile data. For some of this data it is appropriate for it to be pushed to the service and for other data types it is more appropriate for it to be pulled. As a result *it is necessary that the lifecycle account for context data being both pushed and pulled into the system.*

The lifecycle must allow for interaction with third parties, both in the acquisition and provision of context data. Additionally, *An expressive, extensible and commonly understood context data model is necessary* in order to ease importing/exporting of data from/to third parties. Extensibility allows developers to model any concepts which have not been previously modeled within the system.

3   Lifecycles

A substantial amount of related lifecycle work exists which can be leveraged in the development of the WCXMS lifecycle. This section analyses the related work, which is divided into two classifications of lifecycles:

- Enterprise Lifecycle Approaches: Lifecycles which are developed for enterprise applications but which do not explicitly target context data. These lifecycles are robust and well-established industry standard strategies for data management.
- Context Lifecycle Approaches: Lifecycles for managing context data, however they have not undergone the same level of testing as the enterprise approaches.

3.1   Enterprise Lifecycle Approaches

There are several well established data lifecycles approaches in use within enterprise which can influence the WCXMS lifecycle. Enterprise lifecycles are formulated to control the lifecycle of sensitive data in enterprise applications. In comparison to context data, the data stored within the enterprise applications is relatively static. For instance an enterprise application which stores users' contact details is not going to receive as many updates as a context aware application which stores users' location data. However, thanks to commercial support from some of the large software vendors, such as Oracle and Microsoft, enterprise lifecycle approaches are robust and well tested and for those reasons should be analysed to identify any potential relevance to the WCXMS lifecycle. Two of the more popular enterprise lifecycle approaches are Information Lifecycle Management (ILM) [17] and Enterprise Content Management (ECM) [4]. Both ILM and ECM consist of more than just the lifecycle, but also the tools, practices and methods which surround the lifecycle.

ILM is defined by the SNIA Information Lifecycle Management Initiative to consist of *"the policies, processes, practices, services and tools used to align the business value of information with the most appropriate and cost-effective infrastructure from the time information is created through its final disposition"* [17]. The five steps in the ILM are show on the left of Figure 1. ILM is primarily focused on data lifecycles which occur within the same organization; while data may initially be received from a third party, each of the ensuing steps occur within the same organization. As a result the lifecycle is not suitable for the WCXMS application where interaction with third parties is of great importance. However the steps following the data use are relevant as context data must also be maintained and disposed of.

ECM is said to be *"the strategies, methods and tools used to capture, manage, store, preserve, and deliver content and documents related to organizational processes"* [4]. The ECM lifecycle, seen in Figure 1, is not applicable to context data as it is overly focused on the steps prior to data dissemination, whereas ILM is more concerned with the steps after data distribution. The steps within

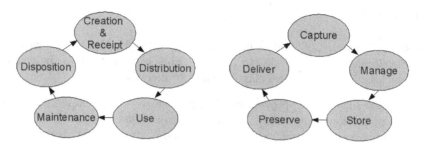

Fig. 1. ILM and ECM Lifecycles

the ECM strategy are prepossessed towards data storage with two entire steps, *Store* and *Preserve*, dedicated to it and a portion of the *Manage* step is also storage related.

Hayden[11] provides an extensive data lifecycle management strategy containing ten steps. Haydens steps, shown in Figure 2, are focused on a distributed enterprise setup which is subject to Federal data retention rules therefore not all of the steps, such as *Transmission & Transportation* and *Retention*, are applicable to a WCXMS. Hayden's lifecycle includes steps to mitigate the impact of users altering data in an unauthorized manner during the lifecycle (*Manipulation, Conversion/Alteration*) this is not an issue for a WCXMS as only the data owner can alter their data. Hayden strikes a balance between ICM and ECM by having a better distribution of steps before and after the *Release* of the data. A *Classification* stage was not present in the previous strategies and is of interest to the WCXMS lifecycle as classification of acquired context data is important due to the variety of context types and the importance of knowing the relationship between different pieces of context data.

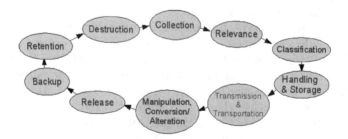

Fig. 2. Hayden's Data Lifecycle

3.2   Context Lifecycle Approaches

Different approaches have been taken to the area of context lifecycle management depending on the application requirements. Chantzara and Anagnostou [7] have identified four separate stages in the lifecycle, shown on the left of Figure 3, and the stages are distributed across three types of actors; *Context Providers*, a

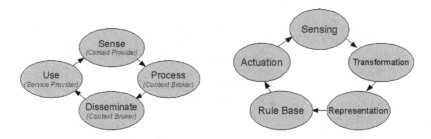

Fig. 3. Chantzara and Ferscha's Lifecycles

Context Broker and context aware *Service Providers*. This approach is of great relevance to the WCXMS lifecycle as the interacting actors in both systems are quite similar. However, the model is overly simplistic, only two stages are handled by the context broker, and would require further elaboration in order for its adoption within the WCXMS lifecycle.

Ferscha et. al. [9] provide details of their lifecycle for context information in wireless networks. They begin with the *Context Sensing* stage, which can be a time triggered or event triggered acquisition of low level context data, followed by the *Context Transformation* stage which involves the aggregation and interpretation of the sensed information, the next stage is *Context Representation*, whereby the transformed context is applied to an ontology to create high level contextual information, *Context Rules* are then applied to the semantic context data which then sends commands to the *Actuation* stage. This lifecycle has more stages than the previous one and it makes use of both ontologies and rules which makes it relevant to the WCXMS lifecycle. The functionality of the *Transformation, Representation* and *Rule Base* stages are of particular interest. Unfortunately there is no distinction between different actors within the lifecycle and therefore it is only applicable for adoption within a controlled environment. Additionally, after the *Actuation* stage the lifecycle restarts and as there are no stages for data storage or controlled disposal of the data, as a result the strategy is incomplete.

As part of the MOSQUITO project Wrona et. al. [21] developed a simple three stage context life cycle which was made up of *"Context Information Discovery"*, *"Context Information Acquisition"*, *"Context Information Reasoning"*. This scheme is incomplete as there is no mention of a stage which uses the context data or a stage which disposes of the data. But the *Context Information Acquisition* stage is applicable to the WCXMS lifecycle as it is more generic than the *Context Sensing* stages used by the other lifecycles and hence applies to pushing/pulling of context data from many different sources, not only sensors.

4   WCXMS Lifecycle

The WCXMS context lifecycle, shown in Figure 4, borrows aspects from many of the above strategies. The lifecyle has been separated between three actors

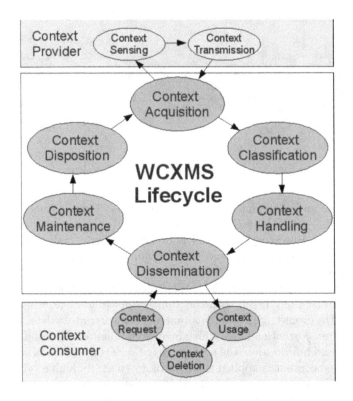

Fig. 4. The WCXMS Lifecycle

in a similar manner to Chantzara and Anagnostou. The *Context Provider* and *Context Consumer* are third party applications, for example, web-applications, smart-spaces, mobile applications which either provide and/or consume context data. The *Context Acquisition* stage, which is inspired by MOSQUITO, provides mechanisms for the pulling and pushing of context data. Two stages overlap with stages in Hayden's approach, *Classification*, which classifies the acquired data using a set of context ontologies, and *Handling*, which expands on the classified data to create associated data with different levels of granularity. Hayden's *Relevance* stage is also integrated into the *Classification* stage as the relevance of WCXMS context data is decided once it once it has been classified.

Context is disseminated in accordance with user defined privacy policies. Users have complete control over their data, i.e. who has access to that data, at what level of granularity and under what conditions. Therefore, once a Context Consumer makes a Context Request for a user's data the user's privacy policy is examined in order to establish what permissions they have been given for that data.The *Maintenance* and *Disposition* stages are borrowed from ILM. The result is a formal context management lifecycle optimized for deployment in a

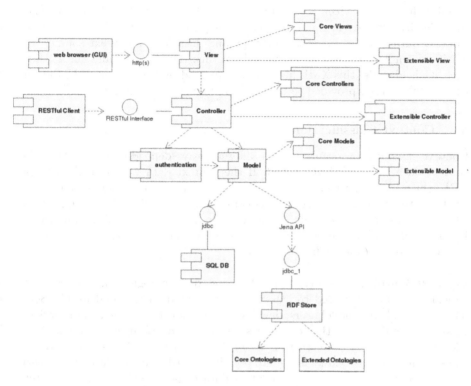

Fig. 5. ConServ Component Diagram

web-based environment. The remainder of this section provides details of a WCXMS lifecycle implementation called ConServ and describes the implementation details of each of the lifecycle steps.

ConServ Overview

ConServ is a REST [10] based web service developed using the model-view-controller (MVC) architectural pattern. ConServ has a core set of ontologies which are tightly coupled to the web-service implementation in order to provide a fast and reliable service for managing popular context data types. The ability to extend the types of context data managed is also provided. By allowing developers to upload additional ontologies to ConServ they can extend the core set of ontologies with any additional concepts which have not been modeled. The component diagram in Figure 5 shows the differentiation between the core and the extensible components, along with the MVC structure of the web-service.

4.1   Context Acquisition

As per the WCXMS lifecycle requirements ConServ can receive context data by pulling or by data sources pushing context data. The *Controller* component handles the *Context Acquisition* stage of the lifecycle. Pushed data can either be manually entered via the web-interface or pushed to the RESTful interface. Context data can also be acquired by pulling data from a context source. Acquiring calendar data is a good example of this; the user provides the URL of their iCalendar file, this XML file is then imported by ConServ and the data in the iCal file is then provided to the classification stage of the lifecycle.

4.2   Context Classification

Context classification occurs in two different ways depending on whether the context data was pulled or pushed. If the context data was pushed then the URL which it was pushed to is decoded into a class and a property for a particular ontology and then the data is converted into RDF before being passed to the *Context Handling* stage of the lifecycle. If the context data is pulled, it is converted to RDF if necessary, then the individual classes are separated and forwarded to the *Context Handling* stage.

Context Ontology Description. A set of core ontologies and related ontological extensions are used to classify the context data acquired by ConServ. The core ontologies model users, devices, policies, locations, events and services. Based on the definition that ontologies are *shared models of a domain that encode a view which is common to a set of different parties* [5] we have opted to use existing popular ontologies where possible in order to ease integration with ConServ and to leverage existing context data rather than create a completely new set of ontologies. The structure of the context ontology is illustrated in Figure 6 and an overview of the key classes is provided below.

Location: The GeoNames location ontology [19] and web service is used as the core of the ConServ location system. The GeoNames ontology is extended to provide a method of modeling buildings, floors, rooms and more. This extension is based on the MIBO [16] building ontology which has been adapted to interoperate with the GeoNames ontology which uses the SKOS [14] ontology.

Person: The FOAF ontology [6] is one of the most commonly used ontologies on the web and therefore was an obvious choice for modeling users within ConServ. FOAF provides many useful of properties for modeling such things as name, date of birth, email address, acquaintances, publications and group memberships to name but a few.

Events: Events are modeled by extending the icaltzd format [20]. Event data can either be imported from an iCal file or manually created using the RESTful interface or the web-interface.

Detection: The detection of a person results in the creation of a detection event. A detection event is associated with a time, location and device; the device is

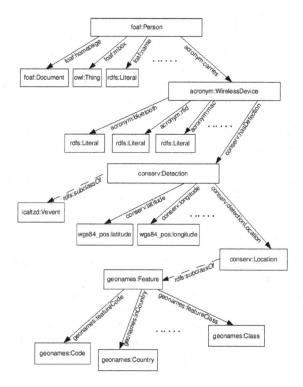

Fig. 6. Structure of the ConServ context ontology

in turn associated with a person. The time at which a detection occurs can be instantaneous or it can be over a period of time, for instance if a person is sitting at their desk for 2 hours, rather than create a new detection every time the person is detected a single detection event can be created with a 2 hour duration.

Devices: Due to the vast array of available personal mobile devices it is difficult to model each individual mobile device and their capabilities and keep the model updated. We have taken the approach of modeling mobile devices based on their connectivity options (Bluetooth, WiFi, RFID). The ACRONYM ontology [15] is used for modeling the devices and it has been extended with the *conserv#hasDetection* property in order to connect devices to detection events.

4.3 Context Handling

The primary function of the context handling step, which occurs in the *Model* component, is to facilitate ConServ's total forward-chained reasoning. ConServ materializes all appropriate location and event data in order to provide access to those concepts at different levels of granularity. Location has thirteen levels of granularity which directly map to levels used in both the GeoNames and MIBO ontologies.

For instance if ConServ is informed that a user, John Smith, is located in the DERI building it then materializes that John Smith is located in Lower Dangan, Galway City, Galway County and Ireland. This allows John Smith to specify at which level he wishes particular context consumers to access his location data. The context granularities are modeled using the SKOS Ontology [14] with the granularities being defined within a *skos#OrderedCollection* which contains a *skos#Concept* for each level of granularity for a particular context type.

There are 3 levels of granularity in event context data. These levels are directly related to the access levels given in online calendar applications. Level 0 does not allow any access to the calendar data, Level 1 allows services to see when the user is either free or busy but it does not provide any details about the events in questions, the final level provides all the available details about the events.

4.4   Context Dissemination

The dissemination of context data to the context consumer is controlled by user defined access policies. The ConServ Policy Ontology, shown in Figure 7, is inspired by the SOUPA Policy Ontology [8] which is in turn based on the Rei policy ontology[12]. Each user has one policy and this policy contains two types of objects, *conserv#AccessRule* and *conserv#AccessRequest*.

Instantiations of *conserv#AccessRequest* are created by services and are used to request access to a particular type of context data. These requests can then

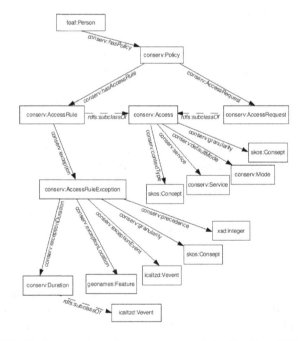

Fig. 7. An overview of the structure of the ConServ Policy

be approved or deleted by the user if they do not wish to allow any access. If the request is approved it is converted into a *conserv#AccessRule* where the user can apply conditions, modeled as *conserv#AccessRuleException*, to when the service can access the data. The *conserv#AccessRuleException* class has a granularity property which sets the granularity at which the context data in question will be accessible to the requesting service.

4.5   Context Maintenance

The context maintenance stage consists of archiving all context data which is more than one month old at the end of each month. This archived data is still accessible to context consumers, however queries on this data are not as fast as the non-archived data which have priority. It is envisaged that a feedback mechanism may also be included within the context maintenance stage in order for the user to provide accuracy ratings for portions of the managed context data.

4.6   Context Disposition

Context disposition is entirely handled by the user. Within ConServ the user is viewed as the owner of all context data which concerns them, therefore they alone have the ability to delete context data. At the moment this is handled via the web-interface, whereby the user selects individual or groups of context data and manually deletes them. In future the users will be able to create rules which would allow for the automatic disposal of their context data according to certain conditions such as time elapsed, location, context source.

5   Proof of Concept

To illustrate how ConServ supports the management of context data throughout the context lifecycle we developed two independent applications; DERI Bluetooth Location System (DBLS) is a *Context Provider* which pushes location data to ConServ and Colleague Finder is a *Context Consumer* which uses the location data provided by DBLS. These two applications illustrate some of the lifecycle requirements implemented within ConServ, in particular the sharing of context data between applications, the enabling of rapid context aware application development, the ability to interact with third parties and the use of privacy policies to protect the user's context data. The evaluation of the remaining lifecycle requirements will be dealt as part of the future work.

The DBLS infrastructure consists of a bluetooth based location scanner deployed in each floor of each wing of the DERI building, as illustrated in Figure 8. The bluetooth scanners are bluetooth enabled Linksys NSLU2s running a modified version of Debian. DBLS monitors the movement of personal bluetooth devices in the DERI building and informs ConServ of any updates. This system enables the locating of a person carrying a bluetooth enabled device to a room within the DERI Building.

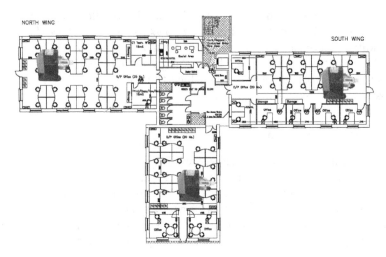

Fig. 8. Linksys NSLU2 Deployment on a Floor of the DERI Building

Fig. 9. User Mark Jones searches for a colleague using "Colleague Finder"

Colleague Finder is a Ruby on Rails web application which allows users to locate a colleague within the DERI building. In the screenshot shown in Figure 9 the user, John Smith, has registered an account with Colleague Finder and added the ConServ URI of his colleague, Mark Jones, to his list of friends. Provided Mark Jones has given Colleague Finder permission to access his location data then John Smith can use Colleague Finder to locate Mark Jones within the DERI building. When Colleague Finder requests location data, ConServ first checks Mark Jones' policy to see what level of granularity was specified for Colleague

Finder. The granularity details are appended to the query, the query is executed and any results are then returned to Colleague Finder. Colleague Finder simply issues a HTTP GET request to ConServ in order to retrieve the context data and the results are returned in XML. Only the HTTP GET request is required to make Colleague Finder context aware as ConServ manages the context lifecycle functionality. At the end of the following month the location data is archived as part of the *Context Maintenance* step and at anytime Mark can *dispose* of his location data within ConServ.

6 Related Work

Recently there have been several efforts to provide web-based context management with the focus primarily being on location data, some examples are FireEagle, Google Latitude, IYOUIT [2] and the applications associated with the OSLO Alliance (Open Sharing of Location Objects) [18]. We will discuss FireEagle due to its early entry into the field, Google Latitude because of its potentially large user base and IYOUIT as a result of its focus on other types of context data rather than just location. Unfortunately none of the three services provide a formal lifecycle which we can directly compare with the WCXMS lifecycle, therefore they will be compared based on the lifecycle requirements outlined at the beginning of this paper.

FireEagle is a location broker which enables users to share information about their location with applications or services in a controlled manner. FireEagle's functionality is limited due to its sole focus on user location data and hence does not fulfill the *extensibility requirement*. It also does not have the ability to *pull location data from third party sources*. However it does provide a strong reference point against which new solutions must be compared and its popularity proves that users have a demand for location aware applications and that users are prepared to provide their location data to web services.

Google Latitude is another example of a location broker which, due to its inclusion in Google's Mobile Maps application, has a large potential user-base. A basic API is provided which allows developers access to a JSON or XML feed containing details of a user's location. Unfortunately, it also suffers from the *extensibility* and *context acquisition* deficiencies of FireEagle and its *privacy policies* are extremely limited as users can only specify full public access or no access at all to their location data.

IYOUIT, developed from the ContextWatcher project [13], is comprised of a mobile phone application which captures as much context data as possible, both automatically and manually, and a web-based context broker which aggregates the data. IYOUIT supports a far greater number of context types than FireEagle and Google Latitude and it represents a significant step towards the creation of a comprehensive personal context data repository. However, IYOUIT currently does not provide access to a developer API, therefore it is not possible to build applications using their data and as a result there is no *interaction with third parties*. An ontology is used to model the context data, however as this ontology had not been made available IYOUIT cannot be said to provide a *commonly understood data model* and thus is not available for reuse or *extension*.

7 Conclusions and Future Work

In this paper we have presented a lifecycle for web-based context management services (WCXMS) and provided details of an example implementation of that lifecycle called ConServ. A set of requirements for a WCXMS were outlined and existing lifecycles were analyzed to establish their applicability, based on this the WCXMS lifecycle was developed. The details of each stage in the lifecycle were then described by giving details of how they were implemented in ConServ.

The purpose of a WCXMS is to encapsulate the context management lifecycle within a web-service which developers can access. This facilitates the rapid prototyping of context-aware applications by removing the necessity for developers to create a context management component for their applications. By providing Context as a Service (CXaaS), WCXMS allows applications access to context data from a wide variety of sources by enabling the sharing of context data between applications. This allows context-aware applications to move beyond the current situation whereby each application is an island of information with little or no interconnecting bridges.

WCXMS lifecycle implementations, such as ConServ, have the potential to increase the number of context-aware applications available to users while still providing the user with authority over their context data. There is a fine balance which must be maintained between supporting the rapid development of context-aware applications and persevering user privacy. It is our belief that the WCXMS lifecycle maintains this balance through the use of, amongst other things, RESTful interfaces and an extensible context models to aid development and the use of detailed privacy policies and providing complete data control from a user's perspective.

At present ConServ's implementation of some of the lifecycle requirements has not been demonstrated and the development of these proof of concept applications is a key part of the future work. The addition of event-driven functionality is also a priority as at present applications must query ConServ frequently to check for new data. Finally the scalability of the web-service must be evaluated.

Acknowledgment

The work presented in this paper has been co-funded by Science Foundation Ireland under Grant No. SFI/08/CE/I1380 (Lion-2) and by the European FP7 project PECES (ICT-224342).

References

1. Google latitude, http://www.google.com/latitude/
2. Iyouit, http://www.iyouit.eu/

3. Yahoo! fireeagle, `http://fireeagle.yahoo.net/`
4. AIIM. What is ecm?
   `http://www.aiim.org/What-is-ECM-Enterprise-Content-Management.aspx`
5. Bouquet, P., Giunchiglia, F., van Harmelen, F., Serafini, L., Stuckenschmidt, H.: Contextualizing ontologies. Web Semantics: Science, Services and Agents on the World Wide Web 10, 325–343 (2004)
6. Brickley, D., Miller, L.: Foaf vocabulary specification,
   `http://xmlns.com/foaf/spec/`
7. Chantzara, M., Anagnostou, M.: Evaluation and selection of context information. In: Second International Workshop on Modeling and Retrieval of Context, Edinburgh (July 2005)
8. Chen, H., Finin, T., Joshi, A. (eds.): The SOUPA Ontology for Pervasive Computing, July 2005. Whitestein Series in Software Agent Technologies. Springer, Heidelberg (2005)
9. Ferscha, A., Vogl, S., Beer, W.: Context sensing, aggregation, representation and exploitation in wireless networks. In: Scalable Computing: Practice and Experience (2005)
10. Fielding, R.T., Taylor, R.N.: Principled design of the modern web architecture. ACM Trans. Internet Technol. 2(2), 115–150 (2002)
11. Hayden, E.: Data lifecycle management model shows risks and integrated data flow. Information Security Magazine (July 2008)
12. Kagal, L., Paoucci, M., Srinivasan, N., Denker, G., Finin, T., Sycara, K.: Authorization and Privacy for Semantic Web Services. IEEE Intelligent Systems (Special Issue on Semantic Web Services) 19(4), 50–56 (2004)
13. Koolwaaij, J., Tarlano, A., Luther, M., Nurmi, P., Mrohs, B., Battestini, A., Vaidya, R.: Context watcher: Sharing context information in everyday life. In: Proceedings of the IASTED conference on Web Technologies, Applications and Services (WTAS), pp. 12–21 (2006)
14. Miles, A., Matthews, B., Wilson, M., Brickley, D.: Skos core: simple knowledge organisation for the web. In: DCMI 2005: Proceedings of the 2005 international conference on Dublin Core and metadata applications. Dublin Core Metadata Initiative, pp. 1–9 (2005)
15. Monaghan, F., O'Sullivan, D.: Leveraging ontologies, context and social networks to automate photo annotation. In: Falcidieno, B., Spagnuolo, M., Avrithis, Y., Kompatsiaris, I., Buitelaar, P. (eds.) SAMT 2007. LNCS, vol. 4816, pp. 252–255. Springer, Heidelberg (2007)
16. Niu, W.T., Kay, J.: Location conflict resolution with an ontology. In: Indulska, J., Patterson, D.J., Rodden, T., Ott, M. (eds.) PERVASIVE 2008. LNCS, vol. 5013, pp. 162–179. Springer, Heidelberg (2008)
17. Peterson, M., St. Pierre, E.: Snias vision for ilm. In: Computerworld: Storage Networking World (2004)
18. Siegler, M.: Oslo alliance wants to share location across networks (February 2009), `http://www.webcitation.org/5i7Kqzj6d`
19. Vatant, B.: Geonames ontology, `http://www.geonames.org/ontology/`
20. W3C. ical schema, `http://www.w3.org/2002/12/cal/icaltzd`
21. Wrona, K., Gomez, L.: Context-aware security and secure context-awareness in ubiquitous computing environments. In: XXI Autumn Meeting of Polish Information Processing Society (2005)

Semantic Annotation and Reasoning for Sensor Data

Wang Wei[1] and Payam Barnaghi[2]

[1] School of Computer Science, University of Nottingham (Malaysia Campus)
Jalan Broga, 43500, Semenyih, Selangor Darul Ehsan, Malaysia
eyx6ww@nottingham.edu.my
[2] Centre for Communication Systems Research, University of Surrey
Guildford, Surrey, GU2 7XH, United Kingdom
p.barnaghi@surrey.ac.uk

Abstract. Developments in (wireless) sensor and actuator networks and the capabilities to manufacture low cost and energy efficient networked embedded devices have lead to considerable interest in adding real world sense to the Internet and the Web. Recent work has raised the idea towards combining the Internet of Things (i.e. real world resources) with semantic Web technologies to design future service and applications for the Web. In this paper we focus on the current developments and discussions on designing Semantic Sensor Web, particularly, we advocate the idea of semantic annotation with the existing authoritative data published on the semantic Web. Through illustrative examples, we demonstrate how rule-based reasoning can be performed over the sensor observation and measurement data and linked data to derive additional or approximate knowledge. Furthermore, we discuss the association between sensor data, the semantic Web, and the social Web which enable construction of context-aware applications and services, and contribute to construction of a networked knowledge framework.

Keywords: Sensor data modelling, Semantic annotation, Linked data, Reasoning, Semantic Web.

1 Introduction

The Internet and the Web are now the most influential communication medium through the world. With the infrastructure of the current Web, most of the information exchange is related to human-created and logical data such as text, image, audio, and video. The current Internet has been less concerned on providing a global solution to sense the physical world incidents, which could facilitate more natural and unobtrusive human-machine interaction. To this end, this vision is closely related to the grand aim of Mark Weiser's "Ubiquitous Computing" [1] which stated that "the most profound technologies are those that disappear, they weave themselves into the fabric of everyday life until they are indistinguishable from it", as well as the recent proposal of "Internet of Things" [2].

P. Barnaghi et al. (Eds.): EuroSSC 2009, LNCS 5741, pp. 66–76, 2009.

Recent developments in sensor technology has made manufacturing low-cost while energy-efficient hardware for sensing devices possible. It in turn leads to a potential interest in adding real world sense to the Internet and various applications and services on the Web. Deployment of (wireless) sensor and actuator networks makes it possible to observe and measure physical phenomena and the obtained information can be further processed to be used in different services and applications.

Universal access to sensor observation and measurement data provides a platform for a wide range of applications in different domains such as geographical information systems, health care, and smart homes. Over the past few years, considerable research effort has been devoted into developing large scale sensor networks such as SENSEI project[1] and SensorWeb[2], and also designing industrial standards for sensor data description such as the Sensor Model Language (SensorML) proposed by the Open Geospatial Consortium (OGC)[3], the Sensor Web Enablement (SWE) activity [3]. The forms of sensor data representation are mostly based on XML data, which has significant limitations in supporting semantic interoperability and linking the described resources to the existing knowledge.

To realise the vision of ambient intelligence, i.e. creating a global (wireless) sensor network and service environment, data collected from heterogeneous wireless sensor and actuator networks have to be integrated and made available to different services and applications. The observation has recently encouraged development of sensor and actuator data representation using semantic Web [4] technologies, for example, the Semantic Sensor Web [5], OntoSensor [6], the SensorData Ontology proposed in [7], and other research works on creating service layers such as [8,9].

In this paper, we continue the discussion on adding semantic Web technologies into the sensor network research. Given the fact that sensor and actuator data representation models using semantic Web technologies have been relatively well developed, we particularly focus on issues related to semantic annotation using domain ontologies based on the "linked data" principle[4]. We discuss associations between the emerging data from sensor networks, the semantic Web and Social Web [10], and describe how semantic reasoning can be further exploited to help discover new knowledge from the annotated sensor data. This will support developments of low-level (i.e. sensor observation, discovery, and retrieval) and high-level services (i.e. service planning and recommendation) which enable construction of a networked knowledge platform [11].

2   Semantic Modelling of Sensor Data

Providing universal descriptions and high-level interfaces for sensor and actuator data significantly ease the tasks for application developers without forcing

---

[1] http://www.ict-sensei.org/
[2] http://research.microsoft.com/en-us/projects/senseweb/
[3] http://www.opengeospatial.org/standards/sensorml/
[4] http://www.w3.org/DesignIssues/LinkedData.html

them to be involved in complex issues related to heterogeneity of the underlying technologies in different platforms. Research in the semantic Web community in the past decade has developed well established standards, i.e. formal knowledge representation framework (i.e. RDF[5], RDFS[6], and OWL[7]) and ontologies. These standard representations are an ideal choice for modelling various sensor data (sensor node and interface descriptions, and also observation and measurement data collected from sensors) at different levels to support interoperability. More importantly, enriched descriptions can be easily integrated with sensor data in forms of semantic annotation, and logical reasoning can be performed over the sensor data to support advanced query and retrieval tasks.

There have been a number of works focusing on the development of representation models for sensor data using ontologies [6,9]. OntoSensor [6] constructs an ontology-based descriptive specification model for sensors by excerpting parts of SensorML descriptions and extending the IEEE Suggested Upper Merged Ontology (SUMO)[8]. However, it does not provide a descriptive model for observation and measurement data. The work presented in [9] proposes an ontology-based model for service oriented sensor data and networks, but how to represent and interpret complex sensor data is not specified. Eid *et al.* [8] propose a universal ontology which includes three sub-ontologies, i.e. extension plug-in ontology, sensor data ontology, and sensor hierarchy ontology. Similarly, the model does not provide details of sensor data specification and relationships between complex sensor data. The SensorData Ontology developed in [7] is built based on "Observations & Measurements" and SensorML specifications defined by the Sensor Web Enablement (SWE) [3].

Sheth *et al* take the research one step further and bring forward the concept of "Semantic Sensor Web" [5]. The idea behind is that with the semantic representation of the sensor observation and measurement model, one could add semantic annotations in terms of time, location, and thematic data into the actual sensor data to facilitate advanced query and reasoning. Collectively, these annotations represent the context data collected from the spatial, temporal, and thematic dimensions. Some application scenarios with reasoning over the semantically annotated sensor data with rules are described in [5,12]. The sensor data is annotated with concepts from the OWL-time domain ontology [12], as such, videos can be retrieved by using (semantic) temporal concepts such as "within", "contains", and "overlaps" when querying with an interval of time. The Semantic Sensor Web also promotes the creation of the so-called "event Web" [13], and supports travelling the semantic Web through space, time, and theme [14].

In the following we focus on the idea of Semantic Sensor Web by extending the discussion of semantic annotation using concepts taken from various domain ontologies. In particular, we propose using "linked data" principle to connect the sensor data to existing knowledge represented in different ontologies. We

---

[5] http://www.w3.org/RDF/

[6] http://www.w3.org/TR/rdf-schema/

[7] http://www.w3.org/TR/owl-features/

[8] http://www.ontologyportal.org/

demonstrate the idea with examples in which semantic reasoning over the sensor data and the existing "linked data" can be performed to deduce new knowledge. Although the sensor data is intended to be primarily utilised by machines, sensor node descriptions and the metadata about the observations and measurement and surrounding environment will be potentially valuable for sensors discovery and their trustworthiness evaluation. With the "collective intelligence", (wireless) sensor and actuator networks can also be linked to the "Social Web" [10], harmonising the Web of data and facilitating creation of real world applications on top of the "Internet of Things" [2].

3   Annotation of Sensor Data Using Linked Data

Utilising metadata and semantic annotations to describe sensor/actuator and in general real world and logical world resources (i.e. "things") in a scalable and heterogeneous platform will enable different communities to exploit the emerging data and exchange information and knowledge in a collaborative environment. Semantic annotations, no matter inferred from the sensor data or provided by users, represent the context data which can be utilised to create context-aware applications.

Previous works in computer science have discussed the representation and modelling of context. Schmidt *et al* emphasises the importance of roles of users in representing context information [15]. They define context as information of users (e.g. knowledge of habits, emotional state, bio-physiological conditions), user's social environment (e.g. co-location of others, social interaction, group dynamics), and user's tasks (e.g. spontaneous activity, engaged tasks, general goals). In service oriented computing context-awareness can refer to including functionalities that make services more dynamic, i.e. to be able to adapt and respond to environment and situation changes [16]. On the other hand, context can be also defined as attributes related to situation of a resource related to physical environment such as location (e.g. absolute position, relative position, co-location), infrastructure (e.g. surrounding resources for computation, communication, task performance), and physical conditions (e.g. noise, light, pressure). An example is Sheth *et al*'s work on Semantic Sensor Web in which the context is modelled as spatial, temporal, and thematic data [5]. In their work, sensor data is annotated with concepts of time, location, and also other domain ontologies. However, the source of these domain ontologies are not specified and the relationship between the Semantic Sensor Web and the existing knowledge is not discussed in detail.

We envision semantic annotations with the linked data principle which is capable of connecting the emerging data from (wireless) sensor and actuator networks to the existing semantic Web. The idea behind the linked data is that the value and usefulness of data increases as it is interlinked with large amount of other data. On one hand, the connection enables qualitative annotations to promote interoperability, avoiding creating repetitive data. Data already published on the semantic Web and widely used by communities can be reused for the sensor data annotation purpose. When annotating sensor observation and

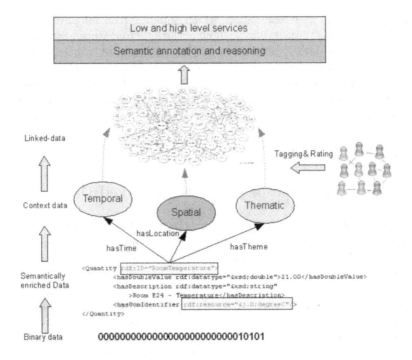

Fig. 1. Integrating sensor data with the semantic Web and linked data

measurement data, or inferred concepts (i.e. a "phenomenon" in Semantic Sensor Web [5]), instead of creating new concepts or instances, one could annotate the sensor data with those concepts on the semantic Web by creating RDF links, i.e. data published by authoritative sources using the linked data principle such as DBpedia[9]. On the other hand, making connections to the linked data also binds the sensor data to potentially endless data or knowledge (provided by authoritative sources). It enables reasoning over the sensor data and the linked data to provide advanced sensor data query and retrieval functions. Figure 1 demonstrates the proposed framework for integrating the sensor network with the semantic Web (and possibly the social Web).

Through the semantic annotation, the real world resources and sensor data can be connected to the existing semantic Web. This associates abundant data and knowledge to the original and inferred sensor data, improving the ways that sensor data is utilised; e.g. the data can be exploited to design enhanced services through the use of reasoning and rules (see Section 4).

4   Reasoning Sensor Data with Context Data

Logical reasoning is a powerful mechanism to derive new and implicit knowledge from semantically annotated sensor data, and to answer complex user queries.

---

[9] http://dbpedia.org/

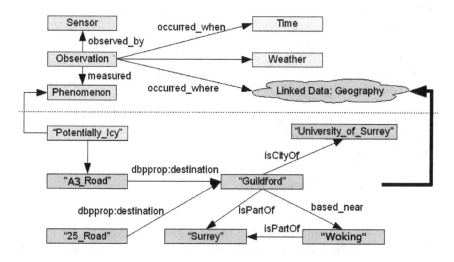

Fig. 2. Associations between sensor data and high-level concepts

The work in Semantic Sensor Web demonstrates some examples (e.g. "Potentially Icy") of using rule-based reasoning to deduce new ontological assertions from known instances [5]. In one of Sheth *et al*'s example, sensor data is first annotated with temporal data extracted from video with respect to a Time domain ontology. Then they present how videos can be retrieved by using semantic temporal concepts such as "within", "contains", and "overlaps". Here we provide an example as an extension to these examples and show how the semantic annotation with the linked data contribute to answering sensor data queries. In particular, we annotate the observation and measurement data by linking it to geographic data published by DBpedia.

As shown in Figure 2, suppose that a number of sensors installed at "A3_Road" provide information on temperature and precipitation, and using rule-based reasoning one infers that the road condition is "Potentially Icy" which is an instance of the class "Phenomenon" defined in the Semantic Sensor Web ontology. The phenomenon is then linked to an instance called "A3_Road" published by the DBpedia through the property "occurred_where". In DBpedia, the instance "A3_Road" is related to many of the other objects, such as it has a destination of "Guildford", which is instance of "City" located in the "Area" of "Surrey" and based near to another instance called "Woking". The linked data enables advanced queries over sensor data, for example, a user might issue a query for all the roads with the condition "Potentially Icy" located in the area of "Surrey". Using the following query one is able to obtain desired results (the query is represented in SPARQL[10] form):

---

[10] http://www.w3.org/TR/rdf-sparql-query/

PREFIX rdf: <http://www.w3.org/1999/02/22-rdf-syntax-ns#>
PREFIX rdfs: <http://www.w3.org/2000/01/rdf-schema#>
PREFIX dc <http://purl.org/dc/terms/>
PREFIX dbpprop: <http://dbpedia.org/property/>
PREFIX dbpedia-owl: <http://dbpedia.org/ontology/>
SELECT ?road
WHERE {
   ?road rdf:type dbpedia-owl:Road.
   ?road dbpprop:destinations ?city.
   ?city rdf:type dbpedia-owl:City.
   ?city dc:isPartOf dbpedia:Surrey.
   ?road ssw:described Potentially_Icy.
}

Without the domain ontology or the linked data it is impossible for applications to answer this kind of queries automatically. Semantic annotation with the linked data reuses the existing information on the semantic Web and eliminates the needs of creating repetitive and redundant data. Making connections from the real world resources to the existing semantic Web ontologies also naturally promotes the idea of traversal of the semantic Web through the dimensions of time, space, and theme [14].

Rule-based reasoning plays important role in sensor data processing as it is one of the most promising means of deriving new and implicit knowledge. Sheth *et al* show that using rules complex queries (e.g. road conditions that are "Potentially Icy" or "blizzard") over simple weather readings can be executed. Rule-based reasoning is also effective to deal with missing data or uncertainty. In some situations, precise answers might not exist due to incomplete information or unavailability of data. However, it is meaningful to provide approximate or indirect answers in responding to user queries. Let's reconsider the previous example as shown in Figure 2: assume that a user is searching the weather condition in "Woking", however, due to the unavailability of sensor observation the query cannot be answered directly. With a domain ontology, e.g. data published in DBpedia, we know that "Guildford" is a town based near to "Woking" area and their distance is less than 20 KM. Moreover, the weather condition in Guildford has been observed, e.g. temperature is 25 degrees Fahrenheit. Using the following rule one could obtain an approximate temperature range for "Woking".

Rule: Approximate Temperature:
   Temperature(?temp_high_Woking)&
   Temperature(?temp_low_Woking)&
   Temperature(?temp_NearCity)&
   City(?city)&
   hasTemperature(?city, ?temp_NearCity)&
   temp_Value(?temp_NearCity, ?temp_NearCity_Value)&

City(Woking)&
hasTemperature("Woking", ?temp_high_Woking)&
hasTemperature("Woking", ?temp_low_Woking)&
basedNear(?city, "Woking")&
distance_Value(?dist, ?dist_Value)&
lessThanOrEqual(?dist_Value, 20)&
sourceArea(?dist, ?city)&
destinationArea(?dist, Woking)&
—>temp_Value(?temp_high_Woking, ?temp_NearCity_Value + 2)
or temp_Value(?temp_low_Woking, ?temp_NearCity_Value - 2)

In the rule, *distance_Value* is a function for calculating the distance between a source area and destination area. The function could be realised using Web services: it takes two cities or coordinates of the cities and returns the geographical distance. Providing approximate answers to queries, especially for service composition in which intermediary results are essential is more desirable when in typical scenarios it return failure or terminates the service execution prematurely.

5   Connecting Real World Resources, Semantic Web, and Social Web

One of the primary visions of providing enriched data for sensor data is to create an infrastructure for networked knowledge [11] that is aware of physical world incidents and enables construction of new services that remove the boundary between the logical and physical world. Today, (wireless) sensor and actuator networks deployed in numerous locations are able to produce multitude of observation and measurements, from simple phenomena to complex events and situations [5]. Semantic Web technologies are ideal choice to represent, manage, store, analyse, and reason over the observed sensor data, enhancing interoperability among heterogeneous networks to build Semantic Sensor Web, and to bring usefulness of the sensor data to its full potential.

We also envision the potential contribution of the social Web [10] to the Internet of Things. Social Web sites such as blogs and wikis allow their users to generate annotations effortlessly through a process of social tagging. The same techniques can be employed in the sensor networks to exploit the "collaborative intelligence". Tags and folksonomies contributed by numerous online users can be valuable information to annotate sensor data and associate them to high-level concepts. In the future, quality and trustworthiness of the sensor data will also have direct impact on real world services that make use of them, for example, user-generated tags and quality ratings can be important factors for evaluation of sensor data.

The main issue in this respect is how to orchestrate annotation process and ontology associations to link the resources to high-level concepts and existing knowledge. Another aspect is using rich-descriptions with automated ontology construction methods to associate the tags to high-level concepts. The annotation of the resources with domain knowledge represented in ontologies facilitates drawing logical reasoning based on the data. This will result in a framework which can "learn" to discover relations between the data and high-level concepts and can "gather" knowledge to perform "adaptable" decision making in dynamic environments. In a recent work, we concentrated on creating ontologies from text using probabilistic methods [17]. In the ongoing work, we also investigate similar approaches to enable (semi-) automated link association to support providing metadata and linked data for the resources on the Internet of Things.

6   Real World Services

The ultimate goal of the Internet of Things is to integrate the physical world into the digital world to support more natural human-computer interaction and to build more intelligent application and services. Real world services utilising sensor data can be generally categorised into two groups: low-level sensor data services (e.g. those provide data integration and semantic reasoning), and high-level services (e.g. context-aware applications, planning, and recommendation).

Typically, low-level services integrate various information from different resources and provide intermediary results or inputs to high-level services and applications (e.g. decision-support systems, planning, and recommendation services). The examples presented earlier in this paper belong to the scope of this service category. In particular, we extend the previous work on Semantic Sensor Web and demonstrate how sensor data can be annotated and enriched using concepts in the spatial, temporal, and thematic dimensions with linked data; i.e. data already exists on the semantic Web. Through rule-based reasoning and using semantically annotated sensor data, additional knowledge and meaningful context data can be derived and used by other applications and services.

High-level services seamlessly integrate the digital world and physical world happenings to create context-aware applications and to support various decision making processes. With the situational knowledge which represented by various sensor data and information gathered from outputs of low-level services, high-level services are able to perceive environment change and autonomously adapt to the new situation. Moreover, they enable personalisation and customisation of contents and services for both human (e.g. planning trips and service recommendation) and machines (e.g. implementation of innovative business applications and semantic Web service composition).

7   Conclusion

Integration of the physical world and the digital world has a wide range of applications such as monitoring, manufacturing, health, tracking and planning. This vision brings forward the issues related to sensor data representation, annotation, sharing, management, and reasoning. Utilising semantic Web technologies, metadata and enriched metadata in particular, to describe sensor data, and more generally real world and logical world resources in heterogeneous platforms enables different communities to exchange information and knowledge in a collaborative environment. More importantly, it facilitates development of context-aware applications to support effective human-machine and machine-machine interaction, moving forward to the grand aims of ubiquitous computing and the Internet of Future.

In this paper we report some preliminary results of an ongoing research on sensor data annotation using the linked data and automated sensor observation using rule-based reasoning. Examples are provided to demonstrate the feasibility of using reasoning mechanisms to infer additional knowledge from semantically annotated sensor data, even in situations with incomplete information. We also discuss the relationships between resources in the Internet of Things, the semantic Web, and the social Web which are usually seen as separated entities. By annotating sensor observation and measurement data using concepts already published on the semantic Web, and user-generated contents such as tags and ratings we envision a fully connected Internet of Things in the future and the great potential to create real world context-aware applications and services. The underlying services will contribute to collect, represent, process, and reason real world and logical world data in a networked knowledge framework.

References

1. Weiser, M.: The computer for the 21st century. Scientific American 265(3), 66–75 (1991)
2. Union, I.C.: The internet of things, iTU Internet Reports, Executive Summary (2005)
3. Botts, M., Percivall, G., Reed, C., Davidson, J.: Sensor web enablement: Overview and high level architecture, pp. 175–190 (2008)
4. Berners-Lee, T., Hendler, J., Lassila, O.: The semantic web. Scientific American 284(5) (2001)
5. Sheth, A.P., Henson, C., Sahoo, S.S.: Semantic sensor web. IEEE Internet Computing 12(4), 78–83 (2008)
6. Russomanno, D.J., Kothari, C., Thomas, O.: Sensor ontologies: from shallow to deep models. In: Proceedings of the Thirty-Seventh southeastern Symposium on System Theory, SSST 2005, Los Alamitos, CA, USA, pp. 107–112 (2005)
7. Barnaghi, P.M., Meissner, S., Presser, M., Moessner, K.: Sense and sens'ability: Semantic data modelling for sensor networks. In: Proceedings of the ICT Mobile Summit 2009 (June 2009) (to appear)
8. Eid, M., Liscano, R., El Saddik, A.: A universal ontology for sensor networks data. In: Proceedings of the IEEE International Conference on Computational Intelligence for Measurement Systems and Applications, CIMSA 2007, pp. 59–62. IEEE Computer Society, Los Alamitos (2007)
9. Kim, J.-H., Kwon, H., Kim, D.-H., Kwak, H.-Y., Lee, S.-J.: Building a service-oriented ontology for wireless sensor networks. In: Proceedings of the Seventh IEEE/ACIS International Conference on Computer and Information Science, ICIS 2008, Los Alamitos, CA, USA, pp. 649–654 (2008)
10. Gruber, T.: Collective knowledge systems: Where the social web meets the semantic web. Web Semantics: Science, Services and Agents on the World Wide Web 6(1), 4–13 (2008)

11. Decker, S., Hauswirth, M.: Enabling networked knowledge. In: Klusch, M., Pěchouček, M., Polleres, A. (eds.) CIA 2008. LNCS (LNAI), vol. 5180, pp. 1–15. Springer, Heidelberg (2008)
12. Henson, C., Sheth, A., Jain, P., Rapoch, T.: Video on the semantic sensor web. In: W3C Video on the Web Workshop (2007)
13. Jain, R.: EventWeb: developing a human-centered computing system. Computer 41(2), 42–50 (2008)
14. Sheth, A., Perry, M.: Traveling the semantic web through space, time, and theme. IEEE Internet Computing 12(2), 81–86 (2008)
15. Schmidt, A., Beigl, M., Gellersen, H.-W.: There is more to context than location. Computers & Graphics 23(6), 893–901 (1999)
16. Vuković, M.: Context aware service composition. UCAM-CL-TR-700, University of Cambridge, Computer Laboratory, Tech. Rep. (October 2007)
17. Wang, W., Barnaghi, P.M., Bargiela, A.: Probabilistic topic models for learning terminological ontologies. IEEE Transactions on Knowledge and Data Engineering (to appear, 2009)

Semantic Rules for Context-Aware Geographical Information Retrieval

Carsten Keßler[1], Martin Raubal[2], and Christoph Wosniok[1]

[1] Institute for Geoinformatics, University of Münster, Germany
{carsten.kessler,c.wosniok}@uni-muenster.de
[2] Department of Geography, University of California, Santa Barbara, USA
raubal@geog.ucsb.edu

Abstract. Geographical information retrieval (GIR) can benefit from context information to adapt the results to a user's current situation and personal preferences. In this respect, *semantics-based* GIR is especially challenging because context information – such as collected from sensors – is often provided through numeric values, which need to be mapped to ontological representations based on nominal symbols. The Web Ontology Language (OWL) lacks mathematical processing capabilities that require free variables, so that even basic comparisons and distance calculations are not possible. Therefore, the context information cannot be interpreted with respect to the task and the current user's preferences. In this paper, we introduce an approach based on *semantic rules* that adds these processing capabilities to OWL ontologies. The task of recommending personalized surf spots based on user location and preferences serves as a case study to evaluate the capabilities of semantic rules for context-aware geographical information retrieval. We demonstrate how the Semantic Web Rule Language (SWRL) can be utilized to model user preferences and how execution of the rules successfully retrieves surf spots that match these preferences. While SWRL itself enables free variables, mathematical functions are added via built-ins – external libraries that are dynamically loaded during rule execution. Utilizing the same mechanism, we demonstrate how SWRL built-ins can query the Semantic Sensor Web to enable the consideration of real-time measurements and thus make geographical information retrieval truly context-aware.

1 Introduction

Information retrieval methods play a crucial role when it comes to organizing and finding relevant information in large collections, potentially spread over thousands of Web servers. This applies also to *geographical* information retrieval (GIR), where innovative approaches are required to turn the vast amount of geo-tagged content and volunteered geographic information [1] into useful information sources. Recent research in information retrieval extends classical methods by employing context information to disambiguate queries [2] and to tailor the results to a user's preferences and her current situation [3].

P. Barnaghi et al. (Eds.): EuroSSC 2009, LNCS 5741, pp. 77–92, 2009.

GIR generally deals with indexing unstructured data sources such as Web pages for detection and disambiguation of place names, document ranking based on relevance with respect to a given query, as well as developmentof user interfaces [4]. Retrieval from the Semantic Web, however, makes use of structured information, i.e., ontologies or resources annotated by means of these ontologies [5]. This structured information is mostly based on nominal symbols encoded in the Web Ontology Language (OWL) [6]. OWL and its theoretic underpinnings in description logics (DL) provide the reasoning capabilities that enable the Semantic Web in the first place. However, they also pose a special challenge for encoding spatio-temporal information, which relies largely on numeric data collected from different kinds of sensors (e.g. for temperature or air pollution) and localized via different positioning techniques such as GPS.

In terms of measurement scales [7], ontologies are built from *nominal* entities and the relationships between them. Context information collected from sensors, in contrast, consists of *ordinal* (e.g. severe weather categories), *interval* (e.g. temperature in centigrades) and *ratio* (e.g. absolute humidity) scaled data. We propose to utilize *semantic rules* for the mapping between these two worlds as well as for the interpretation of the raw values with respect to the current user's preferences. This approach follows the distinction between task model, user model and context model[1] [8]. The Semantic Web Rule Language (SWRL) employed in this paper extends OWL with the first-order logic style rules required for user modelling. Moreover, it provides mathematic functions via *built-ins* – external libraries that are dynamically loaded during rule execution. We demonstrate how this mechanism can be utilized to query sensors on the Web directly from SWRL rules. This allows for a strict separation between static information stored in the ontology and dynamic, frequently changing context information. Moreover, rules can directly access the measured information, so that it is no longer required to manually update the information on individuals in the ontology.

In this paper, we use the task of finding suitable surf spots as a scenario, which is a prime example of a GIR task that cannot be satisfactorily solved without taking context information into account. Whether a spot is appropriate for a specific user depends not only on the user's current location (i.e., her distance to the spot), but also on the current wave and weather conditions, accessibility, crowdedness, and so forth. All of these factors must be regarded with respect to the skill level and personal preferences of the user posing the query: a suitable wave height for one person may be boring for another one, and conditions suitable for experienced surfers may even be dangerous for beginners. While the development of a user interface is out of scope for this research, we have selected four contextual aspects (location, wave height, bottom and crowdedness) that influence a user's decision during the selection of a surf spot. We have developed a prototypical surf spot ontology populated with samples at the central coast in California for demonstration purposes. The insights from this research are not

---

[1] We use the term *model* in the sense of modelling information, not in the strict model-theoretic sense.

specific to the task of selecting suitable surf spots, but can be easily transferred to other highly context-dependent tasks ranking from leisure activities [9] to critical professional applications [10].

The next section introduces related work on ontologies and context. Section 3 outlines the case study, the specific requirements it imposes, as well as the surf spot ontology. Section 4 presents und discusses our rule-based approach for context modelling. Section 5 demonstrates how a novel SWRL built-in can be utilized to process live sensor measurements during rule execution, followed by conclusions and directions for future work in Section 6.

2   Background: Ontologies and Context

This section points to related work in the areas of ontologies for the Semantic Web and context from the perspective of geographical information retrieval.

2.1   Ontologies for the Semantic Web

Research on semantics investigates the meaning of symbols in communication. While views on semantics differ depending on the field of study, information systems research is mostly concerned with the question of how the meaning of pieces of information and ways to interact with them can be described unambiguously. Ontologies as explicit specifications of conceptualizations [11] provide such descriptions by formally constraining the potential interpretations of the symbols used for communication about concepts.

Three kinds of ontologies can be distinguished. *Foundational ontologies* such as DOLCE [12] are "axiomatic theories of domain-independent top-level notions such as object, attribute, event, parthood, dependence, and spatio-temporal connection" [13, p. 91]. While foundational ontologies provide generic specifications on an abstract level, *domain ontologies* specify the shared conceptualization of a specific community, such as the AGROVOC Ontology currently under development by the Food and Agriculture Organization of the United Nations[2] or various ontologies within geographic information science [5,14,15] which is the focus of this research. *Application ontologies*, such as the surf spot ontology introduced in Section 3.3, are the most specific ones, as they specify the conceptualizations that underlie specific applications. In an ideal case, these three groups of ontologies are used in a layered fashion and *semantic interoperability* between all parts of this ontological hierarchy is enabled.

As engineering artifacts, ontologies only become useful through standardized formats. The Web Ontology Language (OWL) is a W3C specification for publishing and sharing XML-encoded ontologies. The OWL DL sublanguage[3] maps to the $\mathcal{SHOIN}$ description logic (DL). A detailed discussion of DL is beyond the scope of this paper – see [16,17] for detailed information on its semantics. The only aspect that needs to be kept in mind here is that the formal semantics underlying $\mathcal{SHOIN}$ maps to set theory.

---

[2] http://www.fao.org/aims/agrovoccs.jsp
[3] OWL comprises the three sublanguages OWL Lite, OWL DL and OWL Full.

2.2   Context in Information Retrieval

From the numerous definitions of context [18], we subscribe to the one by Dey [19, p. 5], who defines context as "any information that can be used to characterise the situation of an entity". This view on context matches both the motivation for this research as well as our case study from geographical information retrieval. Research activities on context-aware information retrieval have increased remarkably in recent years. The ubiquitous and pervasive computing communities have developed numerous approaches to automatically provide users with information and services based on their current situation – see [20] for an overview. Existing context-aware applications range from smart spaces [21] over mobile tour guides [22] to generic prototyping platforms [23]. Gu et al. [24] propose to use an OWL ontology to model the different aspects forming a context. Lawrence [25] provides an overview of the different strategies to make Web search context-aware.

The Semantic Web community has investigated different approaches towards semantic models of context and contextualizing ontologies. CTXML [26] is an XML dialect that enables local, contextualized models within ontologies. It specifies an XML-encoding for contexts as concept hierarchies that can be assigned information on the owner, the groups the context is specified for, and on security and history. Mappings between different contexts based on distributed description logics [27] allow for the identification of different specifications that refer to the same concepts. CTXML eventually merged into C-OWL [28], which is an extension to OWL that enables contextual ontologies via bridge rules that map between the local ontologies. C-OWL thus adds the capability to handle potentially inconsistent knowledge. Korpipää and Mäntyjärvi [29] propose an ontology for contexts based on RDF. It is based on context types (e.g. Environment:Light:Intensity) that can be filled with values (e.g. *Dark*). However, they do not describe how the mapping from the raw sensor data onto the context values (*Dark* in the above example) works.

The use of SWRL for reasoning about context has already been proposed within the A-MUSE project [30]. However, the utilization of SWRL within the project was limited to reasoning about context information in the ontology. For example, SWRL was used to find out whether a person is currently attending a meeting in a certain room based on the property values of the individuals in the knowledge base. We extend this approach by using SWRL to *represent* context (instead of only reasoning about it) and by querying context information directly from a novel SWRL built-in.

3   Case Study: The Surf Spot Finder

This section introduces the case study used in the remainder of this paper. The specific requirements of an application for surf spot recommendation are analyzed and the geographic feature type ontology is sketched.

3.1 Scenario

Choosing a surf spot depends on weather conditions, tide, waves, personal abilities, location and social aspects. All of these characteristics, including their parts, must be rated differently for every surfer. Answering the question "How are the waves?" involves wave height, speed and frequency, but is also strongly tied to the location, type of sea bed and beach accessibility. Although some Web sites provide relevant information for surfers on wave[4] or weather[5] conditions, such information must be rated differently depending on the respective user's personal surfing skills. For example, for an experienced surfer the conditions may be rather rough and in contrast to conditions suitable for a beginner. This leads to the conclusion that there is no generic answer to the question "Where is my optimal surf spot at a given time?". In addition, social aspects play an important role. While a surfer may want to meet a friend to practice, most surfers prefer spots that are not too crowded.

In the remainder of this paper, we will use the scenario of an online surf spot finder service that provides users with surf spot recommendations based on the current conditions and their personal profiles. While the technical aspects of this tool are out of scope for this paper, we investigate the requirements for a representation of contextual factors relevant to this task. As such, the surf spot finder is a prime example of context-aware geographical information retrieval. The insights gained in this study can be transferred to a number of outdoor leisure activities such as hiking, diving and climbing [9], but also to critical applications that depend on the current conditions and skills of the people involved, such as emergency response services [10].

3.2 Requirements

We have selected four contextual aspects to illustrate the modeling challenges with respect to context-aware GIR. The selection also reflects the temporal, spatial and thematic components that characterize geographic information [31]:

1. The *Location* of the surf spot influences the choice depending on the maximum distance the surfer is willing to travel.
2. The current *Wave height* plays an important role with respect to the surfer's skills. This dynamic aspect must be measured by sensors at regular intervals (e.g. those of the Coastal Data Information Program[6]).
3. The *Bottom* points to potential dangers: sandy bottoms are safer for beginners, whereas rocky bottoms can be dangerous, but may be acceptable for experienced surfers.
4. The current *Crowdedness* is a social aspect influencing the decision process, as surfers mostly prefer less crowded spots. Although this aspect is inherently dynamic, real-time measurement seems impractical; we thus model crowdedness distinguishing between weekdays and weekends.

---

[4] http://magicseaweed.com or http://www.wannasurf.com
[5] http://www.windguru.com
[6] http://gcmd.nasa.gov/records/GCMD_SIO_CCS_CDIP_CALSWELLMODEL.html

While these aspects will be covered in the surf spot ontology introduced in the next section, the user models will be specified through SWRL rules as discussed in Section 4. For demonstration purposes, we define two different users with different preferences concerning the four properties of the surf spots described above. In the following, u_{beg} will refer to a user model corresponding to a typical beginner, whereas u_{pro} will refer to the model of an experienced or professional surfer. Table 1 provides an overview of the two user models. We assume that both users are located in downtown Santa Barbara (lat:34.41213°, lon:−119.68913°).

Table 1. Overview of the user preferences to be formalized in Section 4. For reasons of simplicity, the distance to the user's location is expressed in decimal degrees; a representation in km (road network distance) would be required for end users.

	Location	WaveHeight	Bottom	Crowdedness
User u_{beg}	$\leq 0.5°$ away	$< 1.5\text{m}$	Sandy	No preference
User u_{pro}	$\leq 1.5°$ away	$> 2.5\text{m}$	No preference	Low

3.3   Surf Spot Ontology

We have developed a surf spot ontology[7] for this research using the Protégé[8] ontology editor. The ontology consists of a number of concepts such as Surfing (subconcept of Activity), WaveFrequency and RideLength in addition to the four properties of specific surf spots listed in Section 3.2. Figure 1 gives an overview of the concepts specified in the ontology.

4   Representing Context

This section introduces the rule-based mapping approach and presents an implementation of the user models for the surf spot finder case study in SWRL.

4.1   Rule-Based Mapping Approach

Context information only becomes meaningful when it is interpreted with respect to the user. It depends on the user's personal preferences whether a shop has interesting offers, a blog article is worth reading or a surf spot is adequate with respect to the user's expectations and abilities. However, ontologies on the Semantic Web lack support for free variables that are required to express such dependency on the user profile. It is not possible to specify that a user finds surf spots with rocky bottoms too dangerous, or that another one finds waves below 2m unattractive. We propose to utilize the Semantic Web Rule Language

---

[7] Available from `http://ifgi.uni-muenster.de/~lette/resources/surfing.zip`
[8] Protégé is free and open source software; see `http://protege.stanford.edu`

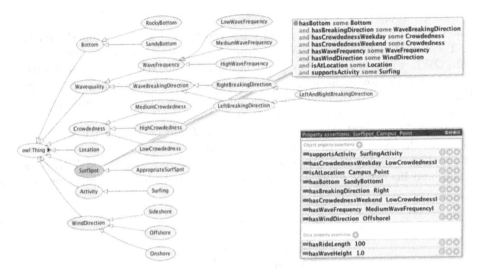

Fig. 1. The graph shows the concept hierarchy of the surf spot ontology. The box on top shows the properties of the central SurfSpot concept. The box at the bottom shows the properties of the SurfSpot individual *SurfSpot_Campus_Point*.

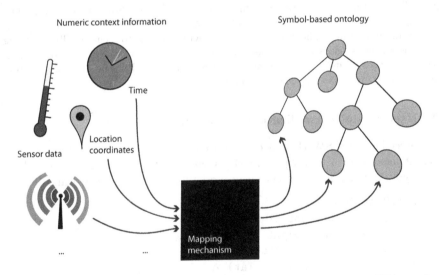

Fig. 2. Context-aware geographical information retrieval on the Semantic Web requires a mapping from the context model (left) to the static ontological information (right)

(SWRL) for personalized mappings between the numeric sensor world and information stored in ontologies, as shown in Figure 2.

SWRL [32] adds rule capabilities to OWL ontologies. SWRL rules are Horn-like clauses [33], consisting of an antecedent (body) and a consequent (head), each containing a set of atoms. For example, the rule hasParent(?x,?y) ∧ hasBrother(?y,?z) → hasUncle(?x,?z)

states that if x has the parent y and y has the brother z, then x has the uncle z. The SWRL submission to W3C introduces a concrete XML syntax for use with OWL, which is achieved by combination with RuleML[9] statements. SWRL can be extended by additional reasoning mechanisms via built-ins. Among the built-ins that have been implemented so far are libraries for mathematics, string handling and date support, enabling rules such as

Person(?p) ∧ hasAge(?p,?a) ∧ swrlb:lessThan(?a,18) → Minor(?p).

Built-ins thus play a central role for the mapping from numeric sensor inputs to ontologies via SWRL. The following section demonstrates how SWRL rules using built-ins can be utilized to represent a user model as shown in Figure 3.

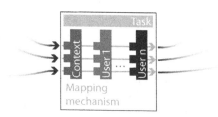

Fig. 3. The contents of the mapping mechanism black box shown in Figure 2: The mapping consists of task model (green, not further specified here), context model (red) and user models (blue). The context model provides access to dynamically changing information from sensors as described in Section 5, which is then fed into the user models. The user models, each consisting of a SWRL rule, filter the incoming context information according to the users' preferences.

4.2   User Model Formalization in SWRL

The antecedent of a SWRL rule can be used to represent a conjunction of the different aspects of a user's preferences. Consider the following SWRL rule in prefix syntax, which is a complete user model for u_{beg} as described in Table 1:

```
01    SurfSpot(?spot) ∧
02    hasWaveHeight(?spot, ?height) ∧
03    swrlb:lessThan(?height, 1.5) ∧
04    isAtLocation(?spot, ?location) ∧
05    hasLatitude(?location, ?lat) ∧
06    hasLongitude(?location, ?lon) ∧
07    swrlb:subtract(?distLat, ?lat, 34.412132) ∧
08    swrlb:subtract(?distLon, ?lon, -119.68913) ∧
09    swrlb:abs(?distLatAbs, ?distLat) ∧
10    swrlb:abs(?distLonAbs, ?distLon) ∧
11    swrlb:lessThanOrEqual(?distLatAbs, 0.5) ∧
12    swrlb:lessThanOrEqual(?distLonAbs, 0.5) ∧
```

---

[9] http://www.ruleml.org/

```
13    hasBottom(?spot, ?bottom) ∧
14    SandyBottom(?bottom)
15    → AppropriateSurfSpot(?spot)
```

The first line constrains the individuals to whom this rule is applied to the ones of the class SurfSpot and assigns the variable name ?spot to them. Lines 2–3 constrain the matching individuals to those that have a wave height smaller than 1.5m. Lines 5–12 take care of the distance calculation of the spots to the user. After assigning variable names to the latitude and longitude of a spot (5–6), the absolute distance to the user's current location is calculated (7–10) to evaluate whether the spot is not further away than the user is willing to travel[10] (11–12). The user preference for surf spots with sandy bottoms is expressed in lines 13–14. Finally, those surf spots satisfying lines 2–14 are reclassified as AppropriateSurfSpot (see Figure 1). Instead of this reclassification, one could also imagine using query built-ins that count the number of spots matching the conditions. The user model for u_{pro} has been defined accordingly:

```
01    SurfSpot(?spot) ∧
02    hasWaveHeight(?spot, ?height) ∧
03    swrlb:greaterThan(?height, 2.5) ∧
04    isAtLocation(?spot, ?location) ∧
05    hasLatitude(?location, ?lat) ∧
06    hasLongitude(?location, ?lon) ∧
07    swrlb:subtract(?distLat, ?lat, 34.412132) ∧
08    swrlb:subtract(?distLon, ?lon, -119.68913) ∧
09    swrlb:abs(?distLatAbs, ?distLat) ∧
10    swrlb:abs(?distLonAbs, ?distLon) ∧
11    swrlb:lessThanOrEqual(?distLatAbs, 1.5) ∧
12    swrlb:lessThanOrEqual(?distLonAbs, 1.5) ∧
13    hasCrowdednessWeekend(?spot, ?crowdedness) ∧
14    LowCrowdedness(?crowdedness)
15    → AppropriateSurfSpot(?spot)
```

This rule implicitly contains temporal information on the weekday in line 13, which could also be integrated automatically via SWRL's date and time built-ins. Either of the two user models can be activated by selecting the corresponding rule. Activation of both rules would find all spots that suit both users. This feature could be used to accommodate the needs of user groups. The SWRL-tab available in the Protégé ontology editor provides a user-friendly way of developing, editing and testing[11] SWRL rules along with the corresponding OWL ontology [34].

---

[10] For a lack of space, distance is calculated separately for latitude and longitude. However, the calculation in Euclidian (or any other) metric is also possible in SWRL.

[11] Using the jess rule engine, see http://www.jessrules.com/

4.3   Discussion

After applying the two rules for the respective user context models, the Jess rule engine correctly reclassified the matching surf spots. For each user, only one of the 15 individuals of the surf spot class satisfied all given requirements. In the following, we discuss the advantages of a rule-based approach and specifically SWRL with its built-in mechanism over other Semantic Web technologies.

As mentioned before, widespread Semantic Web technologies lack support for free variables as required for the representation of a threefold model consisting of task, user and context as shown in Figure 3. This applies both to RDF/OWL (including C-OWL) as well as to alternative approaches such as the ISO Topic Map standard [35]. Although the languages have not been developed to support such functionality initially, these restrictions place constraints on their applicability to real-world problems. Their underlying realist view on semantics [36] ignores the fact that a large number of applications in information retrieval, linguistics or location-based services, for example, can only produce useful results if they take the user's current context into account. Even the context extension to OWL, C-OWL, is limited to fixed contexts (i.e., local micro theories) and mappings between them. It thus cannot live up to the requirements of the notion of *dynamic context awareness* [37] from AI, which heavily relies on sensor input. The same applies to Topic Maps, which allow users to define *scopes* specifying in which context assertions are valid [38]. Scopes form a mechanism that is very useful when stating assertions such as the topic name *München* is only valid in the scope of the German language or the topic name *Jaguar* appears in different scopes (animal, car, operating system). However, same as for C-OWL, scopes neither support rules nor free variables. Overall, these limitations result in the rare use of semantic technologies in context-aware software in AI, which is still largely based on statistics-driven approaches.

As demonstrated above, SWRL helps to overcome these limitations by specifying user models as rules that contextualize OWL ontologies in terms of these models. Moreover, modelling in OWL and SWRL requires a thoughtful separation between the notions modeled in OWL and those modeled in SWRL, forcing clean ontological specifications. For example, consider the data property assertions shown in the bottom right box of Figure 1: any of these could also be modeled as object property assertions. This would require, for example, to define a concept *RideLength* through subconcepts such as *RideLengthMax50m*, *RideLengthMax100m*, and so forth. While this approach appears feasible at first sight, it would render mathematical processing of the actual values impossible, such as checking whether the waves are too high (or too low) for the current user. Hence, our approach forces a clean ontology design based on the distinction between the static information stored in the ontology, and the dynamic aspects which go into the rules. This separation may even become more important when decidability plays a role: since the integration of SWRL renders OWL undecidable [39], it may be desirable to retain the static part of the ontology for reasoning purposes. Nonetheless, context information about individual surf spots is still hard-coded into the ontology. We address this problem in the following section by establishing a link to real sensors.

5 Linking Rules to Real-World Sensors

We have demonstrated how SWRL rules can be employed as user models. Dynamic values, however, still have to be updated manually for an ontology's individuals. In this section, we sketch an approach to this problem that enables querying of sensors from within SWRL rules.

5.1 The SWRL Built-in Bridge

The SWRLTab in Protégé provides a built-in bridge[12], which enables the development of new built-ins, such as for reasoning (temporal, spatial, etc.), mathematical calculations and querying. Technically, new built-ins must be individuals of the class *BuiltIn*, which is defined in the SWRL ontology. This ontology has to be imported to enable the definition of rules. The processing functionality that evaluates the single built-ins (such as *swrlb:lessThan*) must be implemented in Java and is dynamically loaded by Protégé.

As such, new SWRL built-ins bear the potential to link OWL ontologies to external information such as databases – or (geo)sensors [40]. Querying built-ins already exist for (properties of) individuals in the ontology. In the following, we outline the functioning of a new built-in to collect observations from the Sensor Web, which is currently under development. The presented approach can be regarded as a more light-weight variant of the Semantic Sensor Web [41], which builds on fully annotated sensor web services.

5.2 Querying Sensors from SWRL

The Open Geospatial Consortium has introduced a number of service specifications to enable a fully interoperable Sensor Web. One of these standards is the Sensor Observation Service (SOS) [42], which allows clients to request observations for a specific sensor via the `GetObservation` request. Following the idea of "SQWRL for sensors", we are currently developing the `sos:obs` built-in. While the process of service discovery and description (via the SOS' `GetCapabilities` request) is beyond the scope of this paper, Figure 4 shows an overview of the workflow of an SWRL-enabled OWL-ontology using the `sos:obs` built-in. Note that in combination with a user model as implemented in Section 4, the static information about individuals in the ontology is completely separated from any dynamically changing information collected from sensors, as well as the user model.

---

[12] http://protege.cim3.net/cgi-bin/wiki.pl?SWRLBuiltInBridge

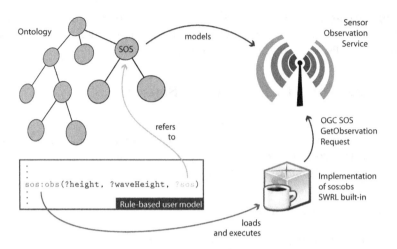

Fig. 4. Workflow of the `sos:obs` built-in: An SOS has to be modeled in the ontology, so that it can be referred to from SWRL rules. During rule execution, the implementation of the built-in is loaded and executed. It queries the SOS and returns the value to the rule engine for further processing.

Using `sos:obs` requires the ontology to contain an individual representing the SOS to be queried, which holds information on the service's capabilities. This instance is an individual of the class generated from the SOS XML schema[13]. The usage pattern for the built-in binds the value observed for the given property (`?observedProperty`) of an SOS individual (`?sos`) to `?observedValue`:

```
sos:obs(?observedValue, ?observedProperty, ?sos)
```

With this built-in, it is possible to remove any dynamically changing information represented from the surf spot individuals. The ontology then only comprises static information about the individual surf spots as well as the sensors measuring the dynamic aspects of the surf spots. The dynamic context information gets requested on demand, i.e. when the rules representing the user model are executed. Accordingly, the user model for u_{beg} is expressed through the following rule (the part of the code not shown here remains unchanged):

```
01    SurfSpot(?spot) ∧
02    hasSOS(?spot, ?sos) ∧
03    hasObservedProperty(?sos, ?waveHeight) ∧
04    sos:obs(?height, ?waveHeight, ?sos) ∧
05    swrlb:lessThan(?height, 1.5) ∧
      ⋮
17    → AppropriateSurfSpot(?spot)
```

---

[13] http://schemas.opengis.net/sos/1.0.0/sosGetCapabilities.xsd

6   Conclusions and Future Work

The Semantic Web is currently based on nominal data and it is therefore inherently difficult to integrate information from the Sensor Web. In this paper, we have demonstrated how semantic rules can be employed to bridge these two worlds to enable context-aware geographical information retrieval from the Semantic Web. Using the Semantic Web Rule Language (SWRL), we showed how the user aspect in a context model can be fully represented in a SWRL rule. SWRL's support for free variables allows for a reclassification of the individuals in an ontology – in our example, surf spots matching the conditions of a user model were correctly reclassified as appropriate with respect to the given user. Moreover, we have outlined an approach to dynamically read observation values from the Sensor Web during execution of a rule based on SWRL built-ins. This approach allows for a strict separation of static knowledge about the individuals in an ontology and any dynamic information through an explicit link to sensors.

Since the built-in is still under development, its completion is the next step in this research. Execution time is thereby a crucial aspect: any rule making use of the built-in will have to wait for the sensor to deliver the data in order to execute the rest of the rule. Caching mechanisms may be required to speed up processing, especially for observed values that do not change very fast. For phenomena such as wave height, hourly observation is certainly sufficient (at least for the surfing scenario; a tsunami warning system, in contrast, would require more frequent updates). Such large-scale systems also raise the question of scalability. Once implemented, a system with a broad user basis could also be employed to apply standard information retrieval measures such as recall and precision.

While our approach to modeling context is independent of the employed information retrieval method, the background for this research is in context modeling for semantic similarity measurement [43,44]. Previous approaches to enable context-aware similarity measurement [45,46] regarded context as a subset of the static information at hand to enhance the cognitive plausibility of the results [47]. Combinations of semantic rules and similarity measurement show promise for adaptation of information retrieval results to the current context that goes beyond previous approaches. One could think of a reclassification of the ontology via rules before measuring similarity, which would put the ontology in the context of the current similarity query. Vice versa, subsets of the ontology which are most similar with respect to a given query could serve as input to rules, which could then adapt these preliminary results to the current context. As such, the approach discussed in this paper is not specific to geographical information retrieval; nonetheless, this field with its broad range of numeric base data provides numerous use cases for its application.

From a theoretical point of view, the problem of monotonicity needs to be addressed: depending on the sensor measurements imported via sos:obs, the same reasoning steps may lead to different results. Concerning SWRL, the number of tools for rule engineering and execution is still very limited. In practice, the rules quickly become verbose, even with the prefix syntax used in this paper. The XML-syntax used for storage is even more extensive, so that neither of the two formats is adequate for interaction of non-experts. These users, such as surfers in our scenario, cannot be expected to edit rules by hand. Instead, user interfaces that hide the complexity of the rules from the user are required.

Acknowledgements

This research is partly funded by the SimCat project (DFG Ra1062/2-1 and DFG Ja1709/2-2), see http://sim-dl.sourceforge.net.

References

1. Goodchild, M.F.: Citizens as voluntary sensors: Spatial data infrastructure in the world of web 2.0. International Journal of Spatial Data Infrastructures Research 2, 24–32 (2007)
2. Kraft, R., Chang, C.C., Maghoul, F., Kumar, R.: Searching with context. In: WWW 2006: Proceedings of the 15th international conference on World Wide Web, pp. 477–486. ACM Press, New York (2006)
3. Brown, P.J., Jones, G.J.F.: Context-aware retrieval: Exploring a new environment for information retrieval and information filtering. Personal and Ubiquitous Computing 5, 253–263 (2001)
4. Jones, C.B., Purves, R.S.: Geographical information retrieval. International Journal of Geographical Information Science 22(3), 219–228 (2008)
5. Abdelmoty, A.I., Smart, P.D., Jones, C.B., Fu, G., Finch, D.: A critical evaluation of ontology languages for geographical information retrieval. Journal of Visual Languages and Computing 16(4), 331–358 (2005)
6. Bechhofer, S., van Harmelen, F., Hendler, J., Horrocks, I., McGuinness, D., Patel-Schneider, P.F., Stein, L.: OWL web ontology language reference. W3C recommendation, W3C (February 2004)
7. Stevens, S.S.: On the theory of scales of measurement. Science 103(2684), 677–680 (1946)
8. Raubal, M., Panov, I.: A formal model for mobile map adaptation. In: Gartner, G., Rehrl, K. (eds.) Location Based Services and TeleCartography II – From Sensor Fusion to Context Models. Selected Papers from the 5th International Symposium on LBS & TeleCartography 2008. Lecture Notes in Geoinformation and Cartography, pp. 11–34. Springer, Berlin (2009)
9. Wilkes, M., Janowicz, K.: A graph-based alignment approach to similarity between climbing routes. In: First International Workshop on Information Semantics and its Implications for Geographic Analysis (ISGA 2008) at GIScience (2008)
10. Rinner, C.: Multi-criteria evaluation in support of emergency response decision-making. In: Joint CIG/ISPRS Conference on Geomatics for Disaster and Risk Management (2007)
11. Gruber, T.: A translation approach to portable ontology specifications. Knowledge Acquisition 5(2), 199–220 (1993)
12. Masolo, C., Borgo, S., Gangemi, A., Guarino, N., Oltramari, A., Schneider, L.: WonderWeb deliverable D17. the WonderWeb library of foundational ontologies and the DOLCE ontology. Technical report, ISTC-CNR (2002)
13. Schneider, L.: Designing foundational ontologies. In: Song, I.-Y., Liddle, S.W., Ling, T.-W., Scheuermann, P. (eds.) ER 2003. LNCS, vol. 2813, pp. 91–104. Springer, Heidelberg (2003)

14. Mark, D., Smith, B., Tversky, B.: Ontology and geographic objects: An empirical study of cognitive categorization. In: Freksa, C., Mark, D.M. (eds.) COSIT 1999. LNCS, vol. 1661, pp. 283–298. Springer, Heidelberg (1999)
15. Frank, A.: Ontology for spatio-temporal databases. In: Sellis, T.K., Koubarakis, M., Frank, A., Grumbach, S., Güting, R.H., Jensen, C., Lorentzos, N.A., Manolopoulos, Y., Nardelli, E., Pernici, B., Theodoulidis, B., Tryfona, N., Schek, H.-J., Scholl, M.O. (eds.) Spatio-Temporal Databases. LNCS, vol. 2520, pp. 9–77. Springer, Heidelberg (2003)
16. Horrocks, I., Patel-Schneider, P.F., van Harmelen, F.: From $\mathcal{SHIQ}$ and RDF to OWL: The making of a web ontology language. Journal of Web Semantics 1(1), 7–26 (2003)
17. Baader, F., Calvanese, D., McGuinness, D.L., Nardi, D., Patel-Schneider, P.F.: The Description Logic Handbook: Theory, Implementation, and Applications. Cambridge University Press, Cambridge (2003)
18. Bazire, M., Brézillon, P.: Understanding context before using it. In: Dey, A.K., Kokinov, B., Leake, D.B., Turner, R. (eds.) CONTEXT 2005. LNCS (LNAI), vol. 3554, pp. 29–40. Springer, Heidelberg (2005)
19. Dey, A.K.: Understanding and using context. Personal Ubiquitous Computing 5(1), 4–7 (2001)
20. Loke, S.: Context-Aware Pervasive Systems: Architectures for a New Breed of Applications. Auerbach Publications (2006)
21. Wang, X., Dong, J.S., Chin, C., Hettiarachchi, S., Zhang, D.: Semantic space: An infrastructure for smart spaces. IEEE Pervasive Computing 3(3), 32–39 (2004)
22. Chou, S., Hsieh, W., Gandon, F., Sadeh, N.: Semantic Web technologies for context-aware museum tour guide applications. In: 19th International Conference on Advanced Information Networking and Applications, 2005. AINA 2005, vol. 2 (2005)
23. Raento, M., Oulasvirta, A., Petit, R., Toivonen, H.: ContextPhone: A Prototyping Platform for Context-Aware Mobile Applications. IEEE Pervasive Computing 4(2), 51–59 (2005)
24. Gu, T., Wang, X., Pung, H., Zhang, D.: An Ontology-based Context Model in Intelligent Environments. In: Proceedings of Communication Networks and Distributed Systems Modeling and Simulation Conference (2004)
25. Lawrence, S.: Context in web search. IEEE Data Engineering Bulletin 23(3), 25–32 (2000)
26. Bouquet, P., Donà, A., Serafini, L., Zanobini, S.: ConTeXtualized local ontologies specification via CTXML. In: AAAI-02 workshop on Meaning Negotiation, July 2002, vol. 28 (2002)
27. Borgida, A., Serafini, L.: Distributed description logics: Assimilating information from peer sources. Journal on Data Semantics 1, 153–184 (2003)
28. Bouquet, P., Giunchiglia, F., Harmelen, F., Serafini, L., Stuckenschmidt, H.: C-OWL: Contextualizing ontologies. In: Fensel, D., Sycara, K., Mylopoulos, J. (eds.) ISWC 2003. LNCS, vol. 2870, pp. 164–179. Springer, Heidelberg (2003)
29. Korpipää, P., Mäntyjärvi, J.: An ontology for mobile device sensor-based context awareness. In: Blackburn, P., Ghidini, C., Turner, R.M., Giunchiglia, F. (eds.) CONTEXT 2003. LNCS (LNAI), vol. 2680, pp. 451–458. Springer, Heidelberg (2003)
30. Zwaal, H., Hutschemaekers, M., Verheijen, M.: Manipulating context information with SWRL (A-MUSE Deliverable D3.12) (2006),
    https://doc.telin.nl/dscgi/ds.py/Get/File-62333/
    Manipulating%20context%20information%20with%20SWRL (last accessed February 22, 2009)

31. Goodchild, M.F., Egenhofer, M.J., Kemp, K.K., Mark, D.M., Sheppard, E.: Introduction to the Varenius project. International Journal of Geographical Information Science 13(8), 731–745 (1999)
32. Horrocks, I., Patel-Schneider, P.F., Boley, H., Tabet, S., Grosof, B., Dean, M.: SWRL: A semantic web rule language combining OWL and RuleML. W3C Member Submission May 21, 2004, http://www.w3.org/Submission/2004/SUBM-SWRL-20040521/ (last accessed February 4, 2009)
33. Horn, A.: On sentences which are true of direct unions of algebras. Journal of Symbolic Logic 16, 14–21 (1951)
34. O'Connor, M., Knublauch, H., Tu, S., Grosof, B., Dean, M., Grosso, W., Musen, M.: Supporting rule system interoperability on the semantic web with SWRL. In: Gil, Y., Motta, E., Benjamins, V.R., Musen, M.A. (eds.) ISWC 2005. LNCS, vol. 3729, pp. 974–986. Springer, Heidelberg (2005)
35. Biezunski, M., Bryan, M., Newcomb, S.R.: ISO/IEC 13250:2000 topic maps: Information technology – document description and markup languages (December 1999), http://www.y12.doe.gov/sgml/sc34/document/0129.pdf (last accessed February 10, 2009)
36. Gärdenfors, P.: Conceptual Spaces - The Geometry of Thought. Bradford Books, MIT Press, Cambridge (2000)
37. Mascolo, C., Capra, L., Emmerich, W.: Mobile computing middleware. In: Gregori, E., Anastasi, G., Basagni, S. (eds.) NETWORKING 2002. LNCS, vol. 2497, pp. 20–58. Springer, Heidelberg (2002)
38. Pepper, S., Grønmo, G.O.: Towards a general theory of scope. In: Extreme Markup Languages 2001, Montréal, Québec, August 14-17 (2001)
39. Horrocks, I.: OWL rules. In: W3C Workshop on Rule Languages for Interoperability (2005)
40. Stefanidis, A., Nittel, S.: GeoSensor Networks. CRC Press, Boca Raton (2004)
41. Sheth, A., Henson, C., Sahoo, S.S.: Semantic sensor web. Internet Computing. IEEE 12(4), 78–83 (2008)
42. Open Geospatial Consortium Inc.: Sensor observation service. OpenGIS implementation standard, OGC 06-009r6. Technical report (2007)
43. Keßler, C., Raubal, M., Janowicz, K.: The effect of context on semantic similarity measurement. In: Meersman, R., Tari, Z., Herrero, P. (eds.) OTM-WS 2007, Part II. LNCS, vol. 4806, pp. 1274–1284. Springer, Heidelberg (2007)
44. Janowicz, K.: Kinds of contexts and their impact on semantic similarity measurement. In: 5th IEEE Workshop on Context Modeling and Reasoning (CoMoRea 2008), Hong Kong, pp. 441–446. IEEE Computer Society, Los Alamitos (2008)
45. Rodríguez, A., Egenhofer, M.: Comparing geospatial entity classes: an asymmetric and context-dependent similarity measure. International Journal of Geographical Information Science 18(3), 229–256 (2004)
46. Janowicz, K., Keßler, C., Schwarz, M., Wilkes, M., Panov, I., Espeter, M., Bäumer, B.: Algorithm, implementation and application of the SIM-DL similarity server. In: Fonseca, F., Rodríguez, M.A., Levashkin, S. (eds.) GeoS 2007. LNCS, vol. 4853, pp. 128–145. Springer, Heidelberg (2007)
47. Janowicz, K., Keßler, C., Panov, I., Wilkes, M., Espeter, M., Schwarz, M.: A study on the cognitive plausibility of SIM-DL similarity rankings for geographic feature types. In: Bernard, L., Friis-Christensen, A., Pundt, H. (eds.) The European Information Society. Proceedings of the 11th AGILE International Conference on Geographic Information Science. Lecture Notes on Geo-Information, pp. 115–134. Springer, Heidelberg (2008)

A Context Provisioning Framework to Support Pervasive and Ubiquitous Applications

Michael Knappmeyer[1,2], Nigel Baker[1], Saad Liaquat[1], and Ralf Tönjes[2]

[1] Mobile and Ubiquitous Systems Group, University of the West of England, Bristol, UK
{michael.knappmeyer,nigel.baker,saad2.liaquat}@uwe.ac.uk
[2] Faculty of Engineering and Computer Science, University of Applied Sciences Osnabrück,
Osnabrück, Germany
r.toenjes@fh-osnabrueck.de

Abstract. Acquisition and dissemination of user and environment context information is critical in development and deployment of context-aware systems. It is fundamental to the success of such systems that they have access to a scaleable, robust and flexible context provisioning framework capable of working across all types of devices and networks. In this paper, we present the design, implementation and experiences of developing a context management system that incorporates these ideas. It is based on a consumer-provider broker model, where providers employ a common context representation format, decoupling various entities involved in the production and consumption of context information. We demonstrate how the idea of independent context providers can aid in end-to-end working of a context management framework. One of the major advantages compared to other approaches is the extendibility of the system. By progressively adding Context Providers to legacy mobile communication systems, new context domains can be added. The system is able to evolve constantly and support a variety of emerging context-aware services and applications.

Keywords: Context-awareness, Context Provisioning, Context Management, Context Provider, Context Broker.

1 Introduction

Being aware of context and communicating context is a key part of human interaction and is a particularly powerful concept when applied to mobile users where network services can be made more personalised and useful. Location and presence are examples of context based services widely deployed today. Harvesting of context to reason and learn about user behaviour will further enhance the future internet vision where services can be composed and customised according to user context. The concept of awareness and context aware applications and systems is a much more difficult proposition. Context awareness refers to the capability of an application, service or even an artefact being aware of its physical environment or situation and responding proactively and intelligently based on such awareness. Context-aware applications, context-aware artefacts or context aware systems are aware of their environment and

P. Barnaghi et al. (Eds.): EuroSSC 2009, LNCS 5741, pp. 93–106, 2009.

circumstances and can respond intelligently. The ubiquity of mobile devices and pro-liferation of wireless networks will allow everyone permanent access to the Internet at all times and all places. The increased computational power of these devices has the potential to empower people to generate their own applications for innovative social and cognitive activities in any situation and anywhere. This wireless connection is not limited to user devices, almost any artefact from clothing to buildings can be con-nected and collaborate. Furthermore new sensor technologies and wireless sensor networks provide environmental intelligence and the capability to sense, reason and actuate. This leads to the exciting vision of the interconnection of artefacts embedded in our real environment, forming a society of "intelligent things" and "smart spaces". This will enable all sorts of innovative interactive pervasive applications as perceived by Weiser [1].

There are many challenges to be overcome to make this vision a reality but crucial in any attempt to do so will require some scalable means of finding and disseminating context. Gathering context about a user or situation is a challenge in itself since a person or object is potentially related in some way to almost an infinite set of objects and characteristics. At best one can expect to gather only a partial incomplete set of context data. However Tobler's Law [2] states that all things are related but near things are more strongly related than those further apart. Therefore things in the near environment will probably be more useful in characterising current context and situa-tion of the user. With the proliferation of mobile and static wireless devices and physical sensors together with virtual sensors (e.g. calendar, weather service) and logical sensors (e.g. databases, user profiles, social profiles) [3] this contextual infor-mation is becoming available. It can be safely estimated that the number of sources from which user and environment context can be acquired will increase tremendously in the near future. This will partly be due to the improved sensing capabilities of user mobile terminals that are increasingly being fitted with GPS modules, accelerometers, magnetometers, light and other sensors. Gathering is just the first step in the context lifecycle. To make use of this raw context it must be found, refined, aggregated, mod-elled and used by appropriate networked reasoning entities to trigger services and applications. The main research questions are: how best to design a scaleable univer-sal distributed context management system?; is it possible to build a scalable distrib-uted reasoning system?; how far can we go in delivering useful context-aware services from partial incomplete context information?

This paper concentrates on the issues surrounding a universal distributed context management system and in particular presents our work on the design of a simple lightweight scalable context provisioning model. Section 2 briefly presents related work. Section 3 defines context and context-awareness while section 4 details the context management design approaches taken in our work before going into more detailed Context Provider design in Section 5. In Section 6 some example Context Providers are described and evaluated. Section 7 concludes with lessons learnt, prob-lems encountered, current status and future work.

2 Related Work

Georgia Institute of Technology elaborated a Context Toolkit [4] offering standard libraries to programmers [4]. Reusable components were designed to assist in the development of context-aware applications. The main limitation of the Context Tool-kit is the lack of a common formal model for context since it is represented by a set of attributes of the context widgets (i.e. the component encapsulating complex sensor functionality) and defined in an ad-hoc manner. The possibility of reconfiguration and extensibility during run-time is therefore not possible. The Context Broker Architecture (CoBrA) developed by the University of Maryland supports context-aware applications in smart spaces. Being based on distributed agents it targets at gathering contextual information from resource limited devices. A Context Broker keeps a shared model of context and represents the entire community of agents. Each is responsible for aggregating and interpreting the raw data and detecting and resolving inconsistency. A rule-based logical inference approach utilised the Web Ontology Language (OWL) [5]. The Context Fusion Network "SOLAR" serves as infrastructure for context acquisition. Based on a graph abstraction of connections between components, their networks provide data fusion services for aggregation and interpretation of sensor data. In order to avoid scalability problems a peer-to-peer model is realised to interconnect several hosts (entitled "Planets") [16]. Sensors need to be controlled by the applications themselves. The PACE (Pervasive, Autonomic, context-aware Environment) project offers functionalities for context gathering, context management and context dissemination, the development of context-aware applications is facilitated [6]. High-level programming abstractions and situation based triggering mechanisms allow for light weight application development. The introduced layered architecture provides an integrated and holistic view. Reconfiguration by the end-user or by the developer during runtime is not foreseen. Another interesting research has been carried out at the University of Berkeley in collaboration with Intel Research and Georgia Tech. Their iCAP system allows for specification of a rule-based reaction for context-aware applications being configured by graphical user interfaces [7]. This approach is hence limited to static and well-specified rules without considering e.g. fuzzy or probabilistic logic. The successor system CAPpella focussed on providing a prototyping environment for recognition-based context-aware applications. It allows for learning user behaviour autonomously. The Service-Oriented Context-Aware Middleware (SOCAM) project provides an architecture for building and rapidly prototyping context-aware mobile services. It concentrates on a central server entitled context interpreter, acquiring context data from distributed context providers [8]. Another example for a centralised middleware approach designed for context-aware mobile applications is the project Context-Awareness Sub-Structure (CASS), allowing for further extendibility.

These are typical examples of middleware solutions and context-aware systems that have been proposed in the last decade. Modularity is partly supported in these approaches but with regard to rich extendibility during runtime, no system provides a ubiquitous "plug and play" like solution. The extensible context provisioning model described here does provide such a generic solution capable of supporting evolving applications and services in a rapidly changing mobile environment.

3 Context, Context-Awareness and Context Management

Context is a form of metadata that is used to describe situations and is most often associated with a temporal event or state. The processing and manipulation of this metadata is fundamental in the design of reactive pervasive services. According to Abowd et al. [4] context can be "any information that can be used to characterise the situation of an entity (person, place, physical or computational object) that is considered relevant to the interaction between entity and application." His definition is by far the most cited in literature. Zimmermann [9] proposes five fundamental categories of context information: time, location, activity, relations, and individuality. Regarding the definition of a situation in context-aware systems, different views exist in the research community. Zimmermann defines it as "the state of a context at a certain point (or region) in space at a certain point (or interval) in time, identified by a name" [9]. Being a structured representation of a part of the context it can be compared to a snapshot taken by a camera. Location and time can be used as spatio-temporal coordinates. With regard to situation-awareness Billings [10] defines a situation as "an abstraction that exists within our minds, describing phenomena that we observe in humans performing work in a rich and usually dynamic environment." In summary, a situation may contain an infinite variety of contextual information.

Machine identification of a situation is difficult but building systems that are automatically aware of situations and responding appropriately is even more of a challenge. Schilit [11] describes this system capability as being context-aware where software adapts according to the location, identities of nearby people, objects and changes to those objects. The primary goal of a context-aware application or service is to be able to change its behaviour in response to a context change. Context-aware applications, context-aware artefacts or context aware systems are aware of their environment and circumstances and can respond intelligently. Adaptation therefore is an essential element of a context-aware system. With the proliferation of wireless sensor-actuator networks there is an increasing interest in context-aware systems that make use of external (physical) context factors such as location, presence, temperature and light information and interact with the environment. This capability to sense, reason and actuate has the potential to imbue the property of awareness into almost any artefact or object.

Engineering a large scale context aware system capable of scaling to the size of an urban cellular network and supporting smart urban type services and applications is a demanding challenge. There are essentially two main parts to any such context-aware system:

- Context Management subsystem concerned with context acquisition and dissemination
- Context Modelling concerned with manipulation, representation, recognising and reasoning about context and situations

Taking into consideration the full sense-decide-actuate cycle of context-awareness then two other subsystems can be identified:

- Sensor and sensor network subsystem: this will include logical as well as physical sensors
- Actuation and Service Composition: Once the system/application becomes aware it adapts by actuating some device/display and or some service is automatically triggered and delivered.

The following sections now discuss the approaches taken in the design of these functional subsystems in the C-CAST project [12] concentrating on the context provisioning aspects.

4 Context Provisioning Framework

There are many research strands in the C-CAST project but the development programme is based on establishing a core context provisioning framework from which more advanced features can be added. The following sub-sections discuss these key features.

4.1 Context Representation

Definition and representation is fundamental in the communicating and processing of context. The difficulty is that communicating simple context over wireless networks between constrained mobile devices requires lightweight representation whereas reasoning about situations and environments requires richer representation and models. Essentially context is metadata so any of the following model categories can be used: key-value, mark-up scheme, graphical, object oriented, logic and ontology based models [3]. For many context-based applications simple matching of context values is sufficient. However as Strang and Linnhoff-Popien [13] observe context representation for more demanding reasoning requires that the modelling approach should be able to: allow for partial validation independently of complex interrelationships; enable rich expressiveness and formalism for shared understanding; indicate richness and quality of information; not assume completeness and unambiguousness.

The approach taken in this work is to define a lightweight Context Meta Language (ContextML) [14] with which to propagate and communicate basic context. More heavyweight database models and reasoning engines also make use of this mark-up scheme to send and receive context. Being based on the Extendible Markup Language (XML) ContextML is used to encode not only the context data but control messages as well. Fig. 1 presents an exemplar ContextML snippet containing the *cell* identifier (scope) of user (entity) *michael*.

```
<ContextML xmlns="http://ContextML/2.0"
   <ctxEls> <ctxEl>
       <contextProvider id="LocationProvider" v="1.0.2"/>
       <entity id="michael" type="username"/>
       <scope>cell</scope>
       <timestamp>2009-05-04T09:00:00+01:00</timestamp>
       <expires>2009-05-04T09:01:00+01:00</expires>
       <state>active</state>
       <QoI>
          <uncertainty>0.02</uncertainty>
       </QoI>
       <dataPart>
          <par n="cgi">222-1-60923-11</par>
       </dataPart>
    </ctxEl> </ctxEls>
</ContextML>
```

Fig. 1. ContextML context update

Besides of the timestamp of creation and an expiration time, some further context meta information has been added to increase expressiveness. A context attribute has been added to reflect the state in the context lifecycle [15] and allow rapid changes between states (e.g. active, suspended). Resolution, accuracy and degree of uncertainty are introduced as optional Quality of Information parameters. Therefore, probabilistic reasoning can be supported where required. The ContextML encoded control messages are explained in the next section.

4.2 Context Management

The basic C-CAST context management architecture is illustrated in Fig. 2 and has been specifically designed to support mobile context based services over any network. The Context Provider-Consumer model together with the Context Broker model allows the system to scale both in terms of physical distribution and in terms of context reasoning complexity.

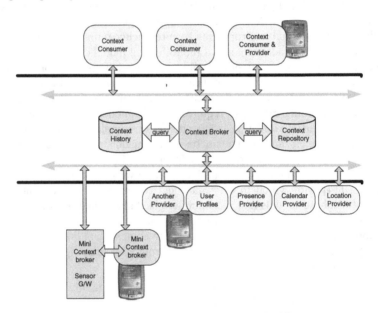

Fig. 2. The C-CAST Context Management Architecture

Network components take the role of Context Provider (CxP) or Context Consumer (CxC) [14][16] and can exchange ContextML in HTTP messages using the Representational State Transfer (REST) interface. Consequently Context Providers and Consumers can be ported onto almost any networked device. The Context Broker (CxB) registers all CxP entities and offers a directory and lookup service so Context Consumers can find and access Providers. Registration and lookup of Context Providers is based on subjects of interests, i.e. context scopes/type (e.g. geographic location) and the entities (e.g. user, terminal) related to the contextual information. Context Providers derive context information from physical, virtual or logical sensors. Each CxP provides a specific type and scope of context information and advertises this to the Context Broker. A CxC may be any kind of application or actuator utilising the context information. Context consumers can query the CxB for a particular type of CxP and, if available, can directly query the CxP for context. This is a 'synchronous' method of communication. Another method of context query by CxC is available which is asynchronous in nature. The CxC subscribes for context information with the CxB. The CxB forwards subscriptions from consumers to all registered providers. When a provider can match the subscription with produced context, it will inform the CxB of the available match and the context is forwarded to the registered con-sumer(s). Fig. 3 shows an interaction sequence between components. The right side parallel life-lines show asynchronous context subscription/notification. For the purposes of this discussion, we will focus on the direct query/response method of communication.

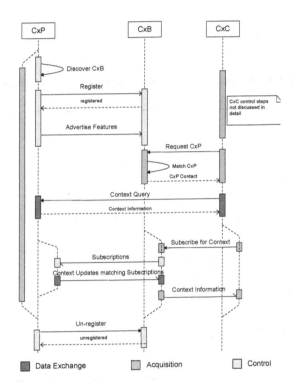

Fig. 3. Typical message sequence chart

Registration of CxP with the CxB takes place in the form of a ContextML adver-tisement message shown in the following snippet (Fig. 4) where a location provider is registering its capabilities and scope(s) at the CxB: It can provide location informa-tion about a user (username) or a device (mobile) based on cell identifier (cell:cgi) or scanned wifi Access Points (wf:wfList). CxC can ask the CxB for a list of providers that can provide location information by invoking:

```
http://cs.com/CB/ContextBroker/getContextProviders?scop
e=position
```

CxC receives the response depicted in Fig. 5 below. To get position context of a particular user, the CxC can issue the following request:

```
http://cs2.com/LP/ContextBroker/getContext?entity=saad&
scopeList=position
```

CxC gets the response listed in Fig. 6. A detailed discussion on our architecture is available in [17].

```
<ContextML>   <ctxAdvs> <ctxAdv>
        <contextProvider id="LP" v="1.2.0"/>
            <urlRoot>http://cs.com/LP</urlRoot>
            <scopes>  <scopeDef n="position">
                <url>/loc/getLocation</url>
                <entityTypes>username,mobile</entityTypes>
                <inputDef>
                    <inputEl name="wf" type="wf:wfList"/>
                    <inputEl name="cgi" type="cell:cgi"/>
                </inputDef>
            </scopeDef>   </scopes>
        </ctxAdv> </ctxAdvs>
</ContextML>
```

Fig. 4. Registration of CxP with CxB, announcing its capabilities

```
<ContextML>
  <ctxPrvEls> <ctxPrvEl>
        <par n="scope">position</par>
        <parS n="contextProvider">
          <par n="id">LP</par>
          <par n="url">http://cs2.com/LP/loc/getLocation</par>
        </parS>
  </ctxPrvEl> </ctxPrvEl>
</ContextML>
```

Fig. 5. CxB informs CxC of a Context Provider matching the criteria given in CxC request

```
<ContextML>
  <ctxEls> <ctxEl dep="gps" p="1.0">
        <contextProvider id="LP" v="1.2.1"/>
        <entity id="saad" type="username"/>
        <scope>position</scope>
        <timestamp>2009-02-17T18:57:30+01:00</timestamp>
        <expires>2009-02-28T18:58:29+01:00</expires>
        <dataPart>
            <par n="latitude">45.11025083333333</par>
            <par n="longitude">7.666810833333334</par>
            <par n="locMode">gps</par>
        </dataPart>
     </ctxEl> </ctxEls>
</ContextML>
```

Fig. 6. Location context information related to an entity, sent from CxP to CxC upon query

5   Context Provider Design

One of the key benefits of this loosely coupled design is that context providers of all types may be added to or removed from the distributed network at any time. Since the main communication transport is HTTP these context providers can operate over a diversity of networks and the simplicity of design ensures they can work on a large

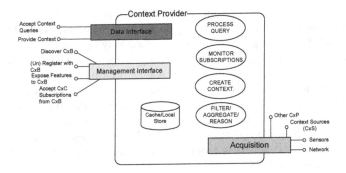

Fig. 7. Context Provider Interfaces & Functions

range of mobile devices. Fig. 7 illustrates the basic functionalities that a context provider may encapsulate together with the main interfaces that it exposes. It is worthwhile mentioning at this point that Context Providers can vary in internal complexity so that some functions may not be implemented.

The main Context Provider features and functions are:-

- *Data Acquisition*: Each CxP is responsible for acquiring the raw information it requires for providing its context information to the system. Sources typically comprise physical sensors (e.g. accelerometers), virtual sensors (e.g. calendar files) and logical sensors (e.g. databases). In addition, context information provided by other CxP(s) may be acquired for further processing and aggregation. Providers may be working on different platforms (user terminals, network servers, etc), and sensors may be attached locally or remotely via wired or wireless communication means and various protocols. Hence, acquisition complexity and heterogeneity is completely hidden to the rest of the context management system.

- *Context Processing*: Each CxP implements one or several of the processing stages for detecting context from real world sensed events. A primitive CxP will most likely focus on sensor data filtering and pre-processing, whereas a high-level CxP will use such primitive context to build more complex inference models on which more powerful processing techniques are applied. The kind of processing is always tailored to the targeted output context information. Produced context information can be kept in a local cache.

- *Context Provider Management*: To ensure a plug and play behaviour, a CxP reports its capabilities to the context management framework by sending an advertisement message to the CxB. Before it can register, at least one CxB entity needs to be discovered. The advertisement message contains information how to access the CxP, its query model and the way context can be accessed. In addition, the CxP indicates whether it provides an internal history or caching service. Optionally, means for controlling and adapting the context processing may be announced, e.g. change of sensor sampling rate.

- *Context Access and Dissemination*: A CxP provides the following access mechanisms: *Synchronous access* is mandatory and allows for handling direct context queries (on demand queries) from other components in the context management framework. The reply contains matching context information if available or a negative acknowledge message. *Asynchronous access* may optionally allow for notifying other components in the context management framework about available context, e.g. upon subscription matching. A CxP offering asynchronous communication is able to accept subscriptions defined by context consumers through the context broker(s). Those providers are able to match produced context against the subscriptions and inform interested parties (context consumers) of available context either directly or through the broker. Whether only synchronous or in addition asynchronous context access is provided is individually reported in the announcement message accordingly.

6 Exemplar Context Providers

A number of different context providers have been designed and implemented, a selection of which are now presented.

6.1 Terminal Capability Context Provider

As rather primitive CxP the Terminal Capability Context Provider offers context information related to the user's mobile device capabilities (multimedia, storage, etc.) and device status (in call, battery life, ringing profile). Some of this information is static and may not change during the life of the device (IMEI number, screen resolution etc.) while some information is dynamic and may change, for example supported media codecs, battery life and ringing profile. This context information may be used by third party services for enhancing delivery of multimedia, advertisements and other services whose content depends on device capabilities.

The Terminal Capability Context Provider makes various scopes related to device information and status available. The current implementation is built on the Android platform. Fig. 8 shows ContextML formatted updates from this provider to a context broker.

```
<ContextML xsi:schemaLocation="http://ContextML/1.6 >
<ctxEls> <ctxEl>
    <contextProvider id="T.C.P" v="0.5"/>
    <entity id="35827901xxxxxxx" type="imei"/>
    <scope>deviceInfo</scope>
    <timestamp>2009-05-04T13:43:48+01:00</timestamp>
    <expires>2009-05-05T13:43:48+01:00</expires>
    <dataPart>
      <par n="vendor">Google Inc.</par>
      <par n="model">Android Dev Phone 1</par>
      <par n="imei">358279XXXXXXXX</par>
      <par n="imsi">234102xxxxxxxxx</par>
      <par n="screenW">320</par>
      <par n="screenH">480</par>
      <par n="screenColorBits">24</par>
    </dataPart>
    </ctxEl> </ctxEls> </contextML>
```

Fig. 8. ContextML formatted updates from Terminal Capability CxP

6.2 Location and Proximity Context Providers

There are two types of context provider that have been implemented under this category: a simple mobile device location provider and a network location provider that gets context from all devices within a zone. As illustrated in Fig. 9 mobile devices act as Context Source (CxS) and push information related to the user and device location to the network Location Provider. This location context (i.e. Cell ID, list of WiFi Access Points in proximity, and/or GPS coordinates) is encoded in ContextML and periodically updated to the provider.

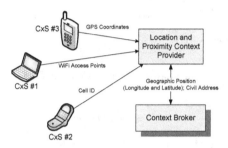

Fig. 9. Location & Proximity Context Provider – Information Flow

The current version of the demo CxS implementation is built on the Android platform [18]. The network location provider has been designed as a Java Enterprise Application running on a JBoss Application server. Amongst other internal databases it also accesses the OpenCellID API [19] to determine the location based on a given cell identifier, the associated civil address is also determined. Applications supporting the CxC interface such as "Where am I" and group multicast perform lookup through the context broker and make use of these context providers.

6.3 Situation Provider

A Situation Provider (SP) is an example of a much more complicated component. In general a provider makes use of several models and abstractions to complete this computational task. The main conceptual layers are illustrated in Fig. 10. The provider finds and subscribes to relevant context sources though the context broker. This is used to update models of the particular situations it is trained to reason about or identify. Various source-context update intervals can be defined: *rapid*, *dynamic* and *static*. These context providers run on servers within the network but conform to the same interfaces as described above.

Fig. 11 illustrates one of the situation providers currently under construction. Using the Context Broker, relevant simple scope-entity context sources are subscribed to and on arrival (in ContextML messages) context is stored inside a logical fact base. The Situation Recogniser applies rule based reasoning and assigns one or more situations to the entity. This information is kept in the Situation Repository and made accessible via the common CxP Interface. For the sake of clarity the arrows in Fig. 11 symbolise the logical context/situation information flow. In addition, a Configuration Interface guarantees the extendibility of the Provider both in terms of the situation

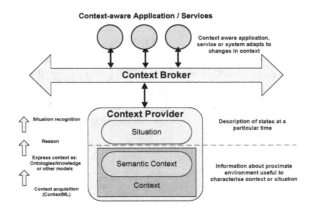

Fig. 10. Conceptual Layers of a more Complex Context Provider

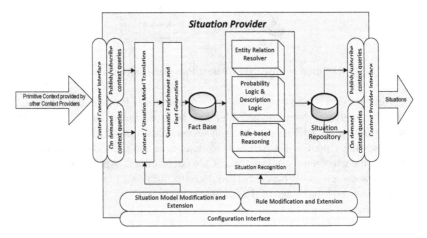

Fig. 11. Situation Provider - implementation features

model and in terms of reasoning rules. Our currently ongoing prototype implementation is based on the Java 2 Enterprise Edition standard. Again JBoss is used as open source application server and JESS (Java Expert System Shell) as rule engine. One of the main goals of the project is to identify situations when multimedia content can be multicast as opposed to unicast to groups of user mobile devices. Consequently identifying group situations is the main task of this provider.

7 Results, Conclusions and Future Work

A first prototype of the context management framework including a query based Context Broker together with a variety of Context Providers has been implemented and trialled over a commercial cellular network and is reported in [14]. The components use REST over HTTP communicating context through ContextML, the XML-based meta language. The results from these trials show that the lightweight context broker architecture performs well in propagating context and is capable of supporting interesting context-based services and applications. The context processing required by the applications is almost exclusively confined to finding and matching context using database queries.

As the number of context providers grow, complexity of finding and accessing relevant context increases. Currently we are experimenting with federated brokers and a publish-subscribe mechanism to enhance the scalability and flexibility of context propagation. One of the main aims of the research was to establish how far we could scale this producer-consumer broker model. Would it be sufficient to support the demands of new mobile context based application and services? Could it be ported on and across a diversity of devices and networks? So far the results are encouraging.

However providing context-aware services is an order of magnitude more complex than offering context-based services. At the moment we tend to conclude that matching and selecting a service or response based on context is probably the best we can achieve. That is to say it is a best effort selection of a response (adaptation) that is likely to lead to a satisfied service user. Context-aware systems attempt to recognise and understand situations in the environment responding appropriately. It has to be accepted that in this endeavour we are attempting to construct and reason about models of the physical world based on partial, uncertain and incomplete information.

How far our concept of enhanced reasoning context providers can be taken is still an open research question. There are many challenges. For example the simple ContextML entity-scope representation is limited in expressing semantically rich context therefore use of other representations is necessary. Valuable information will therefore be lost in translating between representations. This assumes that machine translation is possible. As the context provider models grow so does the computation required to identify situations. The inevitable consequence is that some situations will only be identified some time after the event, of no use to mobile users who in the mean time have moved on. One of the main lessons we have learnt in designing and deploying context-aware applications is the crucial need for social and behavioural studies. In order to help compensate for the partial incomplete context information, gathered behavioural models of the region in which services are to be deployed is mandatory. So for example, if assisting context aware services are to be deployed in a railway station it is necessary to study how the spaces within the building are used and the social behaviour of people who use it at different times of the day and year. In addition to this, as much station and train management information must also be available. So for larger scale situation-aware services the challenges are severe. Our applications are multimedia, so there is limited user dissatisfaction when media streams are out of order, with incorrect colours delivered at the wrong time. In some cases they are still an entertaining media experience.

Acknowledgments

This work has been supported by the European FP7 ICT project C-CAST [12] which aims at evolving mobile multimedia multicasting to exploit the increasing integration of mobile devices with our everyday physical world and environment.

References

1. Weiser, M.: The computer for the 21st century. In: Human-computer interaction: toward the year 2000, Morgan Kaufmann Publishers Inc., San Francisco (1995)
2. Tobler, W.: A computer movie simulating urban growth in the Detroit region. Economic Geography 46(2), 234–240 (1970)
3. Baldauf, M., Dustdar, S., Rosenberg, F.: A survey on context-aware systems. International Journal of Ad Hoc and Ubiquitous Computing 2(4) (2007)
4. Dey, A., Salber, D., Abowd, G.: A conceptual framework and a toolkit for supporting the rapid prototyping of context-aware applications (2001)
5. Chen, H., et al.: Intelligent agents meet semantic web in a smart meeting room. Autonomous Agents and Multiagent Systems, 854–861 (2004)
6. Henricksen, K., et al.: Middleware for Distributed Context-Aware Systems. In: Meersman, R., Tari, Z. (eds.) OTM 2005. LNCS, vol. 3760, pp. 846–863. Springer, Heidelberg (2005)
7. Sohn, T., Dey, A.: iCAP: an informal tool for interactive prototyping of context-aware applications. In: CHI 2003 extended abstracts on Human factors in computing systems, Ft. Lauderdale, Florida, USA, pp. 974–975. ACM, New York (2003)
8. Gu, T., Pung, H.K., Zhang, D.Q.: A middleware for building context-aware mobile services. In: Vehicular Technology Conference, 2004. VTC 2004-Spring. 2004 IEEE 59th, vol. 5, pp. 2656–2660 (2004)
9. Zimmermann, A.: Context Management and Personalisation, PhD Thesis, University of Aachen (2007)
10. Billings, C.: Situation Awareness Measurements and Analysis: A Commentary. In: Proc. Int'l Conf. Experimental Analysis and Measurement of Situation Awareness (1995)
11. Schilit, B.N.: A System Architecture for Context-Aware Mobile Computing, PhD Thesis, Columbia University (1995)
12. Context Casting (C-CAST), European FP7 ICT research project,
    http://www.ict-ccast.eu
13. Strang, T., Linnhoff-Popien, C.: A Context Modeling Survey. In: The Sixth International Conference on Ubiquitous Computing, Workshop on Advanced Context Modelling, Reasoning and Management, Nottingham/England (2004)
14. Moltchanov, B., et al.: Context-Aware Content Sharing and Casting. In: ICIN 2008, Bordeaux, France (2008)
15. Chang, H., Shin&, S., Chung, C.: Context Life Cycle Management Scheme in Ubiquitous Computing Environments. In: International Conference on Mobile Data Management, pp. 315–319 (2007)
16. Ramparany, F., et al.: An open context information management infrastructure the IST-amigo project. In: 3rd IET International Conference on Intelligent Environments (2007)
17. Knappmeyer, M., Tönjes, R., Baker, N.: Modular and Extendible Context Provisioning for Evolving Mobile Applications and Services. In: 18th ICT Mobile Summit (2009)
18. Android, a software platform for mobile devices, initially developed by Google and later by the Open Handset Alliance, http://www.android.com
19. Open Cell, I.D.: open source project aiming to create a complete database of CellID worldwide and assigning them to geographic locations,
    http://www.opencellid.org

Context-Aware Recommendations on Mobile Services: The m:Ciudad Approach

Andreas Emrich, Alexandra Chapko, and Dirk Werth

Institute for Information Systems (IWi)
German Research Center for Artificial Intelligence (DFKI)
Stuhlsatzenhausweg 3, 66123 Saarbrücken, Germany
{andreas.emrich,alexandra.chapko,dirk.werth}@iwi.dfki.de

Abstract. The European FP7 research project m:Ciudad - a metropolis of ubiquitous services - aims at the empowerment of users to create services on mobile terminals. The project demonstrates various scenarios in which users either act as creator of services or interact with the system to search for services or service construction components. The search and recommendation process in the system facilitates retrieval of related entities and shows the results to the users according to their preference and contextual information. The paper demonstrates an approach to integrate contextual information with other search attributes to enable efficient service retrieval and recommendation in mobile user and application scenarios. The specifics of a mobile environment are taken into consideration and are reflected in the design of the m:Ciudad Search and Recommendation Engine. We discuss how context-awareness and proactivity can be implemented and utilised for mobile services.

Keywords: recommendations, mobile services, proactivity, m:Ciudad, user-generated services.

1 Introduction

Nowadays digital information of any type is available at any given time and at almost any given place. At the same time the amount of generated digital information is growing tremendously. The amount of digital information in 2006 was estimated to be 161 billion gigabytes which is about 3 million times the information of all the books ever written [1]. By 2011 the amount is estimated to be 10 times the size it was in 2006 [2]. An unlimited access to an apparent endless amount of digital information demands for highly efficient search mechanisms which incorporate as much information about the user as possible. However, personalized search mechanisms are not sufficient to tackle the issue of information overflow. Personalized and context-aware recommendations are therefore a crucial factor to discover not only the sought-after information but to provide information beyond what is currently being requested by the user.

The search and recommendation engine build in the European funded project m:Ciudad [3] takes the requirements for future discovery tools described in the paragraph above into account. In the following m:Ciudad as a whole and its search and

P. Barnaghi et al. (Eds.): EuroSSC 2009, LNCS 5741, pp. 107–120, 2009.

recommendation engine in particular are described. The search and recommendation engine focuses on how context information of mobile users is incorporated in the search and recommendation processes.

This paper discusses, how m:Ciudad can deal with a large number of short-lived services, and how ontology-based metadata can be used to evaluate services according to their relevance. In the end an outlook is provided which describes how the proposed mechanisms can be evaluated and extended in future work.

2   The m:Ciudad Architecture

The goal of m:Ciudad is to enable mobile users to create services on the mobile device by combining existing service elements. In addition users will be able to provide data for a service, i.e. participating in a multi-provider scenario or using content provided by a service. For all three scenarios a user needs to become a member of the m:Ciudad community by installing the m:Ciudad bundle on the mobile device.

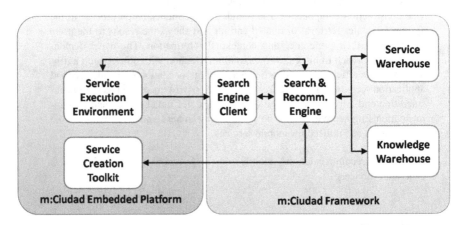

Fig. 1. m:Ciudad Architecture

The architecture of m:Ciudad (see fig. 1) consists of a server part, the m:Ciudad framework and an embedded platform which resides on the mobile device. Due to the limited bandwidth and processing power of mobile devices data storage and processing is conducted on the server side. The most important components on the server-side are the Service Warehouse, the Knowledge Warehouse, and the Search and Recommendation Engine. Information about the created services is stored in the Service Warehouse and the Knowledge Warehouse whereas operational information about the service is stored in the Service Warehouse and meta information about the service is stored in the Knowledge Warehouse. For handling search requests and for the provision of proactive recommendations the Search and Recommendation Engine requests information from the Service Warehouse and the Knowledge Warehouse. On the mobile device the Service Execution Environment is responsible for downloading and running services. Services are created in the Service Creation Toolkit. In the following a more detailed description of the different components is provided.

2.1 The Service Creation Toolkit

The Service Creation Toolkit enables the user to create services. Two approaches for service creation are investigated. On the one hand a question-based approach is analysed. In this scenario the user is asked questions and depending on the answers the service elements are recommended to the user. Technical details of the service creation is transparent for the user. The block-based approach is another approach which is evaluated in the m:Ciudad project. Service creation is based on the logical connections of autonomous black boxes which are high-level parts of a service. It will also feature the annotation of services, which are stored in the Knowledge Warehouse.

2.2 The Service Execution Environment

The Service Execution Environment is the core of the m:Ciudad Embedded Platform and resides on the mobile device. Its main function is to handle the execution of services. Furthermore it interacts with the Service Creation Toolkit and enables testing of new services on the mobile device before publishing them.

2.3 The Service Warehouse

The Service Warehouse is the module in the m:Ciudad Framework which acts as a repository of services and interacts and communicates with several modules both in the Embedded Platform and in the m:Ciudad Framework. Depending on the role of the user, different data is retrieved from the Service Warehouse. In case the user acts as creator of a service, service templates are downloaded from the Service Warehouse. A user interested in providing data for an existing service downloads the full service code from the Service Warehouse. Finally, a user acting as consumer of a service is provided with the User ID of the user providing the service.

2.4 The Knowledge Warehouse

The Knowledge Warehouse is focused on describing services using semantically enriched data. It facilitates search and discovery of services for the m:Ciudad community. This component will be used as a part of the global m:Ciudad architecture in collaboration with the Search and Recommendation Engine to support the service discovery, selection, and creation. The Knowledge Warehouse resides on the server side and is linked to different types of ontologies to represent domain knowledge in different applications. The domain ontologies specify common concepts and their relationships in the domains of application for m:Ciudad (e.g. tourism, traffic, entertainment). However, searching the contents is not the main target in Knowledge Warehouse design. The services and contents are only annotated in a way that supports finding relevant services based on different search criteria. This will be done in cooperation with the Service Warehouse and the Search and Recommendation Engine.

3 The m:Ciudad Search and Recommendation Engine

The m:Ciudad Search and Recommendation Engine (S&RE) comprises a new way for formulating queries, which are used both for search and recommendation scenarios.

Moreover, it supports filtering and ranking based on ontology-based service descriptions. For the ranking and also for proactive recommendations the specifics of the mobile environment are leveraged to boost the quality of search and recommendation results.

3.1 Query Formulation

In m:Ciudad, there are different sources of information that can be leveraged for searches or proactive recommendations:

- *Search items / keywords*: These are terms that are defined by the user and are the only parameters that are explicitly defined by the user. The information is submitted as the user requests information from the system.
- *Context information*: This information is submitted automatically by the mobile device itself. The information includes for example GPS location, the current time, etc.
- *Profile data*: The user profile information is stored on the server-side. It is referred to whenever a user submits a query. For optimization purposes this information is only transmitted if it deviates from the general user profile of the user.

The unique ID of the user is also sent to the system along with the other parameters.

The search mechanism is different from "classic" approaches that rely on a set of search terms. We use the concept of "query extension" [3] to expand the query by adding user-related and contextual information. By this means, we want to achieve a higher quality of search results and provide a personalized and context-aware search mechanism.

For recommendations, there are no explicit search terms. However, there is profile information from the users and contextual data sent by the mobile terminal. The definition of the query is sufficient for both "pull" and "push" recommendations. For "push" recommendations, a background service continually monitors the user's current situation and provides proactive recommendations when a certain "threshold of change" is reached. For "pull" recommendations, the process is similar to a search without any search terms. In this case, the results are suggested by the system based on detected user interests and preferences.

In the following, we consider a query term t to be the atomic part of a search query q:

$$q = (t_1, t_2, ..., t_n)$$

Def. 1. Definition of the Query Formulation

Furthermore, we define a query term t_i as following:

$$t_i = \langle c, n, v, w \rangle$$

Def. 2. Definition of a search term

- c = category of the query term; i.e "keyword", "context-information", or for service creation a "input/output block"
- n = unique name of the query term within a category within a single query; (e.g. "name" for the name of a user, or "name" as the name of the service)
- v = value of the parameter (e.g. the actual name of the user, his current location, the actual search term, etc.)
- w = weight of the query term within the query

As the query formulation shows, also requests from the Service Creation Toolkit can be handled by this generic query formulation. The category can be used to describe, whether the given search term is associated to an input or to an output block. The weight of the query term can be defined by the user, or can be determined by the system. A more detailed description on how these weights are actually defined and used, is provided in the following. When a query is formulated, weights are allocated to the different query terms. This could be done explicitly by users in an advanced search interface or implicitly. Some basic considerations are listed below:

- *Search terms*: If search terms are defined, i.e. we have an actual search and not a proactive recommendation, they should have a rather high weight.
- *User profile information*: a profile can contain the interest of a user, i.e. cooking and football. Users can define weights for different items in their user profile, i.e. cooking → 0.3 and football → 0.5 specifies that a user is more interested in services about football than cooking. When executing a query, the user profile information is matched to the other query terms in order to re-rank the profile information according to their relevance.
- *Context information*: In the following we only elaborate on location and date / time. We will consider these aspects in the design and the latter prototype development. However, context data could include more complex information such as the mood of the user and environment variables. The very generic query formulation as shown above also allows for such scenarios.
  Location: The handling of locations is depending on whether a service is location-based or not. If a service is location-based, another important question is, whether this information is used as a hard criteria, i.e. the specified location MUST be within a certain range, or whether it is a parameter that should be used for the ranking. For the first case, we assume the weight for location to be 1.0, i.e. it will be the most important parameter for selection; if a service is not within the specified range, it will not be selected.
  Date / time: The handling of date and time is depending on whether a service is time-dependent or not. If a service is time-dependent, another important question is, whether this information is used as a hard criteria, i.e. the specified timestamp MUST be within a certain range, or whether it is used as a soft criteria and thus a parameter that should be used for the ranking. For the first case, we assume the weight for location to be 1.0, i.e. it will be the most important parameter for the selection; if a service is not within the specified time range, it will not be selected.

In the following an example of a query is provided. A user enters the terms "cooking" and "football" and assigns the weight 0.3 to cooking and 0.5 to football. The resulting query $\langle t_1, t_2 \rangle$ looks as follows. For t_1 category = keyword, name is empty, value =

cooking and weight = 0.3. For t_2 category = keyword, name is empty, value = football and weight = 0.5.

Overall, there is a need to re-process these weights after the different query terms have been transferred to their ontological representations. We need to re-calcaculate the weights of search terms with respect to their relevance to the other terms in the query. Sections 3.3 and 3.4 describe, how a query is processed.

3.2 Creating the Search Index

To allow for an effective and fast search, we need an infrastructure that holds references to services according to some classification. For our scenario, where we have potentially millions of services, we cannot query the whole semantic infrastructure upon every search request. Therefore we need to build a search index.

This is the basic data structure that allows for a fast filtering. First, all query terms have to be transformed into an ontological representation. Querying for an ontological representation results in a list of service references that match the given ontological representation of query q (see definition 3).

$$f(o_{q,1},...,o_{q,n}) \longrightarrow (s_1,...,s_m)$$

Def. 3. Definition for mapping ontology representations to list of service instances

For the fast and efficient access to service meta data, we hook into the lifecycle events of services in order to create a search index. This search index maps the generic meta data description structure to service instances. The generic meta data description structure comprises a set of ontology classes that have been used throughout the description of the service. When a service is created, all possible combinations of ontological representations will be mapped to the concrete service reference. For instance, a user creates a service named Foodball which is about the best cooking recepies for watching a football match. The most obvious ontological representation for the service Foodball in the search index will be OR_1 = {football, cooking} (see fig. 2). OR stands for ontological representation. However, since football and cooking are part of an ontology, the different super-classes of Football and Cooking have to be considered as well for referencing this service.

The different ontology representations are created according to the inheritance hierarchy of the respective concepts. The ontology representation includes all the references to the contained ontologies (usually a URI – in fig. 2: o1, o2, etc.). Each service will be mapped to the ontology representations which can describe it. In accordance to how many generalization steps have been made, the weight of this representation can be adapted and saved with the representation in the search index, i.e. the more generalization steps have been made, the lower the weight of the respective ontology representation. For instance, OR_2 is not as precise as OR_1, and so on. Many different services can be found according to the ontology representations. The weight of a given ontology representation and service id pair can be used to pre-select appropriate service instances according to their weight. Though we have high costs on the server-side for creating a service, we keep the costs low for the search and recommendation scenarios on mobile devices, as we are able to filter from millions of services to few of them.

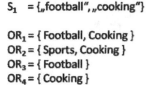

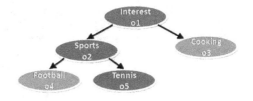

S_1 = {„football", „cooking"}

OR_1 = { Football, Cooking }
OR_2 = { Sports, Cooking }
OR_3 = { Football }
OR_4 = { Cooking }

OR_ID	O_ID
1	o4
1	o3
2	o2
2	o3
3	o4
4	o3

OR_ID	S_ID
1	1
2	1
3	1
4	1

Fig. 2. Search Index Creation

3.3 Filtering

From a process point of view the filtering can be described as follows (see fig. 3). The filtering is triggered with a query and starts the matching of each search term. Having ontologies for each search term an overall ontological representation of the query can be built. This ontological representation is used to query the instance space where each service instance is matched to an ontological representation. At this stage, two types of results are possible: either a list of service instances is found which match the ontological representation of the query. In this case the filtering process ends; Or no services instances are found so that the instance cache has to be queried again with a reduced ontology set. Reduction is conducted by removing the term which has the lowest weight.

The filtering process described in previous sections mainly aims at the discovery of service instances which match the overall search query. For some use cases we need to extend this mechanism with item-based evaluations that have even to be performed throughout the filtering.

For instance, a service might not be valid anymore or the user might not have access rights to the service. Another example is a service which provides information that is outside the physical range of the user.

As these interpretations already contain some information which are needed throughout the ranking, these intermediate results should be cached for the ranking later on. Depending on the search scenarios we have (location-based, time-dependent search, etc.), we need a configuration which describes, which parameters should be evaluated throughout filtering.

For all the different aspects that need an evaluation while filtering, this information needs also to be included in the table that maps ontology representations to service ids. For time-dependent search there could be an additional attribute that can be queried throughout the filtering.

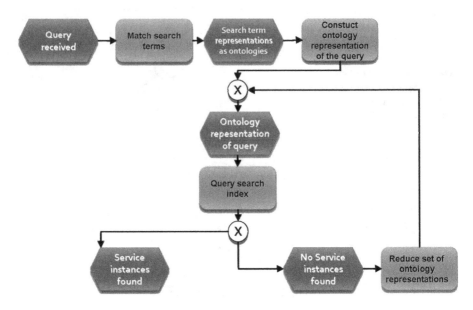

Fig. 3. Filtering in m:Ciudad

3.4 Ranking

The ranking function (see def. 4) is a combination of weights of the different search terms and implicit and explicit user feedback.

$$r(q_s) = \sum_i r(t_i) + \gamma \cdot r(s) + \delta \cdot r(or_s) + \varepsilon \cdot r(inst_s) + \varphi \cdot r(ext_s)$$

Def. 4. Definition of the ranking function

- $r(q_s)$, Overall ranking result of a service s which was returned as a result for query q.
- $r(t_i)$, Evaluation of the search term t_i
- $r(s)$, Feedback about service s
- $r(or)$, Feedback about service description of service s which is represented via its different ontologies
- $r(inst)$, Feedback about how often service s was installed
- $r(ext)$, Feedback about how often service s was extended to a new service
- $\gamma, \delta, \varepsilon, \varphi$, Parameters to emphasize or reduce relevance of function terms of ranking equation

At first the search terms of query q are considered in the ranking function. The sum $\sum_i r(t_i)$ describes the overall evaluation of the different search terms t_i. Each search term is evaluated by its assigned weight and additional parameters. For instance search term t_1 specifies that the desired services should provide information not older than an hour. If the services s meets this requirement the Boolean parameter 1 is assigned, if the services s does not meet this requirement the Boolean parameter 0 is assigned. $r(t_i)$ in this particular example equals 1 multiplied with the weight assigned to term t_1 for the first case and 0 in case service s does not meet the requirement. Hence, $\sum_i r(t_i)$ adds the different evaluations of each search term t_i of query q. $r(s)$ represents the feedback about the service provided by the users. Here, different aspects of feedback are considered, e.g. collaborative or hybrid mechanisms. $r(or)$ is feedback about the description of the service, i.e. whether it was helpful. $r(inst)$ and $r(ext)$ are statistical parameters obtained from the Knowledge Warehouse. $\gamma, \delta, \varepsilon, \varphi$ enable a variation of the relevance of different terms of the ranking function and thus, a variation of order of services in the result list.

Since the list of service instances is a list of ontological representations that matches the ontological representation of the search query, weights of the search terms can be directly used to evaluate the overall ranking of the service instance. Furthermore, parameters $\gamma, \delta, \varepsilon, \varphi$ have to be adjusted in relation to the user role. For instance, if the user searches for services for consumption γ will be assigned a higher value then φ. In the reverse conclusion, φ is assigned a higher value, if the user acts as services creator.

3.5 Enabling Proactivity in a Mobile Environment

The m:Ciudad bundle on the Mobile Embedded Platform includes a browser, which can be used to access to the Search and Recommendation Engine specific URL in order to get the Search and Recommendation Engine main page; when this page is rendered in the user terminal, the user fills in all the parameters (s)he wants to include in the request and then clicks on the "Search" button which sends a request to the Search and Recommendation Engine. However, before this request is really issued, the following information has to be accessed and included in the request:

- *User ID*: The unique user ID to identify the current user
- *Context information*: All capability information by the current device (esp. location[1]; time can be determined in the backend automatically)

The User ID will be part of the user configuration and will be read from the m:Ciudad configuration file but the context information has to be requested from the Capabilities Manager which is accessed through the Service Execution Environment.

---

[1] The option to include information from the network providers about the current location will be analyzed throughout the implementation of the m:Ciudad prototype.

As the search terms and the user profile data can be edited within the Search Client, these should not be provided by the Service Execution Environment. The listed information above will be part of an HTTP session, so the Search Client can use it to load the user profile data from the Service Warehouse (in case of the user ID) and to weigh context data according to their importance.

To enable proactivity in the Search & Recommendation Engine, the Service Execution Environment should also permanently poll the Search & Recommendation Engine for proactive recommendations, as the Search & Recommendation Engine cannot directly address a mobile client without prior request. In this case the same data should be transmitted as with the search request. A response should indicate, whether there are recommendations for the user or not.

In order to keep the user effort as small as possible, the intervals for pushing information from the Search and Recommendation Engine should be quite large. As the Search and Recommendation Engine can keep track of all other parameters all by itself, it only needs to be notified for location changes. For the implementation of the prototype we consider an interval of 5 minutes to be appropriate for this purpose. The option should be investigated, whether the mobile device can determine a certain kind of variation threshold for the parameters location and time. According to that, an update request would be initiated, whenever a certain deviation of the previous location or time has been reached.

An efficient searching interaction between a user and the Search and Recommendation Engine will result in a service being selected for installation and execution on the mobile terminal. At this stage a new interaction between the Search Client and the

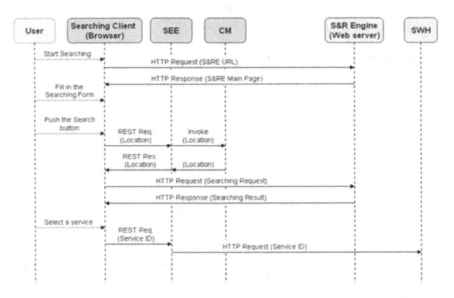

Fig. 4. Interaction between User, the Search and Recommendation Engine, and the Service Execution Environment

Service Execution Environment will be required in order to pass the Service ID of the selected service from the Search Client to the Service Execution Environment; from then on the Service Execution Environment will launch the process of downloading the service from the Service Warehouse and installing it in the terminal.

Figure 4 depicts the main interactions between the Search Client and the Service Execution Environment.

4 An Instance Scenario

A group of friends is having dinner and spontaneously decides to go out afterwards. One of the friends, a member of the m:Ciudad community, starts looking for a service which provides information about cool events. He specifies via an advanced search interface, that the service has to provide information for events that are taking place in a time range of 5 minutes from now. Furthermore, the Search and Recommendation Engine knows from the user's profile that he likes Rock music. Thus, the system starts looking for services that provide information about events which include Rock music. Having found a list of services which match the different criteria, the filtering process removes all services which provide information about events in cities other than the user is in. The ranking function furthermore gives a higher rate to Rock events than to other events. Having filtered and ranked the services the Top 5 services are returned to the user. Figure 5 shows, how this query can be specified on the mobile phone.

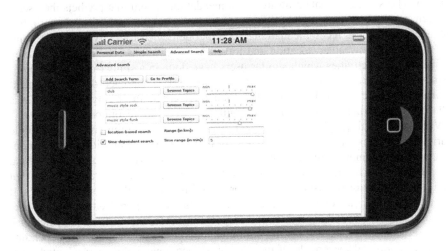

Fig. 5. Sample Screenshot of the Advanced Search Interface

5 Related Work

In recent attempts context-aware recommender systems have been combined with ontologies to further improve the recommendation by adding semantics to the context.

For instance, description of a meeting situation specified in terms of location, time and people can be extended with a qualitative, high-level description such as "Important Work Meeting", "With Friends". In addition, the mobile service description itself can be extended by a service class ontology/taxonomy describing a service as "Real-time Communication Service", "Entertainment Service", "Messaging Service", etc. In other words, service and item representation can be extended across multiple dimensions and taxonomies. Using ontologies, the quality of content description is notably improved for machine processing and reasoning purposes. Domain ontologies enable semantic matching of objects and profiles instead of a simple keyword-based matching or comparison of syntax [5].

In m:Ciudad framework, contextual information such as "location" or "current available bandwidth" is subject to constant and quick changes. Implementation of a context-based recommendation system in a mobile environment is particularly difficult. In the following some of the different approaches of context-based recommender systems in a mobile environment are described.

Woerndl et al. [6] describe recommendation of mobile applications to users based on what other users have installed in a similar context. A hybrid recommender system is created by letting the user select between several content-based or collaborative filtering components. In addition, a rule-based module using information on point-of-interest information in the vicinity of the user is provided. By this means context-dependent information can be recommended to the user, e.g. services of "Real Madrid" can be proposed to the user when he walks in the vicinity of the Bernabeu stadium.

Chen [7] discusses a context-aware recommendation system that predicts the user's preferences on past experiences of like-minded users in "tourist activities" domain. For instance, a user seeks recommendations via a mobile device for activities in the relation to the current weather, location and travelling companions. The recommendation engine suggests activities which similar users have done in a similar context. In comparison to the traditional approaches described above, this approach defines a context similarity measure and includes it in the collaborative filtering rating equation, i.e. a collaborative filtering system is combined with context-aware recommendation.

Van Setten et al. [8] describe a context-aware recommendation engine for mobile tourist applications which uses ontologies. In their approach a hybrid system is constructed by combining a recommender system and a context-aware system. At first, the context item "location" is used as a hard criterion to select relevant services that are in the vicinity of the user. Then, the predicted interest of the user is used as soft criterion to order the remaining services. Requests are triggered either by the user himself or by a detected change of context. For instance, the systems provides proactive recommendations, e.g. nearby buildings, buddies or other buildings, depending on the location and the profile of the user. The recommendations are adapted automatically if the context of the user changes, i.e. if the sensors of the mobile device detects an increase of the user's speed, the application assumes that the user is driving and increases the radius of the area for providing recommendations. For the service description, the semantic web technologies, and in particular OWL, are applied to create additional annotations of service elements, e.g. service type, inputs, outputs which have to be filled in by the service provider.

Zhou et al. [9] developed a recommendation system which is based on user preference, situation context, and capability context for supporting context-aware media recommendation for smart phones. They define a recommendation model for dealing with a wide variety of recommendations. The model provides multimedia recommendations over multiple dimensions to generate multidimensional output. Context is represented via ontology-based context models which include the user's media preferences. For the evaluation of the recommendations three different approaches are combined, namely content-based, Bayesian-classifier, and a rule-based approach. The content-based approach measures the similarity between a media item and the preference of the user then the Baysian Classifier calculates the probability of the item belonging to the situation context, finally a weighted linear combination of the subscores is applied to calculate the overall score.

6 Conclusions and Outlook

This paper discusses how proactive and context-aware recommendations are applied to mobile services in the m:Ciudad Search & Recommendation Engine. Ontologies are used to describe services, users, situations and their domain knowledge. The ontology-based data representations are used as the basis for search and recommendation. The approach for the query formulation is generic and can be used in different service usage scenarios (service creation, service provision, "plain" service usage). Moreover, it serves as internal data structure for both searches and recommendations. The ranking takes specifics of the mobile system into account, e.g., it uses the number of service installations to refine the ranking. Proactivity is enabled by a triggered request for proactive recommendations from the mobile client.

M:Ciudad somewhat differs from the other approaches in similar domains, as it directly addresses a potentially huge number of services and features a filtering method, which allows for highly scalable filtering of millions of services.

Overall, the depicted approach can be used to semantically classify and describe different types of services, items, etc. across the border of a single application. The query formulation is generic and can be adapted to other domains and applications; it is not strictly bound to mobile platforms. Nevertheless, the specifics of a mobile environment are taken into account, and are considered while ranking the different service instances and enabling proactive recommendations in such an environment.

Future work will focus on using the semantics provided by the ontology infrastructure to derive facts from probabilistic measures taken from the user feedback and also the reasoning mechanisms. Moreover, by analyzing the historical data of searches and recommendations, optimization can be learned and reified in the ontology representations, in order to boost the performance of searches and recommendations.

In the m:Ciudad project, the Search & Recommendation Engine will be implemented throughout the next steps. A preliminary set of domain ontologies has been created or reused from existing ontologies, such as FOAF [10] and SKOS [11]. The prototype will be also evaluated against common metrics such as precision, recall and fall-out.

Acknowledgement

This paper describes work undertaken in the context of the m:Ciudad project, m:Ciudad - A metropolis of ubiquitous services (http://www.mciudad-fp7.org/). m:Ciudad is a medium-scale focused research project supported by the European 7th Framework Programme, contract number: 215007.

References

[1] The expanding digital universe, A forecast of worldwide information growth through 2010, An IDC white paper (March 2007),
http://www.emc.com/collateral/analyst-reports/
expanding-digital-idc-white-paper.pdf

[2] The expanding digital universe, A forecast of worldwirde information growth through 2011 (March 2008),
http://www.emc.com/collateral/analyst-reports/
diverse-exploding-digital-universe.pdf

[3] m:Ciudad project homepage, http://www.mciudad-fp7.org/

[4] Pretschner, A., Gauch, S.: Ontology based personalized search. In: Proceedings of 11th IEEE International Conference on Tools with Artificial Intelligence, pp. 391–398 (1999)

[5] Costa, A., Guizzardi, R., Guizzardi, G., Filho, J.: COReS: Context-aware, Ontology-based Recommender system for Service recommendation. In: UMICS 2007, 19th International Conference on Advanced Information Systems Engineering (CAISE 2007) (2007)

[6] Woerndl, W., Schlichter, J.: Introducing Context into Recommender Systems. In: Short Paper, Proc. AAAI 2007 Workshop on Recommender Systems in e-Commerce (2007)

[7] Chen, A.: Context-aware collaborative filtering system: predicting the user's preferences in ubiquitous computing. In: Conference on Human Factors in Computing Systems (2005)

[8] van Setten, M., Pokraev, S., Koolwaaij, J.: Context-Aware Recommendations in the Mobile Tourist Application COMPASS. In: De Bra, P.M.E., Nejdl, W. (eds.) AH 2004. LNCS, vol. 3137, pp. 235–244. Springer, Heidelberg (2004)

[9] Zhiwen, Y., Xingshe, Z., Daqing, Z., Chin, C.-Y., Wang, X., Ji, M.: Supporting Context-Aware Media Recommendations for Smart Phones. IEEE Pervasive Computing 5(3), 68–75 (2006)

[10] http://www.foaf-project.org/

[11] http://www.w3.org/2004/02/skos/

Context Cells: Towards Lifelong Learning in Activity Recognition Systems

Alberto Calatroni[1], Claudia Villalonga[1,2],
Daniel Roggen[1], and Gerhard Tröster[1]

[1] Wearable Computing Laboratory, ETH Zürich, Switzerland
{alberto.calatroni,claudia.villalonga,daniel.roggen,
gerhard.troester}@ife.ee.ethz.ch
http://wearable.ethz.ch
[2] SAP Research, CEC Zürich, Switzerland

Abstract. A robust activity and context-recognition system must be capable of operating over a long period of time, exploiting new sources of information as they become available and evolving in an autonomous manner, coping with user variability and changes in the number and type of available sensors. In particular, wearable and ambient nodes should be trained lifelong, as new context instances naturally arise, and the labeling of the instances should be carried out ideally with no user intervention. In this paper we show by means of an experiment and simulations that we can indeed achieve lifelong learning and automatic labeling by using Context Cells, an architecture capable of sensing, learning, classifying data and exchanging information.

1 Introduction

Research on activity recognition in wearable and pervasive sensor setups has shown that multiple modalities are beneficial to achieve a better accuracy on the recognized activities [1,2,3]. Technical advances and miniaturization are also leading to a continuously and rapidly increasing number of sensors becoming available in the environment, on the user's body [4] and also integrated into smart textiles [5].

These many resources can be exploited in an efficient way to perform activity and context recognition, but challenges arise. In particular, we cannot rely on a fixed sensor setup, since upgrades in the infrastructure can occur and the placement and number of sensors can continuously vary both on the body and in the environment (for example a cell phone can be in different pockets and can have different orientations). In such a scenario where sensors dynamically become available, can be moved etc, it is not possible to train classifiers and map signal instances to activities at design time, like it is done in present activity recognition systems. Traditional activity recognition systems are in fact static, since they feature fixed setups that rely on predefined sensors and machine learning algorithms to achieve their goal and the training of these algorithms is normally done off-line with user-annotated labels [6].

P. Barnaghi et al. (Eds.): EuroSSC 2009, LNCS 5741, pp. 121–134, 2009.

We believe that lifelong incremental learning and automatic labeling are two key features upon which to build in order to obtain a system which can work in a stable way in a dynamical setup, where sensors are opportunistically discovered in the environment or on the user's body. Automatic labeling also brings the desirable property of unobtrusiveness with respect to the user [7]. Instrumental to the labeling and thus to the learning phase is the possibility for sensor nodes to communicate with each other, so that one node trains another node.

In this work we outline the main architectural and operational features that a sensor node should have to achieve incremental learning and labeling. We call "Context Cell" the generic hardware that offers these functionalities and we use a very simple incremental learning algorithm (incremental NCC) to show the main behaviour of our lifelong learning system. We show by means of a real-life experiment that the proposed approach is effective also when dealing with the recognition of fine-grained gestures, which is challenging even for a traditional activity recognition system.

The paper is structured as follows: Section 2 presents the State of the Art; in Section 3 we outline the fundamental architectural and operational features of a Context Cell; in Section 4 we describe in detail the experiment and we discuss the results and in Section 5 we draw the conclusions and outline the future work.

2   State of the Art

Dynamic use of the sensor nodes' functionalities in activity recognition systems has been investigated in the last years and has lead to frameworks like SPINE and Titan.

The SPINE Framework [8] allows health care and assisted living applications to make use of sensor nodes coordinated by a gateway device to detect the patient activity, posture and movements. The framework allows the reuse of nodes that have already been configured in different application scenarios and the easy development of new applications by making services abstract. However, all this composition of services needs to be specified by the service developer. Moreover, this framework has the drawback that the sensor nodes do not classify the activities themselves, in the best case they can extract features, and the activity recognition is done in the gateway, therefore the interaction between nodes serves the purpose of classifying an activity but not to achieve more advanced opportunistic functionalities like training of other nodes.

The Titan framework [9] targets the execution of activity recognition chains in the dynamic and heterogeneous devices available in the environment. The framework knows about the available services in each node and is able to instantiate them at run time depending of the goal that should be achieved by a given recognition chain. The framework provides a good abstraction of the services and cooperation to detect activities, but does not allow advanced opportunistic scenarios like the training of other nodes. Moreover, the definition of recognition chains needs to be foreseen at design time, which does not fit an opportunistic, autonomous scenario.

In the literature we can find some complex classifiers capable of online learning activities, e.g. [10,11,12]. These classifiers could be used as part of an opportunistic system; however, the classifiers alone do not fulfill the requirement of a lifelong learning system since the unobtrusive labeling is not ensured by them and would depend on the implementation of the other components of the system.

In summary, the different approaches described in the literature do not solve one important challenge of an opportunistic system: they do not provide a way to autonomously learn how to map the sensor signals into a set of activities and how to do this over the whole life of the system.

3 Context Cells

A **Context Cell** is a self-contained hardware node that

- exploits sensors to gather information about the physical world;
- is capable of processing and interpreting data to infer context and user activities by using machine learning techniques to classify signals into a set of output classes;
- can cooperate with other Context Cells by exchanging information like the detected context.

Context Cells are heterogeneous, however they can be split in two types following a user centric approach:

- **Wearable Cells** or cells worn by the user;
- **Ambient Cells** or cells that are part of the environment, either embedded in objects or in some infrastructure. Some of these Ambient Cells do not need to implement machine learning algorithms, but just simple signal processing. We call these **Simple Ambient Cells**.

Activity recognition systems based on Context Cells unlock a new set of possibilities, like the long life training of the system with automatic labeling. The Context Cell is in fact capable of adapting its mapping between sensor signals and activity classes incrementally, while operating, through repeated interactions with neighboring cells: this allows the Context Cells to learn about new activity classes, be trained from others, or to train others. The labels used in the learning process are provided by neighboring cells.

3.1 Context Cell Operation

Context Cells interact and collaborate in the task of training activity recognition systems. In order to explain this mechanism, at first we assume that we have two Context Cells, one already capable of recognizing activities and another which needs to be trained. The first cell, which plays the role of the Trainer, detects some change in the context and broadcasts a message with the recognized context. The second Context Cell, that acts as Learner, receives a label

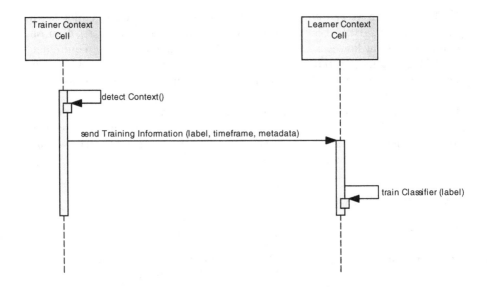

Fig. 1. UML sequence diagram showing the interactions between two Context Cells in the sequential order that those interactions occur: 1) the Trainer Cell detects its context, 2) the Trainer sends the detected label to the Learner Cell, and 3) the Learner trains its classifier using the received label

for the current context and trains the system using that label. This process is shown in Fig.1.

Whenever a cell starts up, it must look for other cells in the neighborhood and synchronize its timer with theirs. Since human activities normally occur within a time span of at least seconds, **synchronization** can be achieved with mild constraints. After the synchronization phase, the cells start buffering data coming from their sensors.

The **learning** process can start as soon as a Trainer recognizes a new context instance. The label associated with this instance is broadcast along with temporal coordinates (e.g. start and finish time of the instance) and optional, complementary data (or metadata). This can include a more detailed description of the instance being recognized and a measure of the the quality of the recognition itself. The temporal information allows the Learner to isolate the correct portion of its input buffer and extract features, which are used to create and store a class model associated with the received label. As more instances are labeled, the Learner's classifier is incrementally trained. In general, the rule with which class models are updated is of the kind:

$$\mathbf{s_c}(n+1) = f(L, \mathbf{s_c}(n), \mathbf{x_c}), \tag{1}$$

where $\mathbf{x_c}$ is the the feature vector extracted from the instance with class label c, L is the learning rate and $\mathbf{s_c}(n)$ denotes the model for class c after having seen n instances of the class (the dependency of n on c has been omitted for a cleaner notation). The choice of L, which takes values between 0 and 1, depends on the classifier used and on the instances acquired before. L could be adjusted depending on metadata provided along with the labels, e.g. higher label reliabilities would imply higher values for this parameter. For a simple incremental NCC, the class model is just the centroid (average) of all received instances. Thus, equation 1 becomes

$$\mathbf{s_c}(n+1) = (1-L)\mathbf{s_c}(n) + L\mathbf{x_c}, \qquad (2)$$

where $L = \frac{1}{n+1}$, for $n = 0, 1, \ldots$. The number n of received instances for each class is stored as an auxiliary parameter.

After enough labeled instances have been stored by a Learner Cell, this cell can also start extracting features from the buffered signal and provide itself output classes that can be sent to other cells, thereby acting as a Trainer. This behaviour of the Context Cells learning and training all life long creates a complex dynamic system.

We have explained the main training with a small example involving only two cells, but in general this is not the case, as many cells interact. Therefore, a Learner Cell receives labels from several surrounding Trainer Cells. Since the Trainer Cells are in general not 100% accurate in the classification, two erroneous situations can occur. First, more Trainer Cells send disagreeing labels at the same time, resulting in a clash at the receiver side. Second, despite an activity occurring, this is not detected by any Trainer Cell, thus no labels are sent. In this latter case the Learner Cell is not trained, because it is not aware of the new activity instance going on, while the former case can be dealt with by simply choosing the first received label. If a reliability measure regarding the labels is also received, the Learner Cell can choose the most likely label received within a certain time slot. Different ways of handling these situations are part of future research directions.

3.2   Context Cell Architecture

Context Cells share common hardware features and each one of them hosts:

- one or more **sensors** which measure the state of the physical world;
- a **computational unit**, which implements feature extraction and machine learning algorithms to detect activities. The complexity of the computational unit can be very different from cell to cell, and it is possible to have a simpler case which only performs basic processing on the sensor signal. An example of computational unit is a microcontroller with DSP functionalities.
- a **radio** for communication purposes; when an activity is detected, a corresponding label is sent along with complementary data through the radio channel to all neighboring cells, which can use the labels to perform incremental training. The radio can also be used to send features or even raw data;
- a **time reference**; when the cell detects the occurrence of an activity, it must record the start and end times for that activity. This information, sent along the label to other cells, will enable them to segment their sensor signal and use the selected part as a labeled training instance;

- a nonvolatile **storage block** where class models can be retained, along with
  auxiliary parameters. For example, if a cell implements a NCC classifier, each
  activity will be associated with a centroid vector and these will be stored in
  the nonvolatile storage block;
- a **temporary buffer**, which is used for the incremental training. The sensor
  signals are stored in this buffer so that if a label is received from another
  cell, the associated time references can be used to extract the correct portion
  of the past sampled data and use it as a training instance. The length of the
  buffer depends on the length of the activities or context instances that must
  be recognized.

4   Experiment and Results

By means of an experiment, we investigate the key algorithmic building block
of Context Cells, namely the incremental learning process performed through
automatic labeling, where several Trainer Cells provide labels with different
accuracies to a Learner Cell.

We study a simple storage management scenario, in which a user opens and
closes drawers in order to store goods in them (e.g., a pharmacist keeping the
medicines in the drawer storage). This scenario could be extended to many real
world activities like the opening of the fridge in a kitchen or the opening of a
closet to store folders in an office.

With this scenario, we want to show that the lifelong training is effective in
a fine-grained setup in which the activities to be recognized are quite similar.
We also want to prove that several Ambient Cells can train a Wearable Cell to
detect user activities.

4.1   Experiment Description

In our experiment we record instances of the fine-grained activity of opening and
closing of 13 drawers in a drawer set. This implies a 26 classes problem, where
classes 1 and 2 represent respectively opening and closing of the topmost drawer,
while classes 25 and 26 concern the bottommost drawer. The distance between
two neighboring drawer handles ranges from 5cm to 15cm, meaning that the
class models are quite similar.

Each of the 13 drawers is instrumented with a USB triaxial acceleration sensor,
which plays the role of a Trainer Ambient Cell. The subject wears three such
sensors on the body and limbs (at the mid-back, shoulder and mid-arm), and
these on-body sensors play the role of the Learner Wearable Cells which are
trained by the Ambient Cells. Fig. 2 shows the experimental setup and the test
subject interacting with one of the drawers.

All the sensors are connected to a PC to allow synchronous recording at 100Hz
sampling frequency. The test subject performs the opening and closing of all the
drawers an average of 10 times in a sequential order, starting from the topmost
and reaching the bottommost. Each instance consists of a rest position (arm

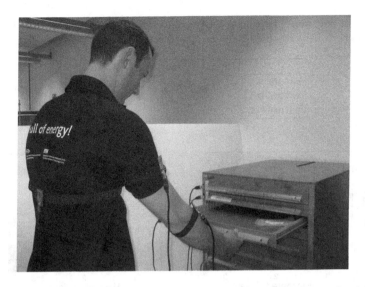

Fig. 2. Experimental setup: drawers equipped with sensors playing the role of Ambient Cells and sensors on the body of the user playing the role of the Wearable Cells

straight parallel to the body), followed by the gesture (opening or closing of the drawer) and ends with the same rest position. This yields a total of 269 instances, that we then randomize in order to have a realistic order of appearance of the instances.

The collected signals are manually labeled and segmented in order to establish the association between the instances and the ground truth labels.

4.2 Simulation of the Automatic Labeling

The collected data is used to simulate the functionality of the automatic labeling, i.e. an Ambient Cell placed on a drawer detects the context of that drawer and this information is used to label the instances with which the Wearable Cell is trained.

In order to do so, the Ambient Cell classifies the instances collected by the sensor into three classes, providing recognition of whether the drawer is being opened, closed, or left untouched (null class).

We extract three different sets of features from the drawer signals and we use the feature vectors to batch-train an NCC classifier for the 3-class problem. The extracted features are:

- Feature set 1: Mean of the magnitude of the acceleration vector in 5 signal windows;
- Feature set 2: Variance of the magnitude of the acceleration vector in 5 signal windows;
- Feature set 3: Variance of the x, y and z components of the acceleration vector in the whole signal.

Table 1. Best and worse accuracies for the detection by the Ambient Cells associated to the drawers, considering the different sets of features

	Best Accuracy	Worse Accuracy
Feature set 1	87.5%	33.3%
Feature set 2	100%	40.0%
Feature set 3	87.0%	45.0%

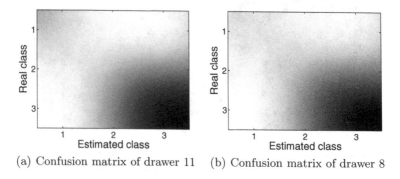

(a) Confusion matrix of drawer 11   (b) Confusion matrix of drawer 8

Fig. 3. Confusion matrix for the classification of the signal of a) drawer 11 and b) drawer 8 using as features the variance of the x, y and z components of the acceleration vector in the whole signal and an NCC classifier

Depending on the set of features extracted from the acceleration signals, we obtain different accuracies for the detection of the opening or closing of a drawer. Since the drawers are not identical, the accuracies are also different for each of them. The reason for accuracies below 100% lies in the mechanical coupling that exists in the drawers, so that an interaction with one generates strong vibrations also in the others. Table 1 shows the best and the worse accuracy obtained by the classifier of the drawer-mounted Ambient Cell with the three different feature sets.

Moreover, Fig. 3(a) shows the confusion matrix for the best performance of the detection using the feature set 3, which takes place for drawer number 11. Fig. 3(b) shows for the same feature set the confusion matrix for the worst detection, which takes place for drawer number 8.

Each time an Ambient Cell detects the opening or closing of the drawer, it sends the label of the detected class together with its own information (e.g. the drawer number) to the Wearable Cell so that the latter can train its classifier using the detected label. Despite the apparent simplicity of the 3-class problem, Ambient Cells make errors in the context detection, as shown by the accuracies obtained above. This causes both clashes in the labels that are received by the Wearable Cell and lack of labels for some of the instances. Fig. 4 shows the labels that are sent over time by each Ambient Cell in the experiment using feature set 1 (light marks for the opening of the drawer and black marks for the closing). In the enlarged view (see Fig. 5) a subset of 30 instances is plotted and the clashing and absence of labels can be seen. The clashes have here been solved by choosing

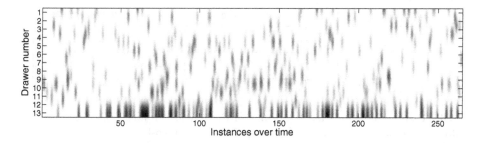

Fig. 4. Automatic labeling for the whole dataset. For each drawer, the detected label for opening or closing of the drawer is shown. A light mark indicates the opening of the drawer, whereas a black one indicates its closing.

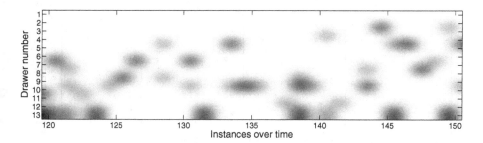

Fig. 5. Automatic labeling for a subset of instances (zoom in Fig. 4). Clashes as well as missing labels can be appreciated.

a label at random among the received ones; in a more advanced system, labels could be chosen according to their reported reliability. For this simulation using feature set 1, the errors in the detection yield 144 label errors and 52 missing labels out of the 269 instances, however better results are achieved using the other feature sets.

4.3 Simulation of the Lifelong Training

The core incremental learning of our Wearable Cell is simulated by the use of a wearable sensor (the mid-back sensor) and an NCC classifier that learns incrementally.

Each simulation run starts with shuffling the available instances and partitioning them into a training and test set (4 to 1). The shuffling accounts for the fact that the order in which instances would appear in a real system is random.

After the randomization, we perform feature extraction on the instances. We use as features the average tilt of the acceleration sensor with respect to the vertical axis in 5 signal windows. The tilt of the mid-back sensor is indeed very informative of the bending that the test subject performs to reach the various

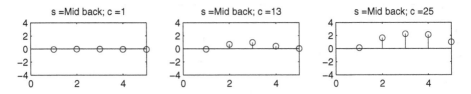

Fig. 6. Feature vector for class 1 (opening of the topmost drawer), class 13 (opening of drawer number 7) and class 25 (opening of the bottommost drawer)

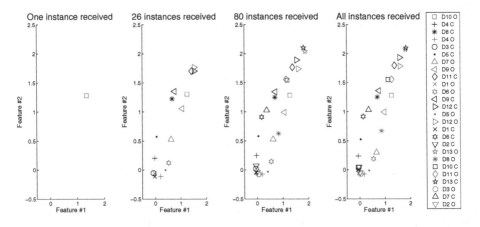

Fig. 7. Evolution of the centroids. 2D projection of the centroids at four moments of the training process. The legend shows the order in which the centroids appear.

drawers. This is apparent in Fig. 6, where the tilt is nearly constant for the topmost drawer, while it exhibits a visible maximum for the bottommost.

Within each simulation run we train the incremental NCC with one training instance at a time. As the first instance is used, a new centroid is added and associated with the ground truth label (see the first plot in Fig. 7). The algorithm also stores the number of already seen instances associated with that label. Upon reception of a following instance, two situations can occur: the label matches that of an already stored centroid, or it has never been seen before by the trainer. In the first case, the centroid position is adjusted according to equation 2. In the second case, a new centroid is created. Fig. 7 shows the evolution of the centroids over time by means of a projection on a 2D space. The initial phases show the appearance of many new centroids and major displacement of existing ones, while as time goes by, the learning rate decreases and the centroids tend to reach stable positions.

In order to evaluate the evolution of the accuracy of the incremental NCC, classification is performed on the test set after each training step and averaged through a 5-fold cross-validation. Since one simulation run only accounts for

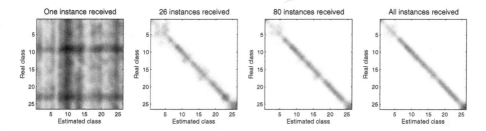

Fig. 8. Evolution of the average confusion matrix. The average performance rapidly converges to that achieved with offline batch training (rightmost plot).

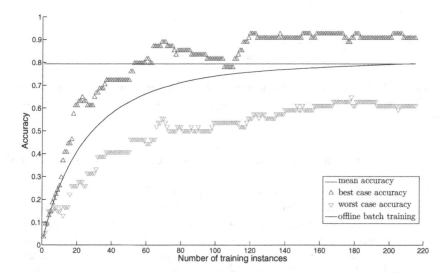

Fig. 9. Evolution of accuracy for incremental training with the ground truth labels. The batch off-line training (horizontal line) serves as a baseline for the maximum accuracy if the classifier would be trained offline. The triangular markers show the best and worst case curves.

one of the many ways in which instances can be ordered, we performed 2000 simulation runs and averaged the obtained accuracies and confusion matrices.

Fig. 8 shows the evolution of the confusion matrix over time. Opening and closing of upper drawers leads to more confusion, due to similar body postures, while performance improves on lower drawers. This can be also seen in Fig. 7, where it is clear how the centroids associated with the opening and closing of the topmost drawers are much closer together than the other centroids.

In Fig. 9 we show the evolution of the average accuracy, along with the best and worst case curves. The exponential nature of the curves shows that the learning is on average quite fast. The difference between the best and worst case

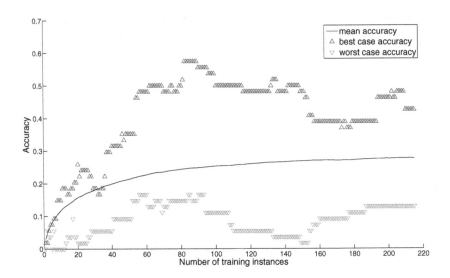

Fig. 10. Evolution of accuracy for incremental training with automatically detected labels for the case of feature set 1. The triangular markers show the best and worst case curves.

curves is due to the randomness with which the training and test sets are formed in each of the simulation runs.

The same 2000 simulation runs are now performed using the automatically generated labels to train the incremental system. The labels are obtained through the use of Ambient Cells using feature set 1 (as explained in Section 4.2). In this paper we do not seek a model for incorrect (or noisy) labels, but research in that direction exists, see for example [13]. The incremental average accuracy is shown in Fig. 10. The performance is much worse than the training obtained with ground truth labels and, in particular, the worst case curve exhibits a really important drop in the recognition accuracy. It is therefore useful that Context Cells work on a lifelong basis, so that they can recover from the effects of training with erroneous labels on the long term.

5   Conclusion

In this paper we have presented the building blocks for context recognition systems that evolve their capabilities over time. We have described with the help of an experiment two essential functionalities of those systems, i.e. lifelong learning and automatic gathering of labels to train classifiers.

We have shown that one way to achieve this is the cooperation between nodes capable of recognizing context (Context Cells). Upon the recognition of a context occurrence by a node, a label is shared with neighboring nodes. Previously untrained nodes can use this label to update their internal state using online incremental machine learning techniques. These nodes gradually learn to recognize these context instances. This training method avoids the large training sets usually needed for the time-consuming offline training and removes the restriction that only the contexts foreseen at design time can be included in the system.

Moreover, we have proposed an automatic labeling process that differs from that used in traditional activity recognition systems, which rely on classifiers that are trained through manually labeled instances.

We have shown an implementation and experimental results based on a simple classifier to validate the principles on a storage management scenario where a set of context-aware ambient-sensors are informing a set of on-body sensors of context occurrences. Through simulations we have got a first understanding of the challenges, limitations and points deserving further research, e.g. how to use information about the reliability of the detected context to improve the learning algorithms in the case of erroneous labels.

While we have shown an example of an AmI environment training a Wearable system, in our future work we also plan to extend the functionalities of the Context Cells in order to allow other uses cases like for example:

- Wearable system classifies activities. A trained wearable system is moved from an instrumented environment into a new environment where no AmI is available and this system is able to continue operating and detecting the learned activities even in this different setup. The user experiences a seamless transition between the two environments.
- AmI environment retrains wearable system. A trained wearable system is moved into a new ambient intelligence environment, there the on-body sensors can learn from the AmI environment the new activities that can be performed in this new setup.
- Wearable system trains AmI environment. A trained wearable system is moved to an environment which is equipped with ambient intelligence but that has not been trained beforehand. Then, the wearable system can be used to train the sensor nodes in the environment and make them capable of detecting context instances.

The ultimate goal is to deploy a complete hardware system based on Context Cells in opportunistic environments.

Acknowledgment

The project OPPORTUNITY acknowledges the financial support of the Future and Emerging Technologies (FET) programme within the Seventh Framework Programme for Research of the European Commission, under FET-Open grant number: 225938.

References

1. Stiefmeier, T., Roggen, D., Ogris, G., Lukowicz, P., Tröster, G.: Wearable activity tracking in car manufacturing. IEEE Pervasive Computing 7(2), 42–50 (2008)
2. Van Laerhoven, K., Gellersen, H.W.: Spine versus porcupine: a study in distributed wearable activity recognition. In: Proceedings of Eighth International Symposium on Wearable Computers (ISWC), pp. 142–149. IEEE Computer Society Press, Los Alamitos (2004)
3. Logan, B., Healey, J., Philipose, M., Tapia, E.M., Intille, S.S.: A long-term evaluation of sensing modalities for activity recognition. In: Krumm, J., Abowd, G.D., Seneviratne, A., Strang, T. (eds.) UbiComp 2007. LNCS, vol. 4717, pp. 483–500. Springer, Heidelberg (2007)
4. Tentori, M., Favela, J.: Activity-aware computing for healthcare. IEEE Pervasive Computing 7(2), 51–57 (2008)
5. Harms, H., Amft, O., Roggen, D., Tröster, G.: Smash: A distributed sensing and processing garment for the classification of upper body postures. In: Third interational conference on body area networks (2008)
6. Bao, L., Intille, S.S.: Activity recognition from user-annotated acceleration data. In: Pervasive Computing: Proc. of the 2nd Int'l Conference, pp. 1–17 (2004)
7. Weiser, M.: The computer for the 21st century. Pervasive Computing 1(1), 19–25 (2002)
8. SPINE: http://spine.tilab.com/ (Last seen May 15, 2009)
9. Lombriser, C., Roggen, D., Stäger, M., Tröster, G.: Titan: A tiny task network for dynamically reconfigurable heterogeneous sensor networks. In: 15. Fachtagung Kommunikation in Verteilten Systemen (KiVS), pp. 127–138 (2007)
10. Zhao, H., Yuen, P.C., Kwok, J.T.: A novel incremental principal component analysis and its application for face recognition. IEEE Transactions on Systems, Man, and Cybernetics Part B 36, 873–886 (2006)
11. Polikar, R., Upda, L., Upda, S., Honavar, V.: Learn++: an incremental learning algorithm for supervised neural networks. IEEE Transactions on Systems, Man, and Cybernetics, Part C: Applications and Reviews 31(4), 497–508 (2001)
12. Freund, Y., Schapire, R.E.: A decision-theoretic generalization of on-line learning and an application to boosting. Journal of Computer and System Sciences 55(1), 119–139 (1997)
13. Angluin, D., Laird, P.D.: Learning from noisy examples. Machine Learning 2(4), 343–370 (1988)

Automatic Event-Based Synchronization of Multimodal Data Streams from Wearable and Ambient Sensors

David Bannach[1], Oliver Amft[2], and Paul Lukowicz[1]

[1] Embedded Systems Lab, University of Passau
{david.bannach,paul.lukowicz}@uni-passau.de
[2] Signal Processing Systems, TU Eindhoven
oliver.amft@gmail.com

Abstract. A major challenge in using multi-modal, distributed sensor systems for activity recognition is to maintain a temporal synchronization between individually recorded data streams. A common approach is to use well defined 'synchronization actions' performed by the user to generate, easily identifiable pattern events in all recorded data streams. The events are then used to manually align data streams. This paper proposes an automatic method for this synchronization.
We demonstrate that synchronization actions can be automatically identified and used for stream synchronization across widely different sensors such as acceleration, sound, force, and a motion tracking system. We describe fundamental properties and bounds of our event-based synchronization approach. In particular, we show that the event timing relation is transitive for sensor groups with shared members. We analyzed our synchronization approach in three studies. For a large dataset of 5 users and totally 308 data stream minutes we achieved a synchronization error of 0.3 s for more than 80% of the stream.

1 Introduction

Multi-modal, distributed sensor systems have been proposed for a variety of wearable and pervasive computing applications. A major practical concern to use such systems is how to temporally synchronize data streams between individual sensors. In particular, methods that rely on sensor fusion (such as computing joint features from several sensors or jointly feeding a classifier) require that sensor signals are well synchronized.

The synchronization problem is a well known and widely studied distributed systems issue [3]. Without precautions, clocks of physically separate processors will run asynchronously [10]. A receiving node observes this as skew and drift in the incoming sensor data stream. Furthermore, networked nodes may startup or resume operation independently. This can causes offsets at stream receivers, similar to not handled data interrupts in wireless links.

Much effort has been devoted to lightweight clock synchronization methods for wireless sensor networks (see related work). In general these methods rely on

P. Barnaghi et al. (Eds.): EuroSSC 2009, LNCS 5741, pp. 135–148, 2009.

elaborate message passing and time distribution protocols among the network nodes. This paper does not aim to compete with, or improve upon this work. While in theory, it may be assumed that a sensor node could receive messages and run such synchronization protocols, in practice many on-body and pervasive sensing setups do not have appropriate capabilities. For one, leaving out the receiving capability reduces power consumption and makes node design simpler. Secondly, systems are often built using nodes from different manufacturers with insufficient built-in synchronization support. It is not common that commercial nodes provide access to node-internal communication routines.

Consequently, we look at a specific problem variation that occurs frequently in wearable and pervasive systems: sensor nodes merely stream data in a hierarchical topology and are not able to communicate with each other. This means that no message passing protocols can be run between the nodes. Instead, the synchronization can rely solely on the content of the data stream.

It is common practice in wearable and pervasive application studies to rely on event-based synchronization of data streams. To this end, 'synchronization actions' are defined, which are periodically performed by a subject during the recording (at least once at the start of a data collection). Such actions are designed to simultaneously activate multiple sensors and provide an easily identifiable data signature. Often encountered examples are clapping, jumping, and hitting a surface. The characteristic signature of a synchronization action can be used to align signal segments from different sensors. Currently, this is typically done through manual inspection of the data streams. This paper investigates a method to automate this process.

It is intuiting to rely on natural activity patterns to synchronize sensor data streams that are performed by users in a pervasive application. However, it is essential to develop a robust synchronization framework in the first place. Hence, we chose validation scenarios for this initial work, in which particularly selected synchronization actions had been inserted into sensor data streams. We subsequently discuss how our concept could extend on natural activities.

1.1 Related Work

Time synchronization is a well known and widely studied problem in wireless sensor networks, in particular for subsequent sensor data fusion. Surveys can be found in [8] and [10]. Typically, the solutions target a network-wide synchronization by aligning the clocks of all physically distributed nodes [10,9]. For this purpose specific messages are exchanged among the nodes.

As detailed above, we target systems where a synchronization based on exchanging messages is not feasible due to unidirectional communication channels. Our approach relies on data signatures (events) embedded in data streams, hence it does not modify the source clocks. However, it ensures a relative synchronization between data sources at the fusion unit.

Instead of establishing a network-wide clock, various communication systems use a source synchronization approach for medium access. These techniques target to align message recipient(s) on a link with the clock provided by the sender, through monitoring packet reception [7] or protocol-specific features, such as a preamble. Our approach is similar to source synchronization, as the fusion unit observes the relative offset in the incoming data streams.

More relevant research looks at correlation of different sensor data streams for various applications. This includes the use of correlations to determine that a set of devices are carried by the same person [5], as well as attempts to use correlation between sounds received by different sensors for indoor location [2].

Many researchers experienced clock synchronization failures in deployed sensor networks due to software bugs, communication failures, and frequent reboots, rendering large parts of data unusable [11,4,6]. Common solutions try to recover corrupted timestamps in a postmortem process. Werner-Allen [11] corrects errors caused by the time synchronization protocol on behalf of a base station that adds its own timestamps to the collected data. They build piecewise linear models to map local node time to global time without utilizing the actual sensor data collected by the nodes. Lukac [6] proposes data driven time synchronization by utilizing background noise in seismic sensing systems. By building a model of the propagation of micorseisms (seismic waves that travel through continents, originated by oceans) they can reconstruct timestamps in large datasets gathered by seismic networks. The Sundial system [4] uses light sensors to detect length of day and noon time and compares them offline with the astronomical model to estimate the correct global timestamps. While this approach is based on a single sensing modality they also apply a method to correlate rain events with soil humidity events for finding the correct day. This is very similar to our approach but we do not rely on additional information about the events to find the correct mapping and we explicitly allow event spotting errors.

1.2   Challenges of Event-Based Stream Synchronization

The conceptual solution for event-based synchronization is straightforward. We assume that each data item is time-stamped with a local clock (or stream sequence number). Once a first synchronization action is localized in all data streams, offsets between the local clocks or sequence numbers are computed. Upon locating a second event, differences between sensor clock frequencies can be computed. Subsequently, the data streams are aligned according to these differences. Additional events may help keeping streams synchronized over time and could increase synchronization accuracy.

In reality, there are a number of problems related to reliable, automatic spotting of synchronization actions. It is well known that recognizing short actions embedded in a continuous stream of arbitrary sensor data is a hard problem. To synchronize data streams based on events, actions must be spotted separately in each data stream. This is even more difficult than under a multi-modal spotting scheme, where signals from several sensors can be combined. Hence actions could be confused with other arbitrary actions. As a consequence, the synchronization algorithm has to cope with deleted (missed) and inserted (wrongly recognized) events in individual streams. Hence it is not a-priori clear which events should be aligned with each other.

Another particular spotting property is the timing variations among retrieved events. For an event-based synchronization approach, this variation can have two origins. On one hand, a spotting procedure can introduce a temporal jitter due to an assumed segmentation. Typically, this jitter is a fraction of the expected event size [1]. Secondly, spotting on independent sensors can impose different event patterns. For example, hitting a table with a fist will generate a short temporal acceleration at the wrist, while the table will vibrate longer with a delayed onset. Thus, even if the synchronization actions are correctly spotted, it is not always clear how to relate events in time.

1.3 Paper Contributions

This paper investigates solutions to the problems described above, facilitating a practical implementation of automatic, event-based synchronization. We demonstrate that synchronization actions can be identified across widely different sensors, such as accelerometers and optical motion tracking systems. We show how using repetitive events can improve synchronization results. Moreover, we show that the timing relation is transitive for sensor groups with shared members. The latter can be exploited for further reliability improvements and to synchronize larger multi-modal sensor networks.

2   Spotting and Synchronization Approach

Our approach consists of two steps. In the first step appropriately defined synchronization actions are spotted in each sensor data stream. Specifically, we spotted hand 'clap', 'push-release' of a button, and arm 'shake' actions as described below. In a second step our online synchronization algorithm is used to establish, which events in two different streams correspond to the same physical action. This step deals with missing and inserted events, as well as temporal jitter. The result of this step is a continuous alignment estimation corresponding to events derived from the participating data streams.

The required synchronization performance is application dependent. For a typical example of motion-related activities in daily life, such as considered in this work, stream alignment should be well below 1 s. Nevertheless, an alignment performance below 0.1 s is typically not needed. In our evaluation we selected a performance of 0.3 s as target alignment.

2.1 Event Spotting

In our approach synchronization actions are associated with a single timestamp from each data stream. Nevertheless, even short physical actions such as a hand clap exhibit a temporal signal pattern. Figure 1(a) illustrates such patterns for acceleration and audio streams. Hence, we specifically modelled a synchronization point in the event patterns using signal features. Two sliding window algorithms were used to spot 'clap', 'push-release', and 'shake' gestures on individual modalities. Figures 1(a)-1(c) show these events on four different sensing modalities (acceleration, force sensitive resistors (FSR), positioning sensors, and audio). Other event types or sensing modalities may require further spotting algorithms, which can be easily designed.

For both algorithms we obtained model parameters manually by analyzing pattern examples. The parameters were chosen to minimize event miss rate. This spotting approach might result in suboptimal event recognition performance. However, it was not the goal of this work to maximize event spotting performance, but to analyze practical operation of our stream synchronization algorithm.

Trailing Edge Detection. The patterns produced by 'clap' and 'push-release' events have similar characteristics. Their signal pattern have a stable phase of "silence" followed by a fast rise or fall (see Fig. 1(a) and 1(b)). The start of a rise/fall phase was considered as the synchronization point. The two events were distinguished by the features: minimal length of silence phase, signal range of silence phase, length of rise/fall phase, and signal range of rise/fall phase.

Shake Detection. The detection of shakes was implemented by tracking peaks (alternating local minima and maxima) over time. The features, minimal peak height, min/max of time between peaks, and number of peaks had been used. The begin and end of shake events may vary between sensing modalities (shown in Fig. 1(c)). Consequently, we defined the center point (midpoint between first and last peak timestamp) as synchronization point for shake events.

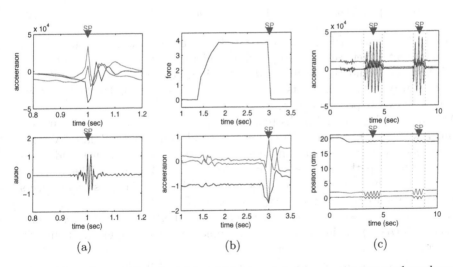

Fig. 1. Aligned sensor signals: (a) hand 'clap' recorded from wrist mounted accelerometers and a microphone, (b) button push followed by sudden release recorded from an FSR under thumb and wrist mounted accelerometers ('push-release'), (c) two 'shake' motions recorded from accelerometers and a camera-based positioning system. "SP" indicates synchronization points returned by our spotting procedure and subsequently used for alignment.

2.2   Event-Based Synchronization

While the event pattern structure (such as signal peaks for 'shake' events) could be used to analyze the synchronization between two sensor streams, we found these patterns to be too variable. Moreover, the patterns may differ between modalities, which would hamper their alignment. Instead our approach relies on a sequence of spotted events from both streams to estimate alignment. In particular, we consider the temporal distribution of the retrieved events as relevant synchronization property. Thus, as long as events do not occur with constant frequency, we expect that a match between event sequences of both streams can be found. Clearly, the probability for a correct event match will increase with the sequence length of matching events.

Algorithm: The synchronization algorithm compares two event sequences $A = \{a_1, \ldots, a_n\}$ and $B = \{b_1, \ldots, b_m\}$ to estimate a sequence match. A sliding window with a size of 30 s was applied on the event sequence for online operation and retain multiple events for alignment analysis at any considered stream position. The procedure can be understood as shifting sequence B in time until an optimal match is found with sequence A.
Let

$$d(i,j) = t(b_i) - t(a_j), \ i \in [1, \ldots n], \ j \in [1, \ldots m] \tag{1}$$

be the n-by-m matrix of timestamp differences between all possible events of sequence A and B, and let

$$P = \{(i_1, j_1), \ldots, (i_k, j_k)\}, \ k > 1, i_l < i_{l+1}, j_l < j_{l+1} \ \forall l \in [1, \ldots k-1] \tag{2}$$

be a matching path of length k between A and B. Each cell (i,j) in path P denotes a match between event a_i and b_j and therefore indicates an offset of $d(i,j)$ between A and B. Matches in P are unique ($i_l \neq i_{l'}$, $j_l \neq j_{l'}$ $\forall l \neq l'$) but not necessarily include all events ($i_{l+1} - i_l \geq 1$, $j_{l+1} - j_l \geq 1$). The latter allows coping with event spotting errors.

We analyze all potential paths (candidate paths) and select the best by applying a weighting function $w(P) = w_K(P) * w_V(P)$ on each candidate. Weights w_K and w_V were defined with an intend to maximize path length k and minimize variance of path distances $v = var(\{d(i_1, j_1), \ldots, d(i_k, j_k)\})$. The synchronization algorithm provides a continuous estimation of relative stream offsets between two sources by selecting $P_{best} = max[w(P)]$.

The path search can be performed incrementally. For a given cell (i_l, j_l) a subsequent cell (i_{l+1}, j_{l+1}) in the path is determined by searching in the submatrix of (i_l, j_l):

$$j_{l+1} = \arg \min_{j' \in [j_l+1 \ldots m]} |d_1 - d(i_l + 1, j')| \text{ and} \tag{3}$$

$$i_{l+1} = \arg \min_{i' \in [i_l+1 \ldots n]} |d_1 - d(i', j_{l+1})|, \tag{4}$$

where $d_1 = d(i_1, j_1)$ denotes a path's starting point. If $|d_1 - d(i_{l+1}, j_{l+1})|$ does not fall below a tolerance threshold this cell is discarded and searching is repeated

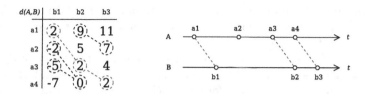

Fig. 2. Two event sequences with the corresponding matching paths highlighted in the timestamp differences matrix (left), and the best path displayed on the timeline (right)

in submatrix $(i_{l+1}, j_{l+1} + 1)$. In our evaluations a tolerance of 0.3 s was used to prune non-relevant paths. Multiple candidates of matching paths are found by starting a new search from each top and left border cell (see Fig. 2.2). This corresponds to shifting sequence B against sequence A.

For path weight $w_K = 1 - e^{-((k-1)/(2-k_E))^2}$ was used where k is the actual path length and k_E denotes the expected path length. As variance weight we used $w_V = 1 - e^{-0.5(v/R)^2}$, where regularizer R serves to control variance weight contribution. Weighting behavior is designed to maximize weight for particular parameter sets. For w_K a maximum is obtained at $k = k_E$, for w_V, variance should be minimized.

Parameters k_E and R can be used to adapt our synchronization algorithm. Expected sequence length k_E depends on the targeted synchronization performance, where larger k_E, hence longer sequences, will result in reduced synchronization errors. Parameter R controls the influence of temporal event jitter in w_V. For this work, we determined $R = 0.05$ in empirical tests and confirmed it in all evaluations discussed in Section 3.

It should be noted that our heuristic algorithm can miss a globally optimal path as Eqs. 3, 4 are sequentially evaluated. We consider our approach as a tradeoff limiting computational complexity compared to a full search which would involve evaluating all potential paths within a submatrix of cell (i_l, j_l). Our evaluation results confirm that this approach is feasible.

2.3 Specific Synchronization Properties

Transitivity. Synchronization alignments, as determined with our approach, are transitive. If relative offsets between data streams A and B and between stream B and C are known, then the offset between stream A and C can be deduced. This transitive property allows that sensors or sensor subnets, which do not share common events with other sensors, can still be synchronized on behalf of mediating sensors. We demonstrate how this property can be exploited by analyzing synchronization pairs in Section 3. Moreover, such dependencies could be used to refine synchronization result, as potentially multiple synchronization sources become available.

Performance Bounds. We analyzed theoretical performance bounds for our synchronization algorithm with regard to event input. In particular, we considered the following essential properties: (1) effect of event sequence timing, (2) impact of the number of synchronization actions, and (3) temporal event jitter introduced through the spotting method.

A sequence of events $a = \{a_1, \ldots, a_n\}$ can be described in terms of time distances between subsequent events $s = \{s_1, \ldots, s_{n-1}\} = \{t(a_2) - t(a_1), \ldots, t(a_n) - t(a_{n-1})\}$. The worst-case scenario for our synchronization algorithm is a monotonous sequence of constant event distances, hence $s_1 = s_2 = \ldots = s_n$. In this specific case, an alignment can not be uniquely identified using our distance approach. However, in practice this situation will be rare and difficult to construct.

If we allow some degree of temporal variance in an input event sequence, we may describe s as a random variable with Gaussian probability distribution $p(s) = \mathcal{N}(\mu, \sigma)$. We denote $\hat{s}$ as an actual distance between spotted events that have jitter $\pm \omega$. Consequently, the probability for obtaining a specific event distance can be derived by:

$$P(s = \hat{s} \pm \omega) = \int_{\hat{s}-\omega}^{\hat{s}+\omega} p(s), \qquad (5)$$

which has its maximum at $s^* = \mu$. Hence, if σ increases, the probability for a unique event match is raised, as $P(s)$ decreases. In contrast, if the temporal event jitter ω increases, $P(s)$ increases as well. This means, that it is more likely to randomly observe a specific event distance.

In the analysis above we considered a distance between two events only, hence $k = 1$. In a more practical setting, however, several synchronization actions may be considered for estimating alignment. Thus,

$$P_{Path}(\omega, k) = P(s_1 = \hat{s}_1 \pm \omega, \ldots, s_k = \hat{s}_k \pm \omega) = \prod_{i=1}^{k} P(\hat{s}_i \pm \omega) \qquad (6)$$

shows the probability for a matching path of constant event distance. Hence, the chance of a random match decreases exponentially with increasing event sequence length k.

3   Evaluation

We performed three experiments to analyze the synchronization performance for different events and sensor modalities. All evaluations use sensor modalities that are relevant in ubiquitous applications and have been used in previous studies. Initially, two experiments where performed to investigate the synchronization approach with different sensor modalities and combinations (force-acceleration-audio, acceleration-positioning). In a subsequent evaluation, we investigate the performance of the synchronization algorithm in a large data set (totally 308 min. of 5 users) that was recorded for activity recognition in daily living scenarios. All synchronization actions were annotated and refined in a post-recording step by visual inspections of the data streams. For all experiments the correct alignment was manually determined from signal inspections. Annotation and alignment information was used as ground truth.

3.1   Evaluation 1: Force-Acceleration-Audio

Data Recording. The dataset was recorded with a single wrist worn motion sensor (Xsens MTx), one FSR on the desk, and an ambient sound microphone. The MTx comprises 3D sensors for acceleration, rate of turn, and earth-magnetic field. In this investigation only 3D acceleration was considered. MTx were sampled with a nominal data rate of 100 Hz, FSR at 16 Hz, and audio at 8 kHz. For FSR and MTx a wireless connection (Bluetooth) was used to transmit data to a computer. Audio was acquired and timestamped on a second computer and streamed to the first computer for archival.

The total recording time was ~20 minutes. During this time five sessions of 'push-release' gestures and six sessions of 'clap' gestures were performed by one person. Each gesture was repeated several times during a session resulting in a total of 20 'push-release' and 24 'clap' gestures. Between the synchronization sessions normal office activities were conducted and several times the wireless connection is intentionally broken by increasing the distance to the recording computer. These link interrupts served to simulate both, connection errors and temporary sensor failures.

Synchronization Procedure. Using the transitive property of our approach, two synchronization pairs were established in this analysis: (1) MTx-FSR using 'push-release' and (2) MTx-audio using 'clap' gestures. The synchronization pairs are illustrated in Figure 3(b). The streams of each synchronization domain were independently aligned using our synchronization algorithm. We used the trailing edge spotting algorithm to recognize both event types in all streams.

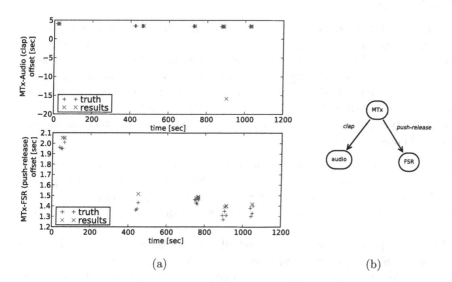

(a)   (b)

Fig. 3. Evaluation 1: (a): Results for the force-acceleration-audio dataset. The offsets indicate the actual (truth) and estimated (result) alignments for the entire dataset. (b): Synchronization pairing scheme.

Results. The event spotting returned 95.5% of the gesture instances correctly. Only 4 instances from the MTx sensor were missed. In total 23 false positives were returned (26.1%), 19 of them by the clap detection on the accelerometer signals, which classified most 'push-release' events as 'clap' events. The remaining false detections were caused by the FSR spotting, which generated insertions at rising signal edges.

Figure 3(a) shows the synchronization algorithm results as a time plot. Green crosses indicate true offsets, manually determined at each event instance. Blue '+' signs mark the offsets estimated by our synchronization algorithm. At least one result was found for each session of 'push-release' gestures with an error of ~0.1 s. One session of clap gestures did not lead to a result because of missed events. This session contained only three annotated event instances, which was also used for k_E. Consequently, if one event was not retrieved by the spotting algorithm, a correct match was no longer possible. The MTx-audio pair incurred one error with an error of -10 s due to event insertions.

3.2 Evaluation 2: Acceleration-Positioning

Data Recording. We attached infrared markers of an optical motion capturing system (Lukotronic) onto two accelerometer-based motion sensors (Xsens MTx). The position data from the Lukotronic system was streamed over a wired network connection (TCP) to the recording computer. The acceleration data from the two MTx sensors was transferred over two independent wireless connections (Bluetooth). All sensing systems sampled with a nominal data rate of 100Hz. A dataset of ~60 minutes was recorded during which individual units and both units together were shaken.

Synchronization Procedure. Three synchronization pairs were established: (1) MTx0-Lukotronic, (2) MTx1-Lukotronic, and (3) MTx0-MTx1. The synchronization pairs are illustrated in Figure 4(b). The streams of each synchronization domain were independently aligned using our synchronization algorithm.

We used the shake detection algorithm to spot 'shake' events for both sensor modalities. As described before, we considered the midpoint of a shake event as synchronization point. This approach compensated varying detections of peak begin and ends on both modalities.

Results. The manual data stream alignment revealed that the camera system had an offset of 8 seconds relative to both accelerometers. This can be explained by different starting times of both system types and by differences in transmission delays. In addition to the stream offset, skew and drift seemed to be marginal for this recording.

The event spotting correctly returned all synchronization actions and did not incur insertion errors. Figure 4(a) shows the synchronization algorithm results as a time plot for all synchronization pairs. The plot can be interpreted as discussed for evaluation 1 above. The algorithm correctly detected that no offset existed at multiple time points on each synchronization domain. The algorithm incurred one error due to a similar event sequence found in one stream.

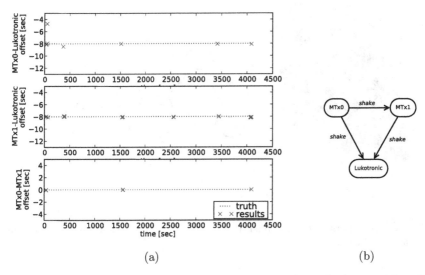

(a)   (b)

Fig. 4. Evaluation 2: (a): Results for the acceleration-positioning dataset. The offsets indicate the actual (truth) and estimated (result) alignments for the entire dataset. (b): Synchronization pairing scheme.

This experiment demonstrates that repetitive gestures (with an extent in time) can be used as synchronization actions. Moreover, it confirms the feasibility to use the transitive property for independent synchronization pairs. Sensors that are members of two independent synchronization pairs could use both to refine alignment results.

3.3 Evaluation 3: Office Scenario

Data Recording. A setup consisting of a motion sensor at the right wrist (Xsens MTx), left wrist (Xsens MTx), and ambient sound microphone was worn by the users. In addition, four FSR sensors were mounted under pads that could sense if household utensils are placed on them were used. The right wrist motion sensor was attached to an Xbus, sampled at 30 Hz and interfaced to a laptop computer using the a wired connection. For the microphone a wired connection at 8 kHz sampling rate was used. The left wrist Xsens was connected through a wireless link (Bluetooth) at 30 Hz. The FSRs were synchronously sampled at 12.5 Hz by another (stationary computer). During the actual study the laptop that interfaced all wearable sensors, was carried by an experiment observer who followed the test person. In total this setup had four unsynchronized data streams recorded by two computers.

Five test person were individually recorded for sessions ~60 minutes. During these sessions the test persons were asked to perform various activities in four

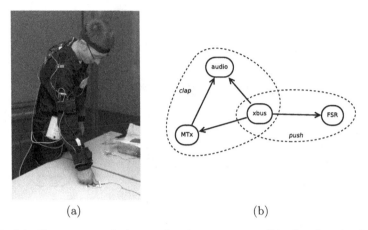

(a)   (b)

Fig. 5. (a): Test person during push-release gesture. (b): Synchronization pairing scheme for evaluation 3.

different scenarios: office (desktop work, printing, using fax), eating (preparing sandwich, making coffee, eating), gaming (installing a Wii console, gaming using the Wii remote), and leisure (reading magazines, speaking at the phoning).

Synchronization Procedure. Three times during the session (beginning, mid-time, end) the test persons were asked to perform synchronization actions consisting of 'push-release' of one FSR pads on the table using the right arm (activation of right MTx and FSR), and 'clap' with both hands (activation of both MTx and audio). Figure 5(a) illustrates the synchronization action for 'push-release'. The synchronization actions were repeated three to four times, resulting in a total of at least 45 relevant synchronization actions per test person (when counted each data streams separately).

Four synchronization pairs were established: (1) right MTx-left MTx using 'clap', (2) right MTx-audio using 'clap', (3) left MTx-audio using 'clap', and (4) right MTx-FSR using 'push-release'. The synchronization pairs are illustrated in Figure 5(b). The streams of each synchronization domain were independently aligned using our synchronization algorithm. We used the trailing edge spotting algorithm to recognize both event types in all streams.

Results. The event spotting algorithm was used with the same parameter set for all test persons. In total for all persons, 83% of the synchronization actions were correctly spotted. The procedure incurred 654 insertion errors (284%) with low inter-person variances. This result should be considered in relation to the recording time (total: 300 minutes), resulting in an average of two insertions per minute. This high insertion rate was expected due to the simple spotting procedure and the limited model training. Elaborate spotting procedures, automated training, and person adaptation could improve the result. However, this was not the goal of this work. Nevertheless, this result represents a hard, real life test condition for our synchronization algorithm.

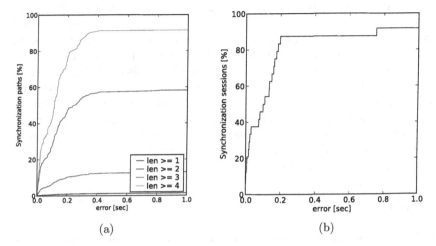

(a)   (b)

Fig. 6. Evaluation 3: Quantitative results of the synchronization. (a): Cumulative distribution results for all candidate synchronization paths and different path length k. (b): Cumulative distribution of synchronization sessions that have at least one alignment estimation result with regard to the synchronization error. The synchronization paths length k was not restricted for this representation.

Figure 6(a) shows the cumulative error distribution for individual synchronization path lengths. This result was obtained by analyzing the synchronization error for all candidate synchronization paths. The result confirms that with increasing path length k the probability for large alignment errors decreases. When considering the targeted alignment error of 0.3 s, ~55% of all cases for $k \geq 3$, and ~90% of all cases for $k \geq 4$ are below this error bar. In contrast, for path length of $k \geq 2$ no useful synchronization performance is obtained. This means that it is very common to find two events in one stream that incidentally have the same distance (time difference) as two events in the paired stream. This observation is related to the relatively high insertion rate for this dataset and the deployed event spotter. However, path lengths of three or four events are sufficient to reach a reasonable synchronization performance. With the simple event spotters considered in this evaluation, we observed that $k = 4$ is needed in many cases.

Furthermore, we analyzed the error distribution with regard to the synchronization sessions that were identified by the event spotting. Figure 6(b) confirms that for more than 80% of the synchronization sessions an synchronization error of less than 0.3 s was achieved.

4   Conclusion and Further Work

Our experiments clearly show the potential of an automatic, event-based approach to synchronize distributed multi-modal sensor systems. We concluded from the results that our synchronization algorithm can achieve the initially set target of 0.3 s synchronization error. However, the evaluations also showed that in realistic scenarios achieving high synchronization performance is not trivial. In evaluation 3, a synchronization path length of four was required to achieve a performance greater than 80% for the targeted error level. This result indicates that an appropriate event spotting and subsequent reasoning across different synchronization pairs is the key to good performance. In addition, more investigation is needed on suitable synchronization actions for different sensor combinations. Our further work will attempt to include natural activities in the event-based synchronization approach. We expect that this step will help to further improve the synchronization performance.

References

1. Amft, O., Tröster, G.: Recognition of dietary activity events using on-body sensors. Artificial Intelligence in Medicine 42(2), 121–136 (2008)
2. Bian, X., Abowd, G.D., Rehg, J.M.: Using Sound Source Localization in a Home Environment. In: Gellersen, H.-W., Want, R., Schmidt, A. (eds.) PERVASIVE 2005. LNCS, vol. 3468, pp. 19–36. Springer, Heidelberg (2005)
3. Coulouris, G., Dollimore, J., Kindberg, T.: Distributed systems. Addison-Wesley, Reading (2001)
4. Gupchup, J., Musaloiu-E, R., Szalay, A., Terzis, A.: Sundial: Using Sunlight to Reconstruct Global Timestamps. In: Roedig, U., Sreenan, C.J. (eds.) EWSN 2009. LNCS, vol. 5432, Springer, Heidelberg (2009)
5. Lester, J., Hannaford, B., Borriello, G.: "Are You with Me?"-Using Accelerometers to Determine If Two Devices Are Carried by the Same Person. LNCS, pp. 33–50 (2004)
6. Lukac, M., Davis, P., Clayton, R., Estrin, D.: Recovering Temporal Integrity with Data Driven Time Synchronization. In: Proc. of The 8th Intl. Symposium on Information Processing in Sensor Networks (2009)
7. MacWilliams, P., Prasad, B., Khare, M., Sampath, D.: Source synchronous interface between master and slave using a deskew latch. US Patent 6209072 (March 2001)
8. Sivrikaya, F., Yener, B.: Time synchronization in sensor networks: a survey. IEEE Network 18(4), 45–50 (2004)
9. Su, W., Akyildiz, I.F.: Time-diffusion synchronization protocol for wireless sensor networks. IEEE/ACM Transactions on Networking 13(2), 384–397 (2005)
10. Sundararaman, B., Buy, U., Kshemkalyani, A.D.: Clock synchronization for wireless sensor networks: a survey. Ad Hoc Networks 3(3), 281–323 (2005)
11. Werner-Allen, G., Lorincz, K., Johnson, J., Lees, J., Welsh, M.: Fidelity and yield in a volcano monitoring sensor network. In: Proc. of The 7th USENIX Symposium on Operating Systems Design and Implementation (2006)

Using Dempster-Shafer Theory of Evidence for Situation Inference*

Susan McKeever[1], Juan Ye[1], Lorcan Coyle[2], and Simon Dobson[1]

[1] Systems Research Group, School of Computer Science and Informatics,
University College Dublin, Ireland
susan.mckeever@ucd.ie
[2] Lero, University of Limerick, Ireland

Abstract. In the domain of ubiquitous computing, the ability to identify the occurrence of situations is a core function of being 'context-aware'. Given the uncertain nature of sensor information and inference rules, reasoning techniques that cater for uncertainty hold promise for enabling the inference process. In our work, we apply the Dempster Shafer theory of evidence to infer situation occurrence with minimal use of training data. We describe a set of evidential operations for sensor mass functions using context quality and evidence accumulation for continuous situation detection. We demonstrate how our approach enables situation inference with uncertain information using a case study based on a published smart home activity data set.

1 Introduction

In the domain of ubiquitous computing, a context-aware system must be able to perceive the state of entities (e.g. users) of interest in the environment, termed situations. A situation is a human-understandable description of an entity state, such as 'user at lunch'. The ability to infer situations, i.e., 'what situation(s) is occurring ' is a critical function for a context-aware system, acting as a driver of adaptive behaviour at the application level. Situation inference is reliant on disparate sensor-based information. This inference process is complicated by the imperfections associated with sensor information, such as problems of noise, breakdown, network delays and user error [3]. Furthermore, observations from multiple sensors can lead to conflicts; for example a user could be detected in two different locations simultaneously. Therefore, inference mechanisms that treat sensor information as evidence of fact, rather than fact, are of particular interest in our work. Situations may continue for a duration of time, and we

---

* This work is partially supported by Enterprise Ireland under grant number CFTD 2005 INF 217a, "Platform for user-Centred design and evaluation of context-aware services" and by Science Foundation Ireland under grant numbers 07/CE/1147 "Clarity, the centre for sensor web technologies", 03/CE2/I303-1 "Lero, the Irish Software Engineering Research Centre", and 05/RFP/CMS0062 "Towards a semantics of pervasive computing".

P. Barnaghi et al. (Eds.): EuroSSC 2009, LNCS 5741, pp. 149–162, 2009.

term these 'time-distributed' situations. In such cases, inference can incorporate time as a factor in the reasoning process.

Bayesian methods, including Bayesian networks [2,11,16] and Hidden Markhov Models [1,14] have been used to infer situations in context-aware systems. These methods demonstrate that with sufficient training data, situations can be recognised from lower level sensor information. Posterior probabilities of situation occurrence are calculated and imperfections of sensor data and inference rules are absorbed invisibly into these probability calculations. *Dempster-Shafer theory* (DS theory), a generalised form of Bayesian theory, is a tool for representing and combining evidence. It offers an alternative to other Bayesian methods when training data is not easily available. It explicitly quantifies ignorance in the face of uncertain or missing data. It does not rely on training data and it offers a range of operations that can be used for propagating evidence from sensor up to situation level in a scrutable manner. We use DS theory to incorporate sensor uncertainty into sensor evidence, and to fuse this evidence in order to infer situations. The novelties of our approach are multi-fold: (1) it explicitly caters for quantified uncertainty for both sensor data and inference rules; (2) domain knowledge is applied in order to minimise or remove dependence on training data; (3) it supports the recognition of time-distributed situations; (4) the inference process from sensor to situation level is scrutable. We demonstrate our evidence-based situation inference process using sample data from a publicly available home activity data set [14].

The remainder of this paper is organised as follows: Section 2 introduces related work by other researchers; Section 3 describes the basic concepts of DS Theory; Section 4 describes situation inference diagrams and the use of DS theory to infer situations. We provide a demonstration of our inference approach in a case study in Section 5. Conclusions and further work are described in Section 6.

2   Related Work

Wu [15] uses DS theory as a sensor fusion model in context-aware systems. Sensor evidence is supplied via DS mass functions and fused using Dempster's rule of combination. Wu's work does not include the propagation of evidence to support higher-level context inference. Wu uses a static weighting on sensor mass functions to indicate evidence reliability. He also introduces a dynamic weighting for evidence sources but his approach requires the availability of ground truth for verification soon after evidence fusion. Closest to our work is Hong et al's [4] work on activity recognition in smart homes. Similar to our work, they use evidence theory to propagate sensor evidence for activity recognition. They use the basic DS theory functions of sensor mass functions, Dempster's combination rule and sensor discounting to process and fuse evidence. They supplement these functions with additional evidential operations to move evidence from sensor level up to activity level. Our work differs from their work in a number of ways: (1) we use context quality information (such as fuzziness and precision) in sensor mass functions to enable dynamic discounting of sensors; (2) we process evidence for time-distributed situations; (3) we use differing evidential operations for evidence fusion.

The application of uncertain reasoning techniques is an active research area within the domain of context-aware computing. In particular, Bayesian methods and fuzzy logic have been used to determine situations from lower level uncertain sensor information. Van Kasteren et al [14] use Hidden Markov Models to successfully determine a person's activity in the home, where inference of high level states (activities), and activity patterns over time are learned from training data. Bayesian networks as used by [2,11,16] are used to determine situations (such as activities in a meeting room) from lower level sensor data. These approaches require training data which can be difficult to obtain in particular environments, such as the difficulties of smart home data collection in real life environments, as noted by Tapia et al [13]. Our approach using DS theory has limited or no reliance on training data, relying more heavily on domain knowledge. Fuzzy sets and fuzzy logic as used by [5,7,11] are used to quantify and reason with imprecise context concepts such as describing the temperature of a room as 'warm' or 'cold'. We incorporate context fuzziness into our evidence-based approach by including fuzzy membership in our sensor mass functions, as described in Section 4.2.

3   Basic Concepts of Dempster-Shafer Theory

Dempster–Shafer theory is a mathematical theory of evidence [12] which is used to combine separate pieces of information (evidence) to calculate the probability of an event. In a DS Theory reasoning scheme, the set of possible hypotheses are collectively called the *frame of discernment*. This frame Θ represents the set of choices $\{h_1, h_2, ... h_n\}$ available to the reasoning scheme, where sources (such as sensors) assign belief or evidence across the frame hypotheses. Let 2^Θ denote the set of all subsets of Θ to which a source of evidence can apply its belief. Then the function $m : 2^\Theta \rightarrow [0,1]$ is called a mass function that defines how belief is distributed across the frame, if the function satisfies the following conditions:

$$m(\phi) = 0 \text{ and } \sum_{A \subseteq \Theta} m(A) = 1$$

Based on these conditions, belief from an evidence source cannot be assigned to an empty or null hypothesis, and belief from the evidence source across the possible hypotheses (including combinations of hypotheses) must sum to 1. The least informative evidence (ignorance) is the assignment of mass to a hypothesis containing all the elements; i.e., $\{h_1, h_2, ... h_n\}$. A crucial part of the process of assessing evidence is the ability to combine evidence from multiple sources. In DS theory, the combination of evidence from two different independent sources is accomplished by Dempster's combination rule:

$$m_{12}(A) = \frac{\sum_{\forall X,Y:X \cap Y=A} m_1(X).m_2(Y)}{1 - \sum_{\forall X,Y:X \cap Y=\phi} m_1(X).m_2(Y)} \qquad (1)$$

where $m_{12}(A)$ is the combined belief for a given hypothesis A. The numerator in equation 1 represents evidence for hypotheses whose intersection is the exact hypothesis of interest, A. The denominator, $1 - K$ is a normalisation factor, where K is a *conflict* factor representing all combined evidence that does not match the hypothesis of interest, A. The value of conflict, K, when combining evidence is indicative of the level of disagreement amongst the sources of their belief in hypothesis A.

In Section 4.2, we explain how we apply the DS Theory concepts of *mass functions, frames of discernment* and *evidence combination* to situation inference.

4   Situation Inference

In this section, we explain how we use Situation Inference Diagrams to capture the inference routes from sensor information to situations. We then explain how basic DS theory (mass functions, evidence combination) and additional evidential operations (context quality in mass functions, evidence transfer, evidence accumulation) are applied to situation inference.

4.1   Situation Inference Diagrams

In order to infer situations using DS Theory, we need to define how evidence is propagated across layers of context, using a multi-layered hierarchy consisting of sensors, abstracted context and situations [8]. We illustrate this hierarchy using a Directed Acylic Graph (DAG) as shown in Figure 1. Sensors are the root nodes at the base of the diagram. Sensor readings are abstracted or mapped to more human-understandable context values. For example, a sensor reading of a user's location may be generated as a set of coordinates '12.4, 10, 5.6, 14:24:08, ID24' and translated using a building layout to a context value of 'Peter hasLocation MeetingRoom5 at 14:24'. Moving up the hierarchy, each context value will be mapped to one or more situations, indicating that the occurrence of a particular context value 'is evidence' of the situation occurring; i.e., an inference rule. Depending upon the complexity and range of situations in the system, higher-level situations may also be inferred from lower level situations. Each solid directed arrow in the graph is interpreted as 'is evidence of'. The full notation for the DAG is shown in Figure 2.

Quantified uncertainty is incorporated into the situation inference DAG at sensor and inference rule level. At sensor level, if sensor reliability is quantifiable, it is included as a sensor discount, as described further in section 4.2. Uncertainty can also be quantified against inference rules. For example, in the home data set that we have examined, a user 'sometimes' uses the microwave when preparing breakfast and this is quantified as 40% of the time, by examining sample occurrences of the 'prepare breakfast' situation in the data. Therefore, a certainty of 0.4 is applied along the edge or inference rule from the context value 'microwave used' to the situation of 'prepare breakfast'.

Situations may be inferred from evidence that does not occur at exactly the same time and we term these 'time distributed situations'. The situation of a

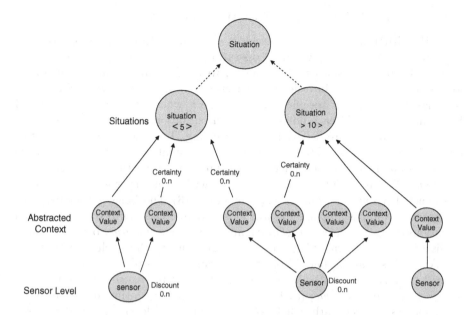

Fig. 1. Situation Inference Diagram

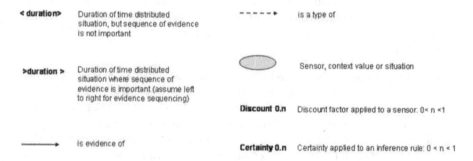

Fig. 2. Situation Inference Diagram Notation

user 'preparing breakfast' may be detected by context values such as the 'plate cupboard used', 'grocery cupboard used', and 'fridge used' over a period of time. We represent evidence that accumulates over time by a time period enclosed in '< >' brackets within the time-distributed situation node on the DAG. This number indicates the typical duration of the situation. Where the actual *sequence* of evidence occurrence is also relevant, the duration is enclosed by '> >' brackets.

Some situations may be detectable by the occurrence of one of a set of situations. For example, a 'busy in kitchen' situation may be declared when either situation 'prepare breakfast' or 'prepare dinner' is occurring. This is indicated on the DAG as 'is a type of'.

4.2   Applying DS Theory to Situation Inference

Once the situation inference hierarchy is determined from sensor to situation level, we can then apply evidential operations from DS theory as described in Section 3, and extensions to DS Theory, to produce and propagate evidence for situation inference. In order to infer situation occurrence, we assess sensor readings or evidence at specific points in time t, where each point is separated by a time gap, $\triangle t$. At each point in time, the situations with the greatest belief (evidential support) are believed to be occurring. To achieve this, a number of evidential operations need to occur from sensor level upwards: (1) At time t, each sensor system defines its belief across the context values for the sensor via a *mass function*; (2) Quality information associated with each sensor is used to modify the belief distribution from its mass function; (3) The belief associated with each context value is mapped upwards along the inference paths to its associated situations using *compatibility relations* and *evidence propagation* between frames of discernment. This mapping process continues up the hierarchy of situations; (4) For each situation, belief from the relevant sources of evidence is fused in order to determine total belief in the situation at time t, using an appropriate *evidence combination rule*; (5) For situations that have a time duration, belief from sources is fused with belief from pre-existing evidence that was captured within the time duration of the situation.

When these steps have been executed, at time t, a separate level of belief is available for each situation. A decision step selects those situations of highest belief, taking into account which situations can occur at the same time. We use examples from an office activity data set and a smart home data set to illustrate the evidential operations.

Sensor Mass Functions.   Mass functions, as explained in Section 3, define how belief from an evidence source (such as a sensor) is spread across a set of choices in a frame of discernment. In our approach, a mass function is required for each sensor, in order to distribute belief for the sensor across the range of possible context values for that sensor, i.e. the frame of discernment for that sensor. In our office activity sensor example, context value 'active' may be defined as any keyboard or mouse activity on the computer within the last 10 seconds. If the sensor at time t has detected a reading 5 seconds ago, the mass function will assign belief across the frame of discernment $\{active, inactive, \theta\}$ as $\{1, 0, 0\}$ respectively. The mass assigned to θ represents ignorance, where belief is uncertain and cannot be sub-divided amongst other elements in the frame.

Using Context Quality in Sensor Mass Functions.   In the real world, absolutely reliable sources are rarely found. 'Discount factors' are an idea that dates back to Shafer's evidence theory work [12] and expanded by Lowrance et al [6]. They can be used to account for the uncertainty due to unreliable evidence sources. However, a variety of additional sensor and context quality metrics such as precision [17] and fuzziness [11] are defined to quantify the imperfections of sensor information. Precision indicates the range within which a sensor reading is correct, for a given accuracy. Fuzziness is used to quantify imprecise context.

If such quality information is available and quantifiable, we propose that it can be incorporated into sensor mass functions in order to provide a more realistic distribution of belief. We illustrate this through a set of examples:

(1) Using precision in mass functions: A location system, Ubisense[1], generates coordinate readings for tags worn for users. The coordinate readings are then mapped to meaningful locations (context values) within the building based on a building map. The measured precisions of Ubisense readings are 3.30 and 2.22 meters along the x- and y- axes respectively, as established using training data in experimental work [17]. When these precisions are used during context abstraction, they form an area around the coordinate reading, and the user/tag may be located anywhere within the area. If this area intersects more than one meaningful space, the proportions of the square in each space can be calculated. Therefore, a reading which is translated to two context values 'desk1, 0.3' and 'desk2, 0.7', means that the sensor is 30% confident that the user is located at desk1 and 70% confident at desk2. The mass function for this sensor based on this coordinate reading will generate belief of $\{0.3, 0.7, ..., 0, 0\}$ for a frame of discernment $\{desk1, desk2, ..., desk_n, \theta\}$.

(2) Using context fuzziness in mass functions: Context values can have imprecise meanings such as 'active' for our activity sensor. The level of imprecision or fuzziness is represented by a membership value, where the fuzzy membership function applies a numerical value from 0 to 1 to each element of the fuzzy set [18]. For our activity sensor, we observe that any keyboard or mouse activity within the last 10 seconds is definitely active. After 10 seconds, the level or membership of 'active' reduces with time, falling to 0 after 60 seconds. The mass function for the activity sensor will include the fuzzy membership values in its calculation of belief assignment to the context values, generating belief distributions such as $\{0.2, 0.8, 0\}$ for the frame $\{active, inactive, \theta\}$, when a reading is more inactive than active.

(3) Sensor discounting: When a quantified measure of sensor reliability is available, it is incorporated into the mass function via a sensor discounting function [12,6]. When a source's evidence is discounted, the remaining evidence is applied to the combination of all options in the frame (i.e., ignorance, θ).

For our Ubisense system, we measured an accuracy of 70% for the precisions described in example (1), meaning that 30% of readings are believed to be incorrect. Using Shafer discounting function, the belief is discounted by 0.7. The remaining 0.3 is attributed to ignorance. Using the Ubisense mass function example from (1) of belief $\{0.3, 0.7, ..., 0, 0\}$ for a frame $\{desk1, desk2, ..., desk_n, \theta\}$, the application of the discount factor will alter the belief distribution to $\{0.21, 0.49, ..., 0, 0.3\}$ where discounting of evidence has resulted in a quantified uncertainty of 0.3.

Reliability of a sensor may be a straightforward measure of physical sensor accuracy as supplied by the sensor manufacturer. However, it may also incorporate additional sources of error such as errors in using a sensor, as described in [9].

---

[1] Ubisense is a networked location system: www.ubisense.net

Evidence Transfer. Evidence propagation through layers of the hierarchy from context value upwards is achieved using compatibility relations and evidential mapping. Compatibility relations [6] define the mappings between the compatible beliefs between two frames of discernment; i.e., the elements from the two frames that can be true simultaneously. We can use compatibility relations to define paths for transferring belief from one layer of the situation hierarchy to the next. For example, a fridge sensor can generate belief across two context values $\{FridgeUsed, \neg FridgeUsed, \Theta\}$. The use of the fridge is indicative of the 'get drink' situation, which has a frame of discernment $\{GetDrink, \neg GetDrink, \Theta\}$. 'Fridge used' is compatible with 'get drink' (i.e. they are both true simultaneously) and so on for the remaining elements in both frames. Having defined the evidence paths using compatibility relations, we use evidence *propagation* [4] to propagate evidence from one frame to another. We apply propagation along the paths defined by the compatibility relations, enabling the mass of compatible elements to be transferred; e.g., mass of 'fridge used' can be propagated to 'get drink'.

Evidence Combination. When each context value has propagated its evidence to situation level, the evidence is combined to produce a final distribution of belief over the choices in the frame of discernment. The basic formalism for evidence combination from two sources is provided in Dempster's rule of combination as described in equation 1 of Section 3. Variations on this combination rule have been introduced in the literature to deal with alternative combination scenarios, such as the use of evidence averaging for unreliable sources when source discounting is used [12] and Murphy's averaged combination rule [10]. Murphy observed that a single piece of evidence can force certainty or overrule a majority when Dempster's rule of combination is used. For scenarios where this may occur (e.g. binary sensors where a single sensor fails to fire), this will distort the evidence, allowing a single sensor to negate evidence from other sources. Murphy's approach is to average the evidence *prior* to combining, thus ruling out the dominance of a single sensor. The averaged evidence is then combined using Dempster's combination rule, applied $n - 1$ times where n is the number of evidence sources. We propose using both averaging as proposed by Shafer and Murphy's alternative combination rule in our work, as demonstrated in section 5, and compare the results in our worked example.

Evidence Accumulation Over Time. In order to accumulate evidence for a situation with a specified duration d, we extend the lifetime of evidence to endure over the duration of the situation, combining later evidence with earlier evidence as if it had occurred at the same time, t. At the first occurrence of evidence of a situation (such as 'grocery cupboard' detected for the 'prepare breakfast' situation), evidence is captured for this time, t. Further evidence for the situation that occurs between time t and $t + d$ is fused with earlier evidence, providing an overall belief in the situation occurrence.

5   Case Study

In this section, we provide a demonstration of our evidence-based situation inferencing approach using a sample of data from Van Kasteren's home activity data set [14]. We explain each of the steps from the processing of sensor evidence up to the fusion of evidence into situation beliefs.

5.1   Data Set Description

The data set was recorded over 28 days in a house where a 26 year old man lives. 14 sensors were places throughout the house. Each sensor generates binary output only, outputting a value of 1 when fired. The data set is annotated with 7 situations or activities, such as 'go to bed', 'take shower', and 'prepare dinner'. None of these activities occur at the same time according to the annotation. In our example, we focus on the three situations that occur in the kitchen: 'prepare breakfast', 'prepare dinner', 'get drink'. Our situation inference DAG for these situations (Figure 3) contains all kitchen-based sensors as root nodes. Because of the binary nature of the sensors, context values for these sensors are very simple; e.g., the grocery cupboard sensor firing indicates 'grocery cupboard used' context. No indication of sensor performance is provided in the data set, so sensor discounting or quality in mass sensor functions cannot be applied. Domain knowledge in this environment for mapping evidence to situations could, in theory, be available from users ('what do you typically do to prepare breakfast?') or from examining small amounts of training data.

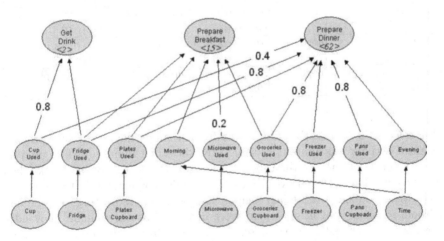

Fig. 3. Situation Inference DAG for kitchen situations: get drink, prepare breakfast, prepare dinner

5.2   Experimental Approach

We used a combination of inherent domain knowledge combined with examination of 5 occurrences of each of the three situations to determine the inference paths for our DAG. This highlighted some uncertainty in the inference rules, such as the occasional use of the microwave in breakfast preparation (20% of the time), or getting cups from the cups cupboard when preparing dinner (40% of the time). Each situation is a time-distributed situation so we estimate situation durations from a combination of data observation and domain knowledge. For instance, the 'prepare dinner' activity lasted an average of 38 minutes for the 5 occurrences we observed, with a standard deviation of 24 minutes so we applied a duration of 62 minutes to capture 'prepare dinner' evidence. We could have used alternative duration calculations such as mean duration, minimum duration or a duration range, depending upon the nature of the situation. From domain knowledge, we included time as evidence to capture the fact that breakfast occurs in the morning and dinner occurs in the evening. 'Get drink' can occur at any time of the day.

Table 1. Evidence and cumulative evidence by time slice for each situation

		Cumulative evidence over situation durations (mins)		
Time	Sensor events	Drink (2)	Prepare Breakfast (15)	Prepare Dinner (62)
9.:49	fridge, plates, microwave	fridge	fridge, plates, microwave (0.2)	fridge (0.8), plates
9:50	groceries	fridge	fridge, plate, microwave (0.2), groceries	fridge (0.8), plates, grocery (0.8)
9:51	none	none	fridge, plate, microwave (0.2), groceries	fridge (0.8), plates, grocery (0.8)
9:52	none	none	fridge, plates, microwave (0.2), groceries	fridge (0.8), plates, grocery (0.8)
9:53	microwave, groceries	none	fridge, plates, microwave (0.2), groceries	fridge (0.8), plates, grocery (0.8)

We selected 5 consecutive time slices from a single day when the 'prepare breakfast' activity was annotated, using time slices of 1 minute (as also used by [14]). Evidence for the five time slices is shown in Table 1, showing the kitchen sensor events that occurred over times 9:49 to 9:53 for one day in the data set. Sensor events outside the kitchen such as 'hall bedroom' indicating that the hall bedroom sensor is still firing (open) were discarded as our domain knowledge suggests that only kitchen based sensors have a direct evidential bearing on kitchen situation occurrence. The evidential calculations for these time slices results in total belief for each of the three situations at times 9:49 to 9:53 as shown in Table 2.

Table 2. Total belief in situations by timeslice using evidence averaging and Murphy's combination rule for 'get drink' (Drink), 'prepare breakfast' (B'fast) and 'prepare dinner' (Dinner) situations

Timeslice	Averaging			Combination Rule					
	Drink	B'fast	Dinner	Drink		B'fast		Dinner	
				Belief	Conflict	Belief	Conflict	Belief	Conflict
9:49	0.5	0.64	0.26	0.63	43%	0.98	22%	0.02	27%
9:50	0.5	0.84	0.37	0.63	43%	1	0	0.2	40%
9:51	0	0.84	0.37	0	n/a	1	0	0.2	40%
9:52	0	0.84	0.37	0	n/a	1	0	0.2	40%
9:53	0	0.84	0.37	0	n/a	1	0	0.2	40%

The process for inferring situation occurrence using sensor evidence is performed by using the following steps for each time slice:

1. Use sensor mass functions to obtain context value beliefs.
2. Propagate the belief from the context values up to the relevant situations, using compatibility relations and evidence propagation as explained in Section 4.2.
3. Obtain total belief for each situation by combining evidence for the situation. We use both basic evidence averaging and Murphy's alternative combination rule, as described in Section 4.2.
4. Select the situation with the highest belief (given that no situations in the data set are co-occurring).

For illustration, we explain these steps for the first time slice (9:49):

(1) Use sensor mass functions for context values
Fridge, plates cupboard and microwave sensors are firing. No sensor discounting is used. The three sensor mass functions assign mass to context values as follows:
   $\{FridgeUsed = 1, \neg FridgeUsed = 0\}$
   $\{PlateUsed = 1, \neg PlateUsed = 0\}$
   $\{MicrowaveUsed = 1, \neg MicrowaveUsed = 0\}$
In addition, the kitchen sensors that did *not* fire are evidential, generating masses as follows:
   $\{CupUsed = 0, \neg CupUsed = 1\}$
   $\{GroceriesUsed = 0, \neg GroceriesUsed = 1\}$
   $\{FreezerUsed = 0, \neg FreezerUsed = 1\}$
   $\{PansUsed = 0, \neg PansUsed = 1\}$
Finally, we are using time as evidence. At 9:49am, the time sensor mass gives:
   $\{Morning = 1, Evening = 0\}$

(2) Propagate the belief from the context values up to the relevant situations
For each situation, propagate context value belief to situations of which that context is evidence, as denoted on the situation inference DAG.

Get drink
$\{FridgeUsed = 1, \neg FridgeUsed = 0\} \rightarrow \{GetDrink = 1, \neg GetDrink = 0\}$
$\{CupUsed = 0, \neg CupUsed = 1\} \rightarrow \{GetDrink = 0, \neg GetDrink = 0.8, \Theta = 0.2\}$

Prepare Breakfast:
$\{FridgeUsed = 1, FridgeNotUsed = 0\} \rightarrow \{Breakfast = 1, \neg Breakfast = 0\}$
$\{MicrowaveUsed = 1, \neg MicroUsed = 0\} \rightarrow \{Breakfast = 0.2, \neg Breakfast = 0, \theta = 0.8\}$
$\{PlateUsed = 1, \neg PlatesUsed = 0\} \rightarrow \{Breakfast = 1, \neg Breakfast = 0\}$
$\{GroceriesUsed = 0, \neg GroceriesUsed = 1\} \rightarrow \{Breakfast = 0, \neg Breakfast = 1\}$
$\{Morning = 1, Evening = 0\} \rightarrow \{Breakfast = 1, \neg Breakfast = 0\}$

Prepare Dinner
$\{FridgeUsed = 1, \neg FridgeUsed = 0\} \rightarrow \{Dinner = 0.8, \neg Dinner = 0, \theta = 0.2\}$
$\{PlateUsed = 1, \neg PlateUsed = 0\} \rightarrow \{Dinner = 1, \neg Dinner = 0\}$
$\{GroceriesUsed = 0, \neg GroceriesUsed = 1\} \rightarrow \{Dinner = 0, \neg Dinner = 0.8, \theta = 0.2\}$
$\{PansUsed = 0, \neg PansUsed = 1\} \rightarrow \{Dinner = 0, \neg Dinner = 0.8, \theta = 0.2\}$
$\{CupsUsed = 0, \neg CupsUsed = 1\} \rightarrow \{Dinner = 0, \neg Dinner = 0.4, \theta = 0.6\}$
$\{FreezerUsed = 0, \neg FreezerUsed\} = 1 \rightarrow \{Dinner = 0, \neg Dinner = 1\}$
$\{Morning = 1, Evening = 0\} \rightarrow \{Dinner = 0, \neg Dinner = 1\}$

Because this is the first time slice, we do not have any cumulative evidence. For the next time slice at 9:50, the sensor events from 9:49 will be assessed as 'still happening' where they contribute to the time-distributed situations, as set out in Table 1.

(3) Obtain total belief in each situation via evidence combination
We calculate total belief in each situation using two different methods: Simple evidence averaging and Murphy's version of the Dempster's combination rule. In the averaging approach, this involves averaging the belief for each separate situation. At 9:49, this gives belief of 0.5, 0.64, 0.26 for situations 'get drink', 'prepare breakfast', 'prepare dinner' respectively as shown in Table 2. For the combination rule, we combine the averaged situation belief n-1 times using the combination rule in equation 1, where n is the total number of evidence sources for the situation. Total belief is shown for the three situations for our time slices in Table 2. We then repeat the steps for the remaining time slices, using new and cumulative evidence from Table 1.

   Looking at Table 2, the situation 'prepare breakfast' is deemed to be occurring at 9:49. As evidence increases for 'prepare breakfast' and 'prepare dinner' (at 9:50) due to the grocery cupboard sensor firing, the belief in these two situations increases. After 9:50, no further sensors fire until 9:53, but the existing evidence endures for time slices 9:51 and 9:52. At 9:53 the microwave and grocery cupboard sensors fire again. However, they do not change the belief because they fired in previous time slices within the system duration so their evidence is still active. For the 'get drink' situation, the situation duration is 2 minutes, so belief drops to zero at 9:51, 2 minutes after the fridge sensor contributed evidence to 'get drink' occurring. For evidence combination, the averaging of evidence provides the same highest belief answer as the combination rule, but the evidence does not converge to the same extent as our combination rule. This is because the combination rule normalises out conflicting evidence and because uncertainty is re-distributed to the two other elements in the frame of discernment. In our example, the three assessed situations cannot be co-occurring (according to the annotations in the published data set). Therefore the selection of 'which situation is occurring' is simply based on the highest belief at time t. In a more complex environment where multiple situations may be co-occurring, we will need to develop heuristics for belief thresholds in order to decide which situations are occurring. We anticipate that use of the conflict metric may be useful in developing decision making heuristics for determining situation occurrence.

6   Conclusions and Future Work

In this paper, we presented an approach to inferring situation occurrence using the Dempster Shafer theory of evidence. Our approach incorporates context quality information into sensor evidence, propagates sensor evidence up to situation level and obtains belief for situations via evidence fusion. We also provided a mechanism to accumulate evidence for time-distributed situations. We demonstrated our approach in a case study, using a sample of time-distributed evidence from a publicly available smart home data set. Our approach enables situation inference with uncertain information, with limited or no need for training data.

Our proof of concept demonstrated the inference of a time-distributed situation using uncertain information, with minimal use of training data. The next stage of our work is to establish inference results for the full smart home data set using our DS theory based approach. As part of our evaluation, we will compare our results against published results for the data set that use alternative uncertain reasoning approaches. We will also test our approach against an intelligent office activity data set that we are collecting in-house. The data set tracks office-based users using a variety of sensors. We expect that it will provide us with richer sensor quality information which we can use to test the impact on situation inference of using context quality in sensor mass functions.

References

1. Clarkson, B., Pentland, A., Mase, K.: Recognizing user context via wearable sensors. Wearable Computers, IEEE International Symposium, 69 (2000)
2. Gu, T., Pung, H.K., Zhang, D.Q.: A bayesian approach for dealing with uncertain contexts. In: Advances in Pervasive Computing, pp. 136–144 (2004)
3. Henricksen, K., Indulska, J., Rakotonirainy, A.: Modeling context information in pervasive computing systems. In: Mattern, F., Naghshineh, M. (eds.) PERVASIVE 2002. LNCS, vol. 2414, pp. 167–180. Springer, Heidelberg (2002)
4. Hong, X., Nugent, C., Mulvenna, M., McClean, S., Scotney, B., Devlin, S.: Evidential fusion of sensor data for activity recognition in smart homes. In: Pervasive and Mobile Computing, Corrected Proof (2008) (in Press)

5. Korpipaa, P., Mantyjarvi, J., Kela, J., Keranen, H., Malm, E.: Managing context information in mobile devices. IEEE Pervasive Computing 2(3), 42–51 (2003)
6. Lowrance, J.D., Garvey, T.D., Strat, T.M.: A framework for evidential-reasoning systems. In: Readings in uncertain reasoning, pp. 611–618 (1990)
7. Mantyjarvi, J., Seppanen, T.: Adapting applications in handheld devices using fuzzy context information. Interacting with Computers 15(4), 521–538 (2003)
8. McKeever, S., Ye, J., Coyle, L., Dobson, S.: A multilayered uncertainty model for context aware systems. In: Adjunct Proc' of the international conference on Pervasive Computing: Late Breaking Result, May 2008, pp. 1–4 (2008)
9. McKeever, S., Ye, J., Coyle, L., Dobson, S.: A context quality model to support tranparent reasoning with uncertain context. In: Proc' of QuaConn, Stuttgart, Germany (June 2009) (to appear)
10. Murphy, C.K.: Combining belief functions when evidence conflicts. Decis. Support Syst. 29(1), 1–9 (2000)
11. Ranganathan, A., Al-Muhtadi, J., Campbell, R.: Reasoning about uncertain contexts in pervasive computing environments. IEEE Pervasive Computing 3(2), 62–70 (2004)
12. Shafer, G.: A mathematical theory of evidence. Princeton University Press, Princeton (1976)
13. Tapia, E., Intille, S., Larson, K.: Activity recognition in the home using simple and ubiquitous sensors. In: Ferscha, A., Mattern, F. (eds.) PERVASIVE 2004. LNCS, vol. 3001, pp. 158–175. Springer, Heidelberg (2004)
14. VanKasteren, E., Noulas, Krose: Accurate activity recognition in a home setting. In: Proc' of 10th Internationall Conference on Ubiquitous Computing, South Korea (September 2008)
15. Wu, H.: Sensor fusion using dempster shafer theory. PhD dissertation, Carnegie Mellon University (2003)
16. Ye, J., Coyle, L., Dobson, S., Nixon, P.: Representing and manipulating situation hierarchies using situation lattices. Revue d'Intelligence Artificielle 22(5) (2008)
17. Ye, J., McKeever, S., Coyle, L., Neely, S., Dobson, S.: Resolving uncertainty in context integration and abstraction: context integration and abstraction. In: ICPS 2008: Proceedings of the 5th international conference on Pervasive services, pp. 131–140. ACM, New York (2008)
18. Zadeh, L.: Fuzzy sets. Information Control 8, 338–353 (1965)

Recognizing the Use-Mode of Kitchen Appliances from Their Current Consumption

Gerald Bauer, Karl Stockinger, and Paul Lukowicz

Embedded Systems Lab, University of Passau
Innstr. 43, 94032 Passau, Germany
www.wearable-computing.org

Abstract. This paper builds on previous work by different authors on monitoring the use of household devices through analysis of the power line current. Whereas previous work dealt with detecting **which** device is being used, we go a step further and analyze **how** the device is being used. We focus on a kitchen scenario where many different devices are relevant to activity recognition. The paper describes a smart, easy to install sensor that we have built to do the measurements and the algorithms which can for example determine the consistency of the substance in the mixer, how many eggs are being boiled (and if they are soft or hard), what size of coffee has been prepared or whether a cutting machine was used to cut bread or salami. A set of multi user experiments has been performed to validate the algorithms.

1 Introduction

Human activity recognition is a key element of many pervasive computing applications [10]. The work described in this paper is part of a large European Union funded project (MonAMI[1]) aimed at the specific application domain of ambient assisted living. As a consequence, our activity recognition research is directed at the monitoring of activities of daily life in the home. An important aspect of the project is large scale deployment in real life environments (planned for hundreds of existing homes). This means that the sensing infrastructure must be cheap, easy to deploy, and simple to maintain. In previous work we have investigated camera based location systems [1] and microphones attached to the plumbing systems [2] as initial components of such a system.

This paper focuses on another component: the analysis of electrical power consumption of different household appliances. To this end we have implemented a simple measuring device (iSensor) which can be inserted between the plug of an appliance and the socket. Multiple devices can be connected to the sensor using a standard multi-plug adapter. It requires no power supply (it is powered from the mains) and no cabled connection (uses a ZigBee transmitter for connection with a gateway). Thus it fulfills the requirement of easy installation and maintenance. At the same time previous work (e.g. by [4] and [3]) has shown that this type

---

[1] www.monami.info

P. Barnaghi et al. (Eds.): EuroSSC 2009, LNCS 5741, pp. 163–176, 2009.

of sensor can detect which device is used when, which in turn is a valuable clue to the recognition of more complex activities. We build on this work to detect **not just which** device is being used, but also **how** it is used. We focus on a kitchen scenario and demonstrate how it is possible to for example determine the consistency of the substance in the mixer, how many eggs are being boiled, what size of coffee has been prepared or whether a cutting machine was used to cut bread or salami.

Related Work. So called infrastructure mediated sensing [9] has recently generated considerable interest as unobtrusive, easy to install and maintain method for activity recognition. Published functionality includes motion tracking through pressure changes in the HVAC system [9], the analysis of water flow in the plumbing [2], [5] and various electric current sensing systems. The latter include different power measuring adapters for the sockets similar to our iSensor device [7,8], the analysis of transient noise to identify different devices [3] and general current consumption based activity recognition [4].

An alternative approach for recognizing interactions with home appliances has been sound analysis (e.g. [6],[11]), and a huge body of research on using different sorts of other body mounted sensors (in particular accelerometers) which will not be listed here, since our work is directed at non body worn approaches. This is because, in our case, the requirements analysis within the MonAMI project has revealed such approaches to be preferred by the users (which is not meant to imply that body worn system are in general less desirable than infrastructures solutions).

Paper Contributions and Organization. The main contribution that this paper makes beyond state of the art described above is to show that power measurements are not only able to determine *what* device is being used, but can also provide relevant information about *how* this device is being used.

The paper starts with an overview of our approach including the description of the iSensor, the scenarios and the principle of our recognition method. We then discuss in detail how the recognition rules are derived from the device signal characteristics. Finally we present an empirical evaluation that includes several devices connected to the same iSensor running simultaneously.

2   Approach Overview

2.1   The iSensor

We have designed and implemented smart wireless sensors, called iSensors, which can be connected to any power socket in a home environment. One or even several different devices can be connected directly or using a multi-contact plug to an iSensor. By analyzing the current consumption the iSensor is able to recognize pre-defined devices when they are in use and also what they are used for. Once a device event (like "toaster on", "bread toasted (brown)") is recognized it is sent via ZigBee to a central home monitoring unit (see figure 1).

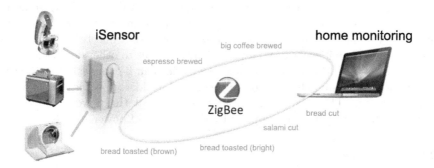

Fig. 1. iSensors send detailed information about activities of several connected devices to a home monitoring unit via ZigBee

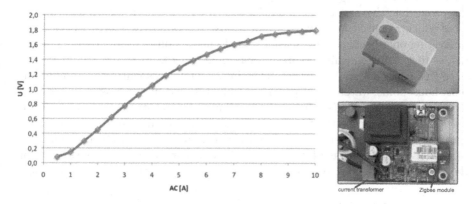

Fig. 2. Left: used ampere value and belonging inductive voltage. Right: iSensor out- and inside.

The current consumption is measured using electromagnetic induction. When devices connected to the iSensor are powered on, the induced voltage is digitalized using an AD converter (ADC)[2]. We used a current transformer which is able to handle devices which need between 0A and 10A. Figure 2 shows the dependency between a device's ampere request and the inductive voltage. As can be seen the resolution is quite good between 1.0A and 7.0A. Unfortunately the used current transformer shows saturation behavior when reaching values higher then 7.0A. Hence when using more devices at the same time a current transformer which provides both higher range and better resolution is needed. To avoid wired connections we used a Jennic ZigBee microcontroller (see http://www.jennic.com/) to send data via ZigBee to a processing unit. The Jennic microcontroller is also powerful enough to do some easy processing tasks. Hence our objective was to implement the later described algorithms using this

---

[2] ADC conversion time: $36\mu s$; feasible voltage range: 0.04V to 2.4V.

microcontroller and to avoid ADC value streaming. Figure 2 shows some pictures of the described iSensor. The iSensor can be integrated in any existing home environment without effort - the sensor is just connected to an existing power socket. The iSensor provides the same interface to other devices as a common power socket. This means that every device can be connected in the same way as without using the iSensor - especially for elderly people this is a quite important fact. There is also no need to care about the power supply of the iSensor - the sensor itself is supplied by the connected power socket.

2.2 Scenarios

Household devices can be assigned to application areas regarding their use. For example there are electric devices for home entertainment (e.g. TV, sound systems, DVD and Blue-ray player or beamer), for kitchen applications (e.g. toaster, coffee machine and egg boiler) or personal hygiene (e.g. electric teeth brusher, fan or electric shaver). In the following we will restrict our experiments to devices which are used for kitchen applications. We found these devices the most interesting ones because they provide lots of functionalities as different operating modes (e.g. coffee machine: espresso or normal coffee).

In this paper we analyze in detail the following devices which can be found in most households: water boiler, egg boiler, mixer, bread cutter, toaster, juicer, coffee machine and fridge (see figure 3). To simulate a realistic kitchen scenario we use a single iSensor for the fridge and connect all other devices to another iSensor using a multi-contact plug. We envision such information to be useful among others for the monitoring of dietary habits and general assessment of stability of daily routines which are both important for ambient assisted living applications.

2.3 Recognition Idea

The general idea is to use ADC peak values (calculated using the last 600 ADC values) as representatives for the current power consumption. After that the last

Fig. 3. Left: Devices that can be found in many common kitchen households. Right: iSensor with several simultaneously connected devices using a multi-plug.

21 representative values are collected and used to calculate the following features: sum, maximum, minimum, average and variance. The resulting feature vector of size five is used to distinguish between different devices and their operating modes. In this way the iSensor provides two feature vectors per second.

The next sections show that we use only simple classification rules based on thresholds which depend on both feature values and the time duration of a specific operation. Such rules can be efficiently implemented in real time on even the simplest microcontrollers as demonstrated by our system.

3 Signal Analysis and Recognition Methods

This chapter discusses the signals measured from different devices when using them in specific operating modes. For each device and each operating mode rules are defined that capture the current consumption characteristics. Impulses which appear when switching on a device are used to distinguish between different device types following a similar method as described in [3]. The description in the rest of the paper will focus on the detection of specific modes of operation assuming that the device has already been identified. All in all we analyzed more then 3600 measurement points for each device. Note: In the following all time axes are in ADC cycles.

Water Boiler. The voltage of the used water boiler ranges from 220V to 240V and its rated power is between 1850W and 2200W. As figure 4 shows the water boiler delivers a constant ADC value of about 2330 when turned on. It can also be seen that the ADC values are independent from the amount of boiled water - only the duration is quite different. The duration feature values are about 469 (1.0l) and 663 (1.5l). As a result we assume that in average 0.002195 liters of water are boiled per calculated feature value. All in all we found thresholds as described in table 1 suitable for recognizing a water boiler device and calculating the about amount of boiled water.

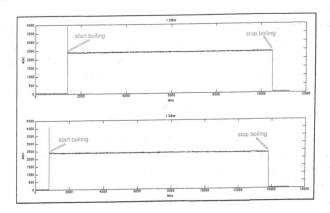

Fig. 4. ADC peak values when boiling 1.0l and 1.5l water

Table 1. Rules: Water boiler

Device:	if $((0 =< variance <= 650)$ and $(2300 =< average <= 2450))$ then $device = waterBoiler$
Boiled water:	$duration * 0.002195l = boiledWater$

Table 2. Rules: Fridge

Activities:	if $((sum > 842) \land (duration == 1))$ then $doorActivity$ if $((sum > 842)$ $\land$ $(duration > 1))$ then $fridgeCooling$ if $(fridgeCooling$ $\land$ $((thr_{powerCooling} - sum) < -70))$ then $doorOpen$ else $doorClosed$

Fridge. When analyzing ADC values generated by a fridge we can detect door opening actions as well as cooling actions. When opening the fridge door, a small light will be turned on, which results in a clearly visible change of ADC value. Unfortunately the fridge light consumes only relatively little power (about 10W, 240V) which is below the minimum power value that can be measured by our ADC (see chapter 2.1). Thus, the current version of our device can detect left open doors only when the fridge is cooling (then the power consumption is above the threshold of our ADC). When analyzing data we found out that the power consumption during a cooling process is mostly constant but varies between different cooling periods. Hence we use the first twenty seconds of a cooling period to calculate the current average power consumption $(thr_{powerCooling})$[3] before we can look for door opening events. The rules, described in table 2, have been derived to detect cooling periods, door opening events and - during cooling periods - door closing events. A visualization of measured ADC values can be found in figure 5.

Bread Cutter. When analyzing the power consumption of a bread cutter it can be seen that resulting ADC values are quite constant and characteristic when the device is powered on and nothing is cut. During cut events the device needs more power and hence ADC values raises a lot while something is cut. As can be seen in figure 6 it is possible to distinguish between bread and salami cuts when analyzing both the maximum adc value and the duration of a cut process. The operating voltage of the used bread cutter is 220V and its rated power 100W. Table 3 shows extracted classification rules.

Juicer. Figure 6 shows ADC values of a common juicer device when extracting juice twice from a half piece of orange. As can be seen ADC values are around 90 when extracting juice. The juicer we used has a voltage of 230V and a rated power of 30W. When analyzing in detail feature vectors of a juicer we found rules as shown in table 4 for detecting juicer activity.

---

[3] Note: During this time door activities cannot be recognized.

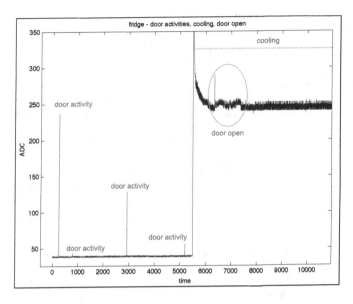

Fig. 5. ADC values indicating fridge events

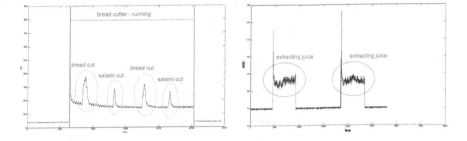

Fig. 6. Left: ADC values when cutting bread and salami. Right: ADC values when extracting juice.

Toaster, Egg Boiler and Coffee Machine. Toaster, egg boiler and coffee machine behave much like the water boiler when turned on. Thus ADC values (current drawn) are used to identify the device and the duration of an operation is used to distinguish between different device actions. In case of a toaster device we are able to differentiate between three toasting levels - bright, brown and dark toast. For egg boiler devices it is possible to recognize if three or five eggs were boiled and if the eggs are soft, medium or hard boiled. In case of a coffee machine we distinguish between a normal size coffee and a big one. Table 5 shows extracted classification rules. Note: The toaster/egg boiler/coffee machine voltage is 230V/220-240V/220-230V and their rated power is 800W/350W/1450W.

Table 3. Rules: bread cutter

Device:	*if* $((0 =< variance < 4000) \quad \wedge \quad (700 < max < 900))$
	then $device = breadCutter$

Activities:	*if* $((variance < 60) \quad \wedge \quad (100 < average <= 250))$ *then* *running*
	if $((32 < variance < 7000) \wedge (130 < average < 600))$ *then* *cutting*
	if $((cuttingDuration < 4) \wedge (maximum < 300))$ *then* *salamiCut*
	if $((cuttingDuration >= 4) \wedge (maximum >= 300))$ *then* *breadCut*

Table 4. Rules: Juicer

Device:	*if* $((0 =< variance <= 16) \quad \wedge \quad (50 =< average <= 90))$
	then $device = juicer$

Table 5. Rules: toaster, egg boiler and coffee machine

Rule toaster:	*if* $((0 =< variance <= 600) \wedge (1100 =< average <= 1250))$
	then $device = toaster$
Activities:	*if* $((110 < duration <= 194)$ *then* *bright* *toast*
	if $((194 < duration < 271)$ *then* *brown* *toast*
	if $((271 <= duration <= 342)$ *then* *dark* *toast*
Rule egg boiler:	*if* $((0 =< variance < 15) \wedge (600 < average < 700))$
	then $device = eggBoiler$
Activities:	*if* $((450 < duration < 650)$ *then* $3eggs$ *soft*
	if $((750 < duration < 850)$ *then* $3eggs$ *medium*
	if $((2000 <= duration <= 2200)$ *then* $3eggs$ *hard*
	if $((250 < duration < 450)$ *then* $5eggs$ *soft*
	if $((650 < duration < 750)$ *then* $5eggs$ *medium*
	if $((1300 <= duration <= 1600)$ *then* $5eggs$ *hard*
Rule coffee machine:	*if* $((0 =< variance < 1000) \wedge (1700 =< average <= 1890))$
	then $device = coffeeMachine$
Activities:	*if* $((25 < duration <= 58)$ *then* *small* *coffee*
	if $((58 < duration < 200)$ *then* *big* *coffee*

Mixer. As can be seen in figure 7 the current drawn by the mixer device depends on the level to which it is set and on the consistency (fluid, medium,creamy) of the substance in the mixer. To recognize mixer devices and to distinguish between different mixing levels and liquids we use thresholds which are shown in table 6. Note: The used mixer has a voltage of 220V to 240V and a rated power of 100W.

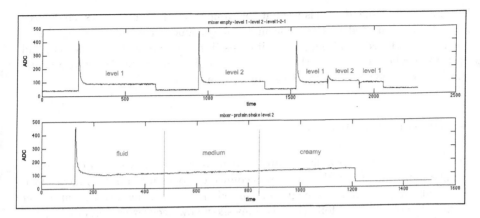

Fig. 7. ADC values of a mixer device: Upper image: Mixer off and on (empty tank - operating level 1, level2, level1-2-1), Lower image: Mixer on (level2) when mixing a protein shake (consistency from fluid to creamy)

Table 6. Rules: mixer

Device:	if	$((0 =< variance <= 30)$	$\wedge$	$(78 =< average <= 150))$
	then	$device = mixer$		

Activities:	if	$(78 =< average <= 88)$	then	mixer	$level1$
	if	$(89 =< average <= 110)$	then	mixer	$level2 - fluid$
	if	$(110 < average <= 125)$	then	mixer	$level2 - medium$
	if	$(125 < average <= 150)$	then	mixer	$level2 - creamy$

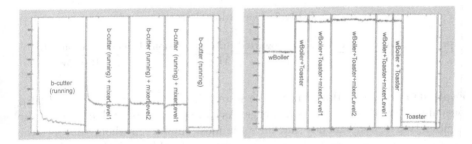

Fig. 8. Simultaneous device usage - Left: bread cutter and mixer; Right: water boiler, toaster and mixer. For each figure the vertical axes specify ADC values and the horizontal ones the time.

3.1   Simultaneous Device Usage

Above we have demonstrated that each of the devices has a characteristic current signature for each of the investigated operating modes. However, so far, we have looked at each device in isolation. In real kitchen environments on the other hand, more then one device is used at the same time. In many cases such devices may all be connected to the same multi-plug connector which is plugged into one iSensor. Hence we also analyzed if it is still possible to recognize devices and operations when using more then one device at the same time. As figure 8 shows thresholds for device combinations can also be found.

4   System Evaluation

During the following evaluation process we connect all devices to one iSensor using a multi-plug (only the fridge was connected to a single one). In most of the cases (about 90%) we can recognize a turned on device using a similar approach as described in [3]. The following sections show how accurate we can distinguish between different device actions when a device was recognized correctly[4].

Evaluation: Mixer. When evaluating a mixer device we tried to distinguish between mixing something fluid and creamy. Hence we asked seven users to prepare both a chocolate milk (250ml milk and two spoons of chocolate powder) and a quark-yoghurt dish (250g quark and 1 yoghurt) using mixing level two. As result 100% of chocolate milks were recognized as fluid and 100% of quark-yoghurt dishes were recognized as creamy. In about 57% of quark-yoghurt dishes we could also see a change from medium consistency to a creamy one.

Evaluation: Juicer. We asked six people to extract juice from two half pieces of orange. Hence twelve juice extractions were performed. As result our system was able to detect 91.66% of performed juice extractions (see table 7).

Table 7. Evaluation: Juicer

performed juice extractions	recognized juice extractions	classification rate
12	11	91.66 %

Evaluation: Egg boiler. Six people were asked to prepare three soft boiled eggs and after that five soft boiled eggs. As can be seen from table 5 this is the combination of usage modes that have the most similar threshold values (=the most difficult recognition task). Still, our system was able to distinguish between the mentioned two types of egg boiling with an accuracy of about 83.33%. As table 8 shows two times three soft boiled eggs were recognized as five soft boiled eggs. This is because some users were not very accurate when filling the required water amount. For other combinations of modes the recognition tends to be better, however, because of the excessive number of eggs needed for the test we did not do a systematic evaluation.

---

[4] For all performed evaluations we stream raw peak ADC values to a processing unit and apply the introduced rules there.

Table 8. Evaluation: Egg boiler

real / recognized	5 eggs soft boiled	3 eggs soft boiled	classification rate
5 eggs soft boiled	6	0	100.00 %
3 eggs soft boiled	2	4	66.66 %
			88.33 %

Evaluation: Toaster. Again we asked six people to evaluate a toaster device. Every person was asked to prepare a bright and a brown toast. Hence users had to choose the time for toasting to get the desired result. As result our system recognized 83.33% of the prepared toasts. As table 9 shows one bright toast was confused with a brown one. In fact there is no clear definition when a toast should be called bright or brown - therefore for some users a light brown toast was still a bright one and the other way round.

Table 9. Evaluation: Toaster

real / recognized	bright toast	brown toast	classification rate
bright toast	5	1	83.33 %
brown toast	1	5	83.33 %
			88.33 %

Evaluation: Coffee Machine. We asked six persons to prepare a double-sized coffee (big) as well as a normal one. As table 10 shows our system could distinguish between big and small coffee brews with an accuracy of about 91.66%. After each brew event the coffee machine is heating its water tank and therefore it consumes the same amount of power as for brewing coffee - but the variance is much higher. Hence we can filter out such water heating events. But every time when the coffee machine is turned on for the first time - which means that both water and heating rods are cold - also the variance of a water heating event is the same as when brewing coffee. Hence our system can't filter out such heating events and a big coffee brew event is wrongly recognized.

Table 10. Evaluation: Coffee Machine

real / recognized	big coffee	small coffee	classification rate
big coffee	6	0	100.00 %
small coffee	1	5	83.33 %
			91.66 %

Evaluation: Water Boiler. As described in section 3 multiplying the time duration which is needed for boiling water with 0.002195 is a good approximation of the amount of water that was boiled. As figure 9 shows this simple formula approximates the real amount of boiled water quite well for the whole water boiler's

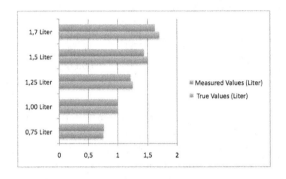

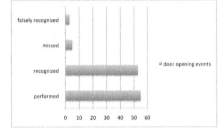

Fig. 9. Left: This chart visualizes the difference between the calculated (measured values) and the real (true values) amount of boiled water for 0.75, 1.0, 1.25, 1.5 and 1.7 liter. Right: calculated amount of water for 1.3liter.

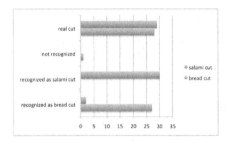

Fig. 10. Left: Evaluation results when cutting bread and salami. One bread cut was not recognized, two salami cuts were recognized as bread cuts and all in all three salami cuts more were recognized as performed. Right: Evaluation results when monitoring a fridge for about 35 hours.

capacity range (0.75 - 1.70 liters). Testing five different water levels (0.75l, 1.0l, 1.25l, 1.5l and 1.70l) the deviation was between 0.006 and 0.076 (average 0.038 liters). In order to see how strong the results vary between different calculation steps, 1.30 liters of water were boiled five times. As figure 9 shows the estimated amount of boiled water is nearly constant and accurate.

Evaluation: Bread Cutter. Figure 10 shows classification results when evaluating a bread cutter device. There six people were asked to cut all in all 28 slices of bread and 29 slices of salami. As can be seen the number of bread and salami cuts is recognized quite well with an accuracy of 96.42% for bread cuts and 93.10% for salami cuts. However there are 10% insertions for salami and 7% confusions between salami and bread. This is because some users had problems when cutting salami/bread and pieces of salami/bread for example clamped between the blades.

Evaluation: Fridge. We monitored a fridge in our lab kitchen for about 35 hours. Our objective was to detect when the fridge door was opened and also to count door opening events. Hence all persons had to note down when and how many times they have opened the fridge door. Figure 10 shows that our system is able to detect nearly 91% of door opening events. As it is mentioned in chapter 3 our system is not able to detect door opening events during the initialization time of a cooling process. Hence we missed 9% of door opening events. Also three door events were recognized two times.

5   Discussion and Future Work

An obvious lesson from the work presented in this paper is that current measurements from household appliances contain more information then just a binary on/off signal. In some cases (e.g. the water boiler) this was to be expected, in others (the consistency of the substance in the mixer or the bread cutter) we found it a bit surprising.

The accuracy of the recognition depends on three things. The biggest factor are variations in how the user operates a device, even when using it in the same mode. This includes the amount of water filled into the egg boiler, or the bread cutter usage. Another source of errors are ambiguities in the definition of the classes (e.g. what is a light and what is a brown toast) In some cases (e.g. like the coffee machine) there are also variations in the way the device works.

Overall the accuracies were in the range of 80% to 90%. Clearly, for applications that require exact counting of individual actions this would not be enough. However, for monitoring trends (e.g. long term nutrition trends or just the stability of a persons routine) or as features in a more complex, multi-modal recognition system it is a reasonable performance.

We have shown that this information can be extracted with an easy to install and maintain sensor and very simple algorithms. In terms of wide scale deployment the biggest problem is the fact that the thresholds have to be tuned to each specific device. A possible way around this problem is to use unsupervised learning techniques during an initial phase of the deployment. In particular in applications where we look for routines or use the information as features for more complex recognition tasks this might be a good solution. In such cases we do not need to know what a certain usage mode corresponds to in real life. It is sufficient to identify that there are different usage modes and be able to spot them.

As next steps we intend to deploy our devices for longer periods of time in real environments (together with our camera based indoor location system [1]) and attempt to recognize the cooking of different meals. This will show how useful the information about the use mode of kitchen appliances really is.

References

1. Bauer, G., Lukowicz, P.: Developing a Sub Room Level Indoor Location System for Wide Scale Deployment in Assisted Living Systems. In: Miesenberger, K., Klaus, J., Zagler, W.L., Karshmer, A.I. (eds.) ICCHP 2008. LNCS, vol. 5105, pp. 1057–1064. Springer, Heidelberg (2008)

2. Ibarz, A., Bauer, G., Casas, R., Marco, A., Lukowicz, P.: Design and Evaluation of a Sound Based Water Flow Measurement System. In: Roggen, D., Lombriser, C., Tröster, G., Kortuem, G., Havinga, P. (eds.) EuroSSC 2008. LNCS, vol. 5279, pp. 41–54. Springer, Heidelberg (2008)
3. Patel, S.N., Robertson, T., Kientz, A.J., Reynolds, M.S., Abowd, G.D.: At the Flick of a Switch: Detecting and Classifying Unique Electrical Events on the Residential Power Line. In: Krumm, J., Abowd, G.D., Seneviratne, A., Strang, T. (eds.) UbiComp 2007. LNCS, vol. 4717, pp. 271–288. Springer, Heidelberg (2007)
4. Berenguer, M., Giordani, M., Giraud-By, F., Noury, N.: Automatic detection of Activities of Daily Living from Detecting and Classifying Electrical Events on the Residential Power Line. In: Proc. 10th IEEE Intl. Conference on e-Health Networking, Applications and Service, HEALTHCOM 2008 (2008)
5. Fogarty, J., Au, C., Hudson, S.E.: Sensing from the basement: a feasibility study of unobtrusive and low-cost home activity recognition. In: Proceedings of the 19th Annual ACM Symposium on User Interface Software and Technology, Montreux, Switzerland (October 15-18, 2006)
6. Chen, J., Harvey Kam, A., Zhang, J., Liu, N., Shue, L.: Bathroom Activity Monitoring Based on Sound. In: Gellersen, H.-W., Want, R., Schmidt, A. (eds.) PERVASIVE 2005. LNCS, vol. 3468, pp. 47–61. Springer, Heidelberg (2005)
7. Logan, B., Healey, J., Philipose, M., Tapia, E.M., Intille, S.: A long-term evaluation of sensing modalities for activity recognition. In: Krumm, J., Abowd, G.D., Seneviratne, A., Strang, T. (eds.) UbiComp 2007. LNCS, vol. 4717, pp. 483–500. Springer, Heidelberg (2007)
8. Lifton, J., Feldmeier, M., Ono, Y., Lewis, C., Paradiso, J.A.: A platform for ubiquitous sensor deployment in occupational and domestic environments. In: Proceedings of the 6th international conference on Information processing in sensor networks, pp. 119–127 (2007)
9. Patel, S.N., Reynolds, M.S., Abowd, G.D.: Detecting human movement by differential air pressure sensing in HVAC system ductwork: An exploration in infrastructure mediated sensing. In: Indulska, J., Patterson, D.J., Rodden, T., Ott, M. (eds.) PERVASIVE 2008. LNCS, vol. 5013, pp. 1–18. Springer, Heidelberg (2008)
10. Schmidt, A., Beigl, M., Gellersen, H.W.: There is more to context than location. Computers & Graphics 23(6), 893–901 (1999)
11. Stäger, M., Lukowicz, P., Tröster, G.: Power and accuracy trade-offs in sound-based context recognition systems. Pervasive and Mobile Computing 3(3), 300–327 (2007)

Wireless Sensor Networks to Enable the Passive House - Deployment Experiences

Tessa Daniel, Elena Gaura, and James Brusey

Cogent Computing Applied Research Centre
Faculty of Engineering and Computing
Coventry University, Priory Street, Coventry, UK
CV1 5FB
t.daniel@coventry.ac.uk, e.gaura@coventry.ac.uk, j.brusey@coventry.ac.uk
www.cogentcomputing.org

Abstract. Finding solutions for the current period of climate change or "global warming" is possibly the most serious and pressing challenge faced by scientists and the wider community today. Although governments are beginning to act, a community wide approach is needed with a large proportion of individuals engaging to reduce energy consumption that depends on fossil fuels. The Passive House (or Passivhaus) standard is an ultra-low energy standard for building construction and design that aims at dramatically reducing energy consumption in the home. While appropriate for new builds, this standard may be difficult to achieve with existing buildings. In this work, Wireless Sensor Network (WSN) technology is examined as an enabling tool to support rapid progression to improved energy efficiency and increased comfort for existing buildings. As with participatory urban sensing, the home occupant could, in the future, take on the role of scientist; developing an awareness of trouble spots in the house would allow them to target problems thus reducing the need for heating and improving comfort. The paper reports on experiences and findings from several residential and commercial environmental monitoring WSN deployments using a WSN developed from off the shelf components. The sensors deployed measure temperature, relative humidity, CO_2 concentration and light. Depending on the size and layout of the space to be monitored, added to the scope of deployment, between 12 and 20 nodes were deployed and the monitoring period was 7-14 days per location. The paper illustrates the value of using WSN technologies as enablers for the amateur eco-home scientist on the path towards reduced energy consumption and increased comfort. It evaluates the suitability of the system for both commercial and residential deployments and shows how large quantities of data can be reduced to meaningful high level information delivered to the user.

1 Motivation

Climate change has emerged as one of the most critical issues facing the world today. It has spawned a movement towards reducing carbon emissions by increasing energy efficiency in a bid to decrease energy consumption. In the UK

P. Barnaghi et al. (Eds.): EuroSSC 2009, LNCS 5741, pp. 177–192, 2009.

alone, the built environment has been identified as being responsible for more than 45% of the energy used [1]. There is a need, therefore, to create new structures that are more energy aware while at the same time improving the energy efficiency of older buildings still in use today. Modern building standards allow for the construction of buildings that follow low energy usage models. The PassivHaus standard [2], for example, is an ultra-low energy standard for building construction and design that aims at dramatically reducing energy consumption (up to 90%) in the home. Passive houses avoid the use of a central heating system by being airtight and using advanced insulation, triple glazed windows and a number of other low energy building approaches.

An urgent problem, however, is the number of older buildings in use today that need to be improved upon. Many of these buildings boast central heating systems but it is doubtful how efficient these systems are, how well the building environment reacts to the energy input and what the optimal amount of heat required is, given a particular occupancy pattern, to create a 'comfortable' environment. As a consequence, a number of energy conservation initiatives have been put forward at a governmental level to encourage commercial entities as well as the population in general to incorporate energy saving measures in their day to day living. These include education and training programs on becoming more energy efficient, funding energy saving home improvements like loft insulation [3] and providing devices like the Smart meter [4] in a bid to provide consumers with more control over their own energy use. The focal point of these strategies is the empowering of consumers to make meaningful changes in their lives. For these strategies to succeed the homeowner must be actively involved. Wireless sensor networks (WSNs) have emerged as a useful tool in pushing such energy conservation strategies forward. Initially aiming at the commercial market they are moving into the residential arena, geared towards indoor environmental monitoring applications.

Generally, WSN technology has prompted the advancement of a number of scientific disciplines and applications by furnishing instrumentation that allows monitoring of phenomena in much greater detail than previously possible. These networks have been used in a variety of application areas like habitat monitoring [5,6] and disaster monitoring [7,8]. The technology allows for monitoring environments at a resolution and density that takes into account the spatial and temporal context of the data as well as the interactions between various parameters within the environment. Such analyses can provide a level of insight previously not possible with other single, point in time and space methods of environment monitoring.

In this study, a WSN system was built from off the shelf components and deployed in a number of residential and commercial buildings. The goal of these deployments was to determine, from a user and technical perspective, the suitability of the system for both commercial and residential monitoring and to identify the data and information representation needs of various user types. The users' needs as well as their control over the environment and comfort settings are different in the residential and commercial contexts. Moreover, a variety of stakeholders exist for data and information generated by these monitoring and analysis systems. For example, a house occupant may simply want to know which room is most comfortable on a given day while a building manager may want to know which offices in a building are using the heating least efficiently. Both want to assess the 'health' of the building but the most expressive way to furnish that information may be very different. Different user requirements translate to different application requirements, such as: the data rates, duty cycles and timeliness of the data and information (real-time vs post-deployment analysis and data delivery). It is therefore important to assess WSN systems in both types of spaces to determine how well-matched such systems are for a host of applications and a host of users.

The residential deployments focused on assessing the WSN system from the point of view of the home occupant and the housing association who constructs and maintains the structure. Could the system be used to obtain useful, actionable information about the general quality of the building and its indoor environment? (The quality of a building refers to the integrity of the physical structure as well as the state of the environment within the structure [20].) Could space usage patterns and problem areas within the home be identified?

The commercial deployments focused on assessing the system from the point of view of the building manager and users in a multi-occupancy open-plan office. Could spatial and temporal patterns and environmental trends be detected within those spaces and could the system provide high level information that was both useful and easy to understand for both stakeholders?

The hypotheses emerging from these test cases were as follows:

1. The WSN system can be a useful tool for assessing the quality of the building.
2. The system can be used to identify waste.
3. The system can be easily used to infer high level, relevant information.

The remainder of this paper is organized as follows: Section 2 describes some related work in the area of WSNs for environmental monitoring with Section 3 providing a brief description of the deployed WSN system. Section 4 provides an analysis of the results obtained and Section 5 concludes the paper with some lessons learned.

2   Related Work

Building monitoring is a fast growing application area for wireless sensor networks with systems being deployed for structural monitoring, emergency response and building climate control. Ji-Hye et al. discuss the development of MONETA, an embedded monitoring system aimed at indoor environment monitoring [9]. The system uses a remote shell to obtain device status information and to send control data, while a web-based user interface allows display of and interaction with sensor data. It is unclear, however, what sensors were used in the system and whether or not the system has been deployed. Song et al. describe a hybrid home monitoring sensor network comprised of static and mobile nodes [10]. Nodes form a multi-hop mesh network with each node capable of collecting and routing data. The system is suitable for building control applications and has been validated in a testbed setting.

In the area of indoor environmental monitoring research has looked at some specific application areas in which microclimate monitoring is critical. The microclimate in a building refers to the variations in localised climate within the building envelope [11]. This microclimate impacts the energy performance of the building and is affected by factors like: the orientation of the building (which affects solar access), the surrounding landscape (is there shading provided by trees) and the shape of the building (which can determine the quantity of solar radiation falling onto the external surface area which in turn can increase savings in heating for example.) Studies have shown that there can be considerable variation within a building's environment.

Monitoring and control of indoor climate conditions is critical to preserving art as they are affected to a great degree by fluctuations in temperature and relative humidity (RH). Fluctuating levels of RH cause materials to corrode, shrink, swell, or warp [12]. Researchers used piezoelectric quartz crystal sensors to measure the RH and temperature gradients across a painting located at the Sandham Memorial Chapel [13]. Temperature and RH measuring circuits were connected to a computer using a cable and data collected showed that abrupt changes could occur in the microclimate surrounding the painting and that these changes over time could lead to cracking and damage.

In another study [12] researchers deployed a wireless sensor network to monitor temperature and RH in an art gallery. The design of the system allowed for lower power consumption and was evaluated in terms of cost, range, power consumption and packet error rate.

More recently, however, there has been a proliferation of building environmental monitoring systems on the market aimed at commercial organizations. These systems are marketed as commercial products and aim at facilitating a number of building control functions including: lighting monitoring and control systems, heating, ventilation and cooling (HVAC) systems and energy consumption monitoring [14,15,16,17,18,19]. The study here used one such off-the-shelf system to test the hypotheses outlined in Section 1.

3   System Description

The Arch Rock platform [14], is an off the shelf wireless sensor network system that enables the development of a variety of WSN applications. The system brings together the power of embedded systems, flexible web service architectures and makes use of industry-standard multi-hop mesh networking protocols. It allows energy-efficient, reliable data collection, routing and dissemination over industry standard links like IEEE 802.15.4.

3.1   Network Architecture and Hardware

An IP-based server attaches to a local area network (LAN) and provides access to the sensor network through a router which connects to nodes in the wireless mesh network via IEEE 802.15.4 low-power radio. The IPSensor node platform is the Telosb mote, an open source platform produced by Crossbow. The mote consists of a IEEE 802.15.4 Zigbee compliant RF transceiver, a 250 kbps high data rate radio, 1MB external flash for data logging and uses a Texas Instrument MSP430 microcontroller with 10kB RAM. The node runs the open source TinyOS 1.1.10 operating system, and is powered by 2 AA batteries. Each node contained a number of integrated sensors: a Sensirion SHT-11 sensor provided temperature ($\pm$ 0.5°C accuracy) and relative humidity ($\pm$ 3.5% accuracy) measurements; a Hamamatsu S-1087 light sensor for photosynthetically active radiation (wavelength 350 to 700nm), a Hamamatsu S-1087-1 light sensor for total solar radiation (wavelength 320 - 1000 nm).

Fig. 1. IPSensor node with attached CO2 sensor is shown on the left and the weather-proof box is shown on the right

IPSensor nodes were integrated with CO2 sensors (shown in figure 1), this is discussed in greater detail in Section 3.2. Nodes which had to be deployed outdoors were housed in a weatherproof box (shown in figure 1.)

3.2   Attaching External Devices to the Node

IPSensor nodes have a number of expansion ports which allow the integration of binary devices such as high/low voltage switches, analog devices such as variable voltage sensors and actuators such as relays. The node allows the attachment of up to 5 external devices. This facility is useful as it allows the expansion of the sensor load, increasing the scope of possible applications that can be created using the platform.

An external ELT B-530 CO2 sensor ($\pm$ 30ppm precision) was integrated in-house using the available ADC and VPU0 connectors. Given the power requirements of the sensor, the node had to be powered using a separate battery pack of 8 AA batteries. Cost was a constraint so the lowest priced CO2 sensor on the market was selected, at the expense of dealing with a shortlived, relatively large sensor with a large power source footprint.

The CO2 sensor had to be interfaced using a relay to provide a duty cycle of 3s warm-up/10seconds sample collection and reading/ every 5 minutes (which was the sample rate for all sensors in the system). This ensured the optimal functionality with respect to both overall data collection requirements and minimizing CO2 power consumption. The Arch Rock web interface allows sensor calibration coefficients to be set and the ADC0 port to be activated. From then on, the system deals with the external sensor readings in an identical way to the internal ones. A node with an integrated CO2 sensor is shown in figure 1.

3.3   Software

The Arch Rock system provides a web services API that allows interaction with sensor nodes and server for retrieving data, metadata and node statistics, sending commands and setting variables. API calls operate on a set of event channels, remote procedure calls, and attributes provided by the embedded application. A web-based interface allows access to the nodes, server, router as well as statistics and logs generated by the system. A local datawarehouse is available for persistent data storage.

3.4   Ease of Configuration and Deployment

Deploying the Arch Rock system is straightforward and entails assigning the server an IP address, connecting and registering the router to the server and then linking nodes to the deployment. Once a deployment is up and running additional routers can be added either to support an existing network or to connect a separate network. The ease of setup and configuration means that very little time is lost in actually deploying the system. A number of 'drop-and-go' deployments (numbering between 10 and 20 nodes) have been carried out using the system. Set up time is usually between 30 minutes to an hour.

3.5   Flexibility

The Arch Rock system allows the creation of single to multi network, multi-location applications. The server is configured to manage as many routers as required and routers can be placed in any location as long as they can connect to the server. This in theory means that there is no limit to the size of the network that can be deployed.

The system is also amenable to integration with other devices to extend its capability. In addition to the CO2 sensor integration described in Section 3.2 a message logging system using 3G technology was developed to allow remote access to the deployment. Each message contains information about the quantity of data collected and the system status including: what nodes are down or not sending data and detecting if the server or router is down. The remote connection will also allow download of data and logs which will allow troubleshooting if any problems arise.

3.6 Robustness and Reliability

Links may experience errors due to interference and obstructions and limiting hop length is essential for limiting energy consumption to maximize node lifetime. The Arch Rock system allows any node to act as a router thereby relaying data hop-by-hop along a reliable path. Routing paths are adapted through continuous network monitoring services and reliability is enhanced by link, network, and transport level techniques [14]. A number of power management techniques are used to reduce energy spent during communication without relying on complex preplanning and scheduling that reduce the flexibility of the network.

In addition, secondary routers can be added to a deployment as an alternative communication route in and out of the network. This ensures that if one router fails a backup router is available to take over. This increases redundancy and reliability of the system.

3.7 Connectivity

Given the need to deploy the system in a number of different building layouts a number of connectivity tests were carried out. These were used to inform the locationing of nodes within future deployments in terms of density and distances required from nodes, router and server to ensure maximal connectivity.

Table 1. Connectivity test results

Obstruction	Maximum radio range
None	30m
1 wall	18.9m
2 walls	11.9m
wooden door	22.5m
1 floor	4.6m
PC system	22.8m

The results showed that a maximum distance of 30m between nodes allows for optimal connectivity in an open space. The impact of multipath fading, however, causes radio range between nodes to vary depending on the type, location and number of obstructions (table 1 shows the results.) Tests also showed that to ensure reliable connectivity, nodes should be deployed so that each node can connect to more than one node.

3.8 Deployment Density

It is important to note that the deployment density required for connectivity is not necessarily adequate to allow meaningful observations to be made. Experiments were carried out in the office deployments to determine what a suitable density was to allow meaningful trends in the data to be recorded. Nodes were initially deployed in Office A at a density of 1.5m to 2.5m and then more nodes added for a 1m-1.5m density. Evaluation of temperature across the office showed greater variability with the more dense deployment (over 6°C) compared to 1.5°C for the more sparse deployment . The denser deployment also allowed a problem hotspot in the office to be identified and isolated.

Given these findings, nodes were initially deployed at a 1m-1.5m density in Office B and then increased to a 0.5m-1m density. Variability of temperature showed little difference (less than 1°C) between the two densities. Based on the test results a density of 1m-1.5m was selected for both office deployments.

3.9   Deployments

Residential
House A is a 2 floor, 5 bedroom, early twentieth century terraced house occupied by a family of four (2 adults and 2 children). There is old double glazing on most of the upstairs windows with single glazing on downstairs bathroom and kitchen windows and secondary glazing in the living and dining rooms. The central heating system is over 20 years old. 18 nodes were deployed (at a height of between 1m and 2m), one node per room with additional nodes at the entrance and the closet in Bedroom 2 (this was at the request of the homeowner who identified those locations as possible problem areas.)
House B is a 2 floor, 4 bedroom, early twentieth century terraced house with 5 occupants (all university students). All windows are double glazed and the house has a new central heating system. 13 nodes were deployed (at a height of between 1m and 2m) with 1 node per room and an additional node at the window in Room 1 which was identified as a potential problem area.

Commercial
The building consists of regular offices, seminar rooms and lecture rooms distributed over five floors. The two open-plan office spaces (**Office A** and **Office B**) monitored in this exercise were both located on the ground floor with double glazing and centrally controlled heating systems. Nodes were distributed throughout the offices at a 1m to 1.5m density and positioned opportunistically (for example, on desks and shelves).

4   Evaluation

4.1   Hypothesis Testing

Hypothesis 1: The WSN system can be a useful tool for assessing the quality of the building.
Patterns in temperature, humidity and CO_2 can be useful indicators of the condition of properties that affect a building's quality. Presenting time series graphs for each sensor and location over the deployment period, the modus operandi for the majority of off the shelf systems, is not adequate for a number of reasons:

1. with the sheer volume of data generated, it is difficult to identify trends and patterns in the data without in-depth analyses (12 nodes, for example, each with five sensors enabled and a sampling period of 5 minutes would generate over 480,000 data points over a 2 week deployment.)
2. it is challenging for the user to translate parameter readings to meaningful building health indicators. For example the user may see that temperature is rising but what does that imply?
3. Multi-variable correlation is required but difficult to do with time series data for multiple nodes and multiple parameters.

The key here is that the information presented reflects the needs of the particular stakeholder, giving an indication of how well his home is performing in terms of the properties described above. In the next section, some example analyses are discussed to show how the data was used to derive meaningful conclusions which were presented to the home occupant.

Findings
Analysing heating efficiency
By assessing the impact of heating on indoor temperature profiles, conclusions can be made about the insulation and heat retention properties of the home.

House A
Figure 2 shows the temperatures recorded over a typical 24 hour period for House A. There were two heating periods, 5:30am for 2 hours, and again at 3:00pm for approximately 5 hours. For the first heating period, the overall increase in temperature in all rooms was between 2°C - 3°C with the exception of the entrance way and loft spaces which did not appear to be affected by the heating. Once the heating was switched off there was an almost immediate decrease in temperature over a 2 hour period till it returned to pre-heating levels.

During the second heating period the increase in temperature was about 5°C over the four hours of continuous heating. Again, there was a steady decline as soon as the heating was turned off. An interesting note here was the almost 3°C difference between temperature measurements in Bedroom 2 and a closet in the same room.

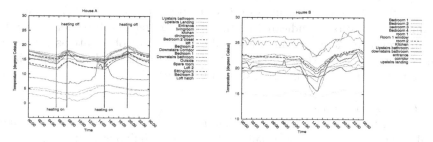

Fig. 2. A graph of temperatures recorded at various rooms in House A over a 24 hour period is shown on the left, House B temperature recordings are shown on the right

Conclusions for the home occupant
General insulation and heat retention problems are evident throughout the house, with marked problems in the entranceway and loft spaces. A possible draft exists in the Bedroom 2 closet which would warrant special attention. For this purpose the visualization tool provided by the Arch Rock system was sufficient.

House B
Figure 2 shows daily temperatures measured at various locations in House B over a 24 hour period. Temperatures remain relatively constant within each room throughout the day with a loss of almost 5°C over a four hour period before the temperature again starts to rise when the heating is turned back on at approximately 3pm. Two exceptions are the node at the window in Room 1 and the node in Bedroom 1 whose readings both show relatively small changes. Although the window in Room 1 had double glazing, it shows consistently lower temperatures (between 4 and 7°C) than another more centrally located node in the same room.

Conclusions for the home occupant
Insulation is good throughout the house with the exception of Bedroom 1 and the window in Room 1. There is a possible heat leak at the Room 1 window and heat retention problems exist in both bathrooms. Again the Arch Rock system's visualization functionality was sufficient to allow these inferences to be made.

Users rarely want to look at data in isolation. If we imagine two home occupants in different houses using the WSN system it is more interesting to make comparative assessments to determine how well one house is performing vis-a-vie another. The Arch Rock system would need additional functionality, however, to be able to make these more complex analyses. The next section is a comparative assessment of heating efficiency in the two houses.

Comparing heating efficiency across houses
Figure 3 compares and contrasts the average temperatures between House A and House B for each day over the deployment period.

In general, the average temperatures at House B were higher than at House A with differences of 3-7°C calculated. When the dispersion of temperature data between the two houses was analysed (see figure 3) it showed higher minimum, maximum and average (indicated by the black bar) temperatures for House A. The difference in energy consumption could explain these observations as the gas consumption in House B was over 70% higher than House A. It is also possible, however, that House B is better insulated than House A.

Identifying dampness
Excess moisture due to high relative humidity can lead to mould, mildew and wood rot which can cause permanent damage to a building structure. One of

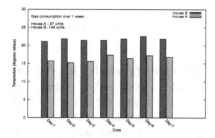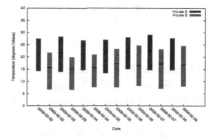

Fig. 3. A comparison of daily average temperatures in House A and House B is shown on the left; a comparison of daily minimum, maximum and mean temperatures in House A and House B

the causes of dampness is condensation which can result from poor insulation or poor ventilation. Figure 4 shows relative humidity readings taken over a 24 hour period in House A. The graph indicates that both bathrooms have potentially problematic relative humidity readings (above 65%). The Arch Rock system was therefore successful in allowing the flagging of these areas for closer inspection.

In order to determine to what degree this humidity is actually a problem, however, further correlation analyses between humidity and temperature must be carried out. The dewpoint is the temperature at which water condenses and the closer the air temperature is to this dewpoint the more likely condensation will occur. Therefore, by monitoring for periods where the dewpoint and air temperature are close we can isolate problem areas. The graph in figure 4 shows the difference between the air temperature and the dewpoint in different locations in House A.

In the upstairs bathroom the difference in the two temperatures falls just below 3°C and remains consistently at that level for the entire period. This means that if the temperature in that room were to drop by that figure condensation would likely occur.

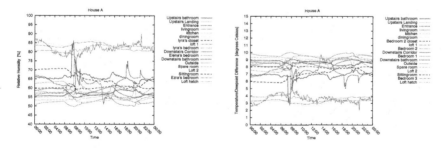

Fig. 4. The leftmost figure shows humidity measurements in House A over a 24 hour period, a graph of the difference between temperature and dewpoint measurements over a 24 hour period is shown on the right

Conclusions for the home occupant

Although there was high humidity observed in both bathrooms, damp is a more pressing issue in the upstairs bathroom.

Hypothesis 2: The system can be used to identify waste. Improvements in energy efficiency is the key promise of many of the off-the-shelf systems being sold today. It is therefore important to determine whether the data collected by these system can provide insight on 'wasteful' behaviours within the home. Providing time series data by itself is clearly not adequate, rather, the data gathered has to be linked to the behaviour of the home occupant in order to provide easy to understand, meaningful information that can be acted upon.

Findings
Identifying light usage

A good indicator of waste is the amount of electricity that is used within the home. By selecting time periods when lights should be off in particular rooms, and calculating summaries of time for which lights remain on during these periods, we can assess electricity waste by looking at the light usage figures. Comparing real occupancy with apparent light usage may act as a prompt to perhaps change behaviour in an effort to reduce waste. Again, the information has to be easy to understand.

The graph in figure 5 shows the total number of hours lights stayed on during the night hours (10pm to 6am) over the entire deployment period in House B. Areas that are likely to be unoccupied and/or not being used were ideal places to examine more closely.

An interesting observation from the graph is the pattern of usage of areas like the bathrooms and bedrooms during the night/early morning hours. The downstairs bathroom shows 27 hours of usage over the 7 day deployment, an average of almost 4 hours for each 8 hour 'night' period (10pm to 6am). An inference can be made that the lights are being left on for extended periods, rather than that the bathroom is actually being used for that long. Bedroom 2 also shows high usage with 20.3 hours over the deployment period. In this case, the occu-

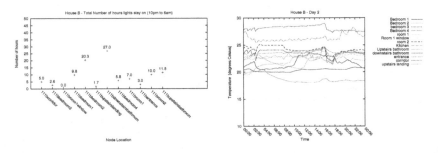

Fig. 5. A graph showing the total number of hours lights stayed on from 10pm to 6am over the deployment period in House B is shown on the left; Temperatures recorded over a 24 hour period in House B is shown on the right

pant of the room has to determine whether the light usage pattern matches up with the actual occupancy and use of the room. (Does the occupant, who is a student, sleep with the lights on? Is the occupant in that room studying at that time of the night?) More importantly, is the room not receiving enough essential daylight, important for health?

Identifying heating waste
Another good indicator of waste is the amount of heat used within the home. Is the heat on when no one's home? Is the heat being used efficiently? Again, it is incumbent upon the occupant to link the information presented to his behaviour to be able to make meaningful changes that can help reduce waste.

Figure 5 shows the temperatures recorded over a typical day in House B. It shows relatively constant temperatures in each of the rooms with a range of 20°C to 28 °C across different rooms. This is with outside temperatures between 4°C and 5 °C for that entire day. It is clear from time series that the heat is turned on throughout the day. However, the following questions require in-depth analyses which the off the shelf system does not provide. Would the benefit to the occupants be similar if the heat is turned on an off periodically? Can the thermostat be turned down once the room heats up to a comfortable temperature level? The information given here is designed to get the occupant to first think about what they are doing in order to effect change in their behaviour.

Hypothesis 3: The system can be used to infer high level, relevant information easily.

Monitoring comfort. Many commercial systems are able to generate large quantities of data cannot reduce this data into usable information. In this first example, the stakeholder is the building manager who wants to know what the comfort levels are within the monitored office at any moment in time. In addition, the building manager wants to track the comfort within the space over time. There is, therefore, real-time, spatio-temporal requirements that are not supported by the Arch Rock system.

An application was created and integrated with the Arch Rock system to monitor comfort levels within different spaces. Comfort can be calculated by correlating temperature and humidity at points in time to determine what the comfort index is at that point. Using temperate and humidity data gathered by the system, comfort indices were calculated for each of the nodes and used as input to an interpolation algorithm to generate a live comfort field map of the monitored offices. The application run in real-time and showed the user, 'at-a-glance', the comfort variation across the office as well as changes in the measurements over time. Figure 6 shows a section of a comfort map generated for Office A.

Another important stakeholder is the office occupant who needs to be assured that conditions in the offices are optimal. Simplicity is key and so charts clearly showing the comfortable and uncomfortable zones (during the occupant's time in the space) can give a clear indication of the state of the office environment. Again

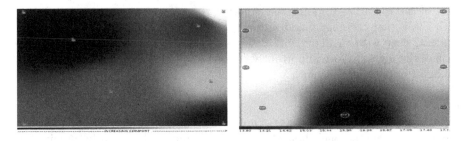

Fig. 6. A comfort map of Office A is shown on the left and a thermal map of the livingroom in House A is shown on the right

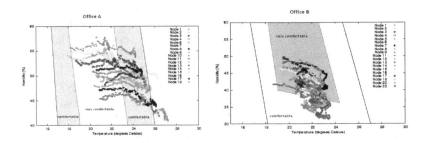

Fig. 7. Comfort chart for Office A (on the left) and Office B (on the right)

these charts required analysis and visualization beyond the facilities provided by the off the shelf WSN system. Some examples of comfort charts for Office A and Office B are shown in figure 7.

Locating poor insulation sites

Time series data allowed rooms with poor insulation to be identified, however, the ability to drill down into the area in order to localize the problem is important. By deploying a larger number of nodes in the room, gathering the necessary data the problem area was located and visualized in an easy to understand format.

Figure 6 shows some interpolated maps generated from temperature data collected by a custom-built component. The maps make it easier to visualize the parameter field over the space. In this example, the heating was turned on in the room with a fire lit in the fireplace (the white area on the left). The poorly insulated area is clearly distinguishable as the dark area at the bottom of the map.

5   Concluding Remarks

WSNs are increasingly being used in the area of indoor environmental monitoring with systems being marketed as energy saving enablers. In this paper, the authors discuss a case study in which the suitability of an off the shelf WSN system was assessed in the context of both residential and commercial deployments. It is clear that the system has some value: it facilitates reliable, robust gathering of data; it allows flexible deployment configurations and it also provides data that can be useful in giving a degree of insight into the state of the building environment. The study clearly showed, however, the limitations of such a system in terms of the lack of higher level information (beyond time series) that it provides.

In order to be of any value in answering serious questions about the building indoor environment, the system has to be transformed from a data collector to an information generator. Moreover, it has to take into account the various stakeholders for whom the information is being generated and cater the representation of that information to the particular stakeholder. Granted, the examples described in Section 4 are amenable to post analysis, but this is not always desirable and it is often necessary that information be generated in real-time. Therefore, the authors propose the creation of a real-time indoor environmental monitoring system. The system will exploit the benefits of off-the-shelf components while incorporating high level information generating and visualization tools. The hope is that the system will be of benefit in a number of indoor environmental monitoring applications for a variety of stakeholders.

Acknowledgements

The authors would like to thank Dr. Xiang Fei for his contributions to this paper.

References

1. Technology Strategy Board (n.d.) (June 15, 2009),
   http://www.innovateuk.org/_assets/pdf/tsb_ddtoolfor
   lowimpactbuildcompflyer.pdf
2. Passive House Institute (n.d.) Passive House Institute (June 11, 2009),
   http://www.passivehouse.com/
3. Department of Energy and Climate Change (n.d.) Home Energy Meter (June 2, 2009),
   http://www.decc.gov.uk/en/content/cms/what_we_do/consumers/
   home_energy/
4. Department of Energy and Climate Change (n.d.) Smart Meter (June 2, 2009),
   http://www.decc.gov.uk/en/content/cms/what_we_do/consumers/
   smart_meters/
5. Mainwaring, A., Culler, D., Polastre, J., Szewczyk, R., Anderson, J.: Wireless Sensor Networks for Habitat Monitoring. In: Proc. of WSNA, pp. 88–97 (2002)
6. Tolle, G., Polastre, J., Szewczyk, R., Culler, D., Turner, N., Tu, K., Burgess, S., Dawson, T., Buonadonna, P., Gay, D., Hong, W.: A macroscope in the redwoods. In: Proceedings of the 3rd international Conference on Embedded Networked Sensor Systems, SenSys 2005, San Diego, California, USA, November 02 - 04, pp. 51–63. ACM, New York (2005),
   http://doi.acm.org/10.1145/1098918.1098925

7. Suzuki, M., Saruwatari, S., Kurata, N., Morikawa, H.: A high-density earthquake monitoring system using wireless sensor networks. In: Proceedings of the 5th international Conference on Embedded Networked Sensor Systems, SenSys 2007, Sydney, Australia, November 06 - 09, pp. 373–374. ACM, New York (2007), http://doi.acm.org/10.1145/1322263.1322301

8. Werner-Allen, G., Lorincz, K., Welsh, M., Marcillo, O., Johnson, J., Ruiz, M., Lees, J.: Deploying a Wireless Sensor Network on an active volcano. IEEE Internet Computing 10(2), 18–25 (2006)

9. Bae, J.-H., Lee, K.-O., Park, Y.-Y.: MONETA: an embedded monitoring system for ubiquitous network environments. IEEE Transactions on Consumer Electronics 52(2), 414–420 (2006)

10. Song, G., Wei, Z., Zhang, W., Song, A.: A Hybrid Sensor Network System for Home Monitoring Applications. IEEE Transactions on Consumer Electronics 53(4), 1434–1439 (2007)

11. Energy Systems Research Unit (n.d.) Energy Systems Research Uni (June 10, 2009), http://www.esru.strath.ac.uk/

12. Lee, A.M.C., Angeles, C.T., Talampas, M.C.R., Sison, L.G., Soriano, M.N.: Philippines Univ., Quezon. MotesArt: Wireless Sensor Network for Monitoring Relative Humidity and Temperature in an Art Gallery. In: Proc. of IEEE International Conference on Networking, Sensing and Control, 2008 (ICNSC 2008), April 6-8, pp. 1263–1268 (2008)

13. Odlyha, M., Foster, G.M., Cohen, N.S., Sitwell, C., Bullock, L.: Microclimate monitoring of indoor environments using piezoelectric quartz crystal humidity sensors. Journal of environmental monitoring: JEM. 01/05/200005/2000 2(2), 127–131 (ISSN: 1464-0325)

14. Arch Rock (n.d.) Solutions (June 9, 2009), http://www.archrock.com/

15. SensiNode (n.d.) SensiNode (June 8, 2009), http://www.sensinode.com

16. SpinWave (n.d.) Spinwave Systems (June 8, 2009), http://www.spinwavesystems.com

17. MicroWatt (n.d.) Power Manager (June 8, 2009), http://www.microwatt.co.uk

18. Sentilla (n.d.) Products (June 9, 2009), http://sentilla.com/

19. MillenialNet. (n.d.) MeshScape (June 9, 2009), http://www.millennial.net/products/meshscape.php

20. Ilozor, B.D., et al.: Understanding residential house defects in Australia from the State of Victoria. Building and Environment 39(3), 327–337 (2004)

21. Oak Ridge National Laboratory (n.d.) Defining and Rating Commercial Building Performance (June 15, 2009), http://eber.ed.ornl.gov/commercialproducts/CWB.htm

Mobile Context Toolbox
An Extensible Context Framework for S60 Mobile Phones

Jakob Eg Larsen and Kristian Jensen

Technical University of Denmark,
Informatics and Mathematical Modeling,
Richard Petersens Plads, Building 321,
DK-2800 Kgs. Lyngby, Denmark
{jel,krije}@imm.dtu.dk

Abstract. We describe an open framework utilizing sensors and application data on S60 mobile phones enabling rapid prototyping of context-aware mobile applications. The framework has an extensible layered architecture allowing new sensors and features to be added to the context framework as they become available on mobile phone platforms. The framework provides access to multiple sensors to derive user context, and we present results from experiments with two prototype applications built using the toolbox. Initial experiments have been carried out to validate the data obtained by the tool. In the experiments 14 participants have been continuously using a Nokia N95 mobile phone with a *context logger* application for an average of 48 days per user and covering 70% of the time. The study has provided valuable insights into the performance issues of the system in real-life usage situations, including the stability of and power consumption in the system.

Keywords: context, context-awareness, mobile, framework, toolbox, application prototyping.

1 Introduction

Context-awareness and context-aware applications have gotten much attention for more than a decade. With the advancements in mobile platforms, such as mobile phones the potential for developing novel context-aware mobile applications is increasing. Standard off-the-shelf mobile phones now have several built-in sensors, such as, GPS, accelerometer, light sensor, proximity sensor, microphone, camera, as well as multiple network connectivity options, such as, GSM, WLAN, and Bluetooth. However, utilizing these sensor inputs for developing context-aware mobile applications is a complex task. The complexity of development include:

Abstraction level: low-level sensor information has to be translated into higher-level information in order to be useful in the application. For instance a GPS coordinate being translated into human-readable place descriptions.

P. Barnaghi et al. (Eds.): EuroSSC 2009, LNCS 5741, pp. 193–206, 2009.
© Springer-Verlag Berlin Heidelberg 2009

Multiple sensors: are available which can potentially supplement each other (information fusion) in order to deal with the uncertainty of the information read from individual sensors.

Dynamic environment: readings from sensors will change dynamically according to changes in the environment.

We therefore propose an open extensible framework for developing context-aware mobile applications. The framework has a layered architecture, which abstracts the complexity of multiple low-level sensors from the application programmer. Sensors is interpreted broad, as it includes built-in sensors such as accelerometer, microphone, camera, etc, as well networking components, phone application data (calendar, address book, phone log, etc), and phone state (profile, charge level, etc). Our current implementation exploits the potential of using such sensors in modern off-the-shelf S60 mobile phones for novel applications.

The focus has been on the assessment of the potential for such a framework taking into consideration the increased performance requirements in such system due to the additional CPU, memory and power consumption introduced. An initial deployment of the system included continuous use by 14 participants, which were provided with a standard mobile phones (Nokia N95) which had the Mobile Context Toolbox installed along an application that would continuously log the data acquired from all sensors currently supported by our framework. The experimental results from real-life use of the device for a period of time have provided interesting insights into the potential of such a system as well as information about the additional CPU, memory and power requirements.

2   Mobile Context Toolbox

Mobile Context Toolbox is based on the Symbian OS running on Nokia N95 smart-phones. The reason for choosing this platform is the wide array of built in sensors as well as the relatively easy access to them. At the time of development the standard operating system for Nokia N95 phones is the Symbian OS S60 3rd Edition and the tool is developed in Python for S60 [1].

2.1   Mobile Phone Sensors as Context Sources

In principle, mobile devices can acquire context data through a large variety of sensors embedded in the device and in the surrounding environment, as well as from online sources.

GPS provides an absolute localization system which was designed for surveying tools and navigation aids with global coverage. Typically, the accuracy on low cost devices ranges between 5–20 meters [2]. While having a high availability measured by the geographical coverage, GPS receivers require a clear view of the sky and thus do not work well indoors or under cover. They also perform poorly in cities where tall buildings form the so called urban canyons and block parts of the sky, thus preventing the devices from obtaining locks on enough satellites to calculate a position.

Identifying the cell that is being used by the phone in cellular networks is the most basic method of localization, also it is the most imprecise as the granularity will only be the same as the cell size. Experimental analysis performed by Trevisani et al. [3] in urban, suburban, and highway environments showed that directly associating the device's location with that of the **Base Transceiver Station** covering the current cell resulted in average differences of 800 meters or more, compared to the actual location recorded via GPS. In the programming interfaces available for these experiments only information about the currently active cell is provided and not to all visible base stations. However, [4] observed that if a user spent enough time in one place, improved location estimates could be produced from the probability density function of nearby base stations.

For more fine grained localization **wireless access points** might be used when available. Similarly to base transceiver stations, access points are typically affiliated with a place, such as *Home*, *Office* or even *Train*. Wireless access points also have unique MAC addresses, also called Basic Service Set ID (BSSID), which makes them an excellent radio beacon. Compared to the area covered by a base transceiver station, the reach of a wireless access point is significantly smaller, especially indoors. Therefore, by applying the same principles as mentioned above, it is possible to use wireless network signatures to identify places more precisely than with base transceiver stations.

Bluetooth devices are not well suited to be used directly as beacons for places in the same way as base transceiver stations and wireless access points because of their nomadic behavior [5]. Bluetooth was primarily designed to enable wireless headsets or enable laptops to connect to mobile phones and typically have a reach of 5 - 10 m. However, as a by-product devices are becoming aware of the presence of other Bluetooth-enabled devices. As Bluetooth capability is often embedded in wearable devices, they can be used as electronic representatives for people. The ability to infer which context two people share can provide insights into the nature of their association, for example associating a person to a certain place, or time of day.

While scanning for Bluetooth-enabled devices provides a profile of the physical nearby surroundings, the obtained results may not be an accurate reflection of the user's social relations. If it is assumed that the most important individuals in a person's social settings are also people that the user contacts or is contacted by, this will be reflected in the devices **correspondence logs**. If there exists a correlation between the time or whereabouts of the user and correspondences, it can be used to stipulate in which context a social relation exists based on the number of calls and/or messages, their frequency and time. This can for example be used to deny incoming calls from friends when at work, or to sort the contacts in the contact list by the current context rather than simply alphabetically.

There have been approaches to infer activities based on **accelerometer** sensor readings [6], but most of them have required a rather high sampling rate and extensive data processing. However, computationally simple and low sample based activity detection might very well be interesting, for example to turn costly services on and off, to adjust other sensor sampling rates or simply to differentiate between the phone being *Idle* or *Moving*. For low sample rate based approaches it is most likely not possible to track or recognize the users movement patterns, nonetheless approaches based on sample differences are still possible. The accelerometer available in Nokia N95 phones is a 3-axis accelerometer which includes the gravitational acceleration. The output from the accelerometer is a three dimensional vector, $A = (a_x, a_y, a_z)$, indicating the acceleration in each spatial direction. In situations with low acceleration, the gravitational force will be dominant, from which the device's orientation can be obtained. If a device is moved sporadically and only in short intervals, which often is the case when it is being handled, it is most likely not possible to measure any significant difference in the magnitude of the acceleration, thus an orientation based approach is more appropriate. If the device is kept in the users pocket or purse, the orientation may not show any significant change between samples, in which case it is more appropriate to observe the differences in the magnitude of the acceleration vector, expressed as $|A| = \sqrt{a_x^2 + a_y^2 + a_z^2}$.

In [7] a system is described where readings of ambient **audio and video** are clustered into events, such as walking through a door or crossing a street. These events are then hierarchically clustered into higher level scenes, such as visiting a supermarket or walking down a busy street.

The **system state** of a mobile phone can be a valuable source of contextual information. For instance, the volume of a mobile phone can be an indicator of the user's context. In most cases when a mobile phone has the volume turned down, it could mean that the user is not available to talk, and that a discrete message might be the appropriate way to contact him. Furthermore, by automatically learning when to turn down the volume and acting on behalf of the user, unseemly situations can be avoided. Reading if the device is in power saving mode or currently in active mode can be a valuable context, as this knowledge can be used to activate other more expensive sources of context, for example gesture recognition, or prefetching online resources relevant to the current context, etc. By reading the battery state it is possible to decide if it is appropriate to start a job or if some precautions must be made.

Information entered by the user himself is probably the most precise indication of his contextual state available. Examples of such sources are the calendar, where future objectives, social meetings and whereabouts in many cases is readily available. The Smart Location Bar on modern webbrowsers applies the webbrowser history for adapting the presentation of available options. Instead of merely adapting the presentation, a more active approach could be taken. For example, prefetching online information or even automatically launching the browser based on the history of visited websites, music played, etc.

2.2   Architecture

The system is built in layers (as depicted in Fig. 1) on top of the Nokia S60 platform using Python for S60 (PyS60) with a set of extensions for accessing low-level sensors and application data. The adapters layer provides interfaces for the low-level sensors, whereas the context widgets uses one or more adapters to infer higher-level contextual information. Finally the application layer utilize contextual information inferred from context widgets and/or directly from context adapters. The inspiration for taking this approach is the framework of context widgets described in [8] where the emphasis is on a clean cut between system resources, inferring contextual information and applications using it. Taking this approach simplifies the process of aggregating sensor data into higher-level contexts, as-well as making the framework extensible and adaptable to changes in the underlying platform.

As described in Sec. 2.1 there is an abundance of possible sources of contexts on the S60 platform devices, such as the Nokia N95, and naturally not all of them have been included in the initial version of the Mobile Context Toolbox. The first version's main objective was to be applied in a survey where the emphasis was on studying the data available for services running continuously on mobile phones. Therefore, support for all of the major mobile phone sensors as discussed in Sec. 2.1 has been included in the toolbox, with the exception of audio and video. Furthermore, an analysis of social relations was also one of the survey goals and a very valuable source of social insight is from the Correspondence Logs, which is also recorded.

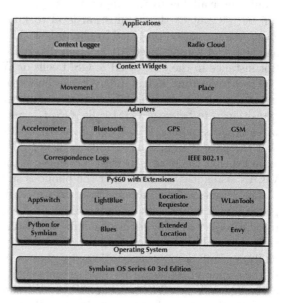

Fig. 1. Mobile Context Toolbox architecture. The bottom two layers show Symbian, PyS60 and extensions to PyS60. The Adapters and Context Widget layers encapsulate system dependencies and inference logic and provide resources that the Application layer utilizes.

2.3 Sensor Adapters

In the bottom two layers in Fig. 1 the vendor software is found, in our case Symbian OS and Python for S60 with a set of extension modules [9]. A layer of adapters provides access to all vendor specific resources and serves as the base for the rest of the system. If the vendor software is changed at a later point in time or if the survey application will run on different devices, only the adapters will need to be replaced.

2.4   Context Widgets

The aim of introducing Context Widgets [8] is to enable the application developer to work at a higher abstraction layer. The context widget mediates between the application and the underlying sensors and mobile operating system, by abstracting the complexity of the sensors and the context information, as well as provide a set of building blocks for the application programmer. Thus the widgets (or combinations of widgets) can be re-used in multiple applications. As pointed out in [10], the underlying complexity and details of the sensors should be available to the applications using them if needed. For instance, it can be relevant at the application level to know the accuracy of for instance location information provided by the widget. This accuracy may vary depending on the set of sensors used for location determination in the underlying widget (for instance in the case of GPS, GSM cells or WLAN access points).

The **Movement** widget differentiates between the user being stationary, moving at a moderate pace and moving at a significant pace. The widget follows the transition rate between GSM cells, GSM_{tr}, and the change in observations of wireless access points, $WLAN_{change}$. If GSM_{tr} exceeds a threshold it is assumed that the pace is significant. Similarly, if $WLAN_{change}$ exceeds a threshold, it is assumed that the pace is at least moderate. If there is little change in GSM and WLAN scans it is assumed that the phone is stationary.

The **Place** widget incrementally creates and maintains WLAN profiles for places that the user spends time in. Each profile is automatically established and recognized without any requirement for user interaction. Firstly, a filter is applied such that only access points, APs, continuously observed are considered. Secondly, a graph is constructed with edges between APs which have been observed in the same WLAN scan. By applying a weight, $w_{AP1,AP2} = p(AP2|AP1)$, on each edge, it is possible to group APs by the similarities of their edges.

As the framework has been designed with the aim to be open and flexible it is possible for the application programmer to add new sensor adapters and context widgets, for instance to infer context information based on new or combined sensors or to aggregate available context information into higher-level contexts.

2.5   Applications

Applications are the top-level software modules in the architecture that make use of context information received either directly from adapters or from widgets. There are two examples of applications provided in the toolbox. The *Context Logger* application implements the subscriber interface and provides the means to subscribe and record events from adapters or widgets. The *Radio Cloud* is an example application, which gets it's input directly from the WLAN and Bluetooth Adapters and visualizes the observed surroundings in a *Tag Cloud* manner where the size is determined by the number of observations in the last 20 minutes, as seen in Fig. 2.

Fig. 2. Radio Cloud

2.6   Event Driven System

It is vital that no unnecessary queries of sensor data are made and that all sensor readings are utilized. Approaches where the upper layers poll for sensor data are therefore not practical, as making a new scan for each poll as-well as unnecessary polling and subsequent data analysis pose an unwarranted strain on the battery. For example, if several context widgets make use of the WLAN interface, it is not suitable for each of them to generate individual scans. In order to ensure that all sensor readings are perceived and utilized, two design patterns are used. Firstly, all entities encapsulating a system resource are used as singletons, which simply means that there are shared and global points of access to all system resources. Secondly, the system is based on propagation of events, which means that when a resource is updated, modules relying on this resource will be notified, as shown in Fig. 3.

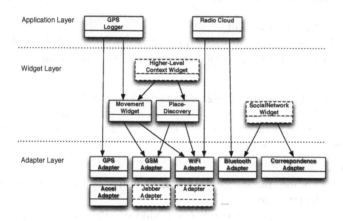

Fig. 3. Event dependency structure in the Mobile Context Toolbox. Arrows indicate event subscriptions. Modules with solid borders are currently provided by the toolbox.

3   Experiments

The availability of real-world data is crucial when designing and testing prototypes for mobile phones. In order to make such data available a survey has been conducted where 14 people volunteered and were provided with a Nokia N95 mobile phone, which was used as their regular mobile phone for a period of five weeks or more. The phone had the *Context Logger* application installed in order to continually record sensor data from the phone. The goal of the survey was first and foremost to provide material in the study of which data is available to applications running continuously on mobile phones and under which circumstances this data is available.

As the survey is completely dependent on the cooperation of the participants and due to increased use of sensors, the lack of battery time was considered a risk in terms of participants leaving the survey. To get a better understanding of the power requirements, a set of experiments measuring power consumption were made using the Nokia Energy Profiler application [11].

3.1 Recorded Data Sources

The data sources that were recorded in this survey include:

Accelerometer
Data Captured: Time stamp, and x- y- z- values of the accelerometer.
Sample Rate: Every 2 seconds.
Comment: The data was sampled every 30 seconds where 15 readings were done every 2nd second.

GSM
Data Captured: Time stamp, country code, operator code, location area code, cell ID.
Sample Rate: Every 60 seconds.
Comment: The phone software API only allow reading the CellID of the GSM base transceiver station to which the phone is currently connected.

GPS
Data Captured: Time stamp, longitude, latitude, altitude.
Sample Rate: Varies. GPS is activated when movement is detected.
Comment: GPS is by far the most expensive sensor in terms of energy consumption.

Bluetooth
Data Captured: Time stamp, Bluetooth MAC address, Bluetooth friendly name, Bluetooth device type.
Sample Rate: Approximately every 1.5-3 minutes. The sampling rate varies as the Bluetooth discovery time increases with the number of Bluetooth devices available within discovery range.
Comment: Continuous discovery of Bluetooth devices is performed by the mobile device. A discovery of a device will always produce the unique MAC address of the device, however lookup of the Bluetooth "friendly name", and device type might fail, as more time is required to obtain that.

WLAN
Data Captured: Time stamp, AP MAC address, SSID, RX level.
Sample Rate: Every 60 seconds (varies with a few seconds).
Comment: Continuous discovery of WLAN access points (AP's) are performed. RX level (in dBm - power ratio in decibels) is a measurement of the link quality.

Phone Activity
Data Captured: Time stamp, activity type, phone number, direction.
Sample Rate: Whenever phone activity occurs.
Comment: Currently captured phone activity data includes SMS, MMS and calls made.

3.2   Ground Truth

A survey as the one conducted here require ground truth from users in order to cross check assumptions about the data. For this purpose, it is made possible for the user to manually label his present context (location and activity), which simply records a key-value pair along with a time-stamp. This mechanism is further enhanced with the ability to automatically poll for labels. The initial settings of the manual logging mechanism is to ask the users to manually log their location or activity.

Ground Truth

Data Captured: Time stamp, type, text label.

Sample Rate: User may enter a label at any point in time and the app will also prompt the user to label a location and activity every 3:5 hour.

Comment: The context discovery application can prompt the user to provide feedback by showing a simple popup menu where the user can indicate a current state. In the current version of the tool two types of information can be provided:
  - Location information (such as, home, work)
  - Activity information (such as working, having dinner, running)

4   Results

The survey started October 28, 2008 and ended January 7, 2009 and resulted in approximately 472 days worth of mobile data recordings. The average duration in which data was recorded was 48 days and the average coverage was 70% of the time. Table 1 provides an overview of the number of records for each user.

The coverage is calculated based on the time stamps of the recorded data, where it is assumed that whenever the phone is active data is being recorded. The unique values should be read as unique for each user and not globally. The bottom row indicate the unique values across all participants, which confirms that the participants where located in the same geographical area.

4.1   Power Considerations

For the purpose of the survey software, the aim was to only require the phone to be recharge once per day. To document the power consumption of the different sensors, a set of measurements were made of the power consumption while making use of the phone's sensors.

The results show that when the device has no application running or only the Python for S60 environment loaded, the energy consumption is approximately $0.05W$. Furthermore, the tests also confirmed that retrieving Base Transceiver Station information does not pose any extra load on the device. The GPS-AGPS measurements indicated that there is no difference in the energy load when they are active. The energy consumption is in both cases approximately $0.41W$, which roughly corresponds to 11 hours of usage. This strongly suggests that GPS is not

Table 1. Overview of the number of recordings made for each participant in the survey in the following order: Participant, Accelerometer, Bluetooth, Unique Bluetooth devices, GPS, GSM, Unique GSM cells, Manually entered labels, Phone Activity, Wireless Access Points, Unique Wireless Access Points, Duration of Survey in days, Coverage (percentage of the time recordings were made)

Part.	Accel	BT.	BT.*	GPS	GSM	GSM*	Man.	PA.	WiFi	WiFi*	Days	Cov.
1	1474480	54349	2846	516	69458	529	533	544	224101	6387	71	68%
2	2045773	38028	2478	1514	75669	603	596	1062	364272	6040	66	80%
3	318597	27329	790	12	37217	98	222	21	125600	630	31	83%
4	875287	7880	743	2	17750	228	134	620	186421	2394	52	24%
5	1117147	13575	2373	4058	56206	227	386	277	251016	2347	48	81%
6	711490	23702	1141	95	51702	235	82	839	92396	2119	50	72%
7	1184457	13327	1765	3	45826	955	272	581	139466	4017	46	69%
8	700258	42346	2080	614	74250	172	212	74	154108	3359	41	61%
9	1101926	42346	1050	119	37393	100	104	497	104576	1804	38	68%
10	1103086	21676	2104	419	63937	419	414	116	192338	2650	48	93%
11	1122315	12492	655	929	46158	929	163	121	295716	2286	47	68%
12	796452	30610	2317	40	51548	40	143	151	97769	2403	50	72%
13	1024276	27550	1741	1114	49349	1114	137	949	171951	5463	51	68%
14	971558	21502	1303	44	40017	44	149	686	118687	1263	36	77%
Total	14547102	350879	20408	9479	716480	2837	3547	6538	2518417	28110	48.2	70%

suitable to continually run in the background. The measurements while scanning for wireless networks resulted in spikes of energy consumption and otherwise no further load on the device. When using the *lightblue* python API, the minimum length of the Bluetooth scanning period is 15 seconds and cannot be modified. During scanning the energy consumption is approximately $0.23W$. However, as the length of each scan varies with the number of visible bluetooth-enabled devices, the additional load of constantly scanning also increases.

4.2   Sensor Readings

Fig. 4 plots a typical day's worth of observed wireless access points and GSM cell ID's, as-well as inferred output from the Movement and Place widgets, as described in Sec. 2.4. The readings are visualized by assigning each wireless access point and GSM cell a unique color. The size of each bar in the WLAN BSSID stack bar chart is defined by the normalized response rate histogram for access points in a sliding window of 3 min.

It is evident that the Place widget infers which WLAN profile the phone observes and does so consistently. The output from the widget is an ID, that was randomly generated during the creation of the profile, and is made available to modules that subscribe to the widget.

The Movement widget outputs 0, 1 or 2 for stationary, moderate, significant movement. When the rate of transitions between GSM cells reaches a certain threshold the widget assumes that the user is moving at a significant pace.

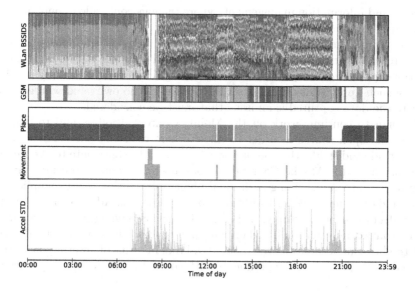

Fig. 4. WLAN BSSIDs shows the availability of WLAN access points, GSM shows the variation in GSM cells, Place shows places recognized based on observations of wireless access points, Movement is detected based on both observations of wireless access points as-well as GSM cells and Accel STD shows the standard deviation of the magnitude of the acceleration vector calculated every 30 seconds from samples made every two seconds

Similarly, if the WLAN scans contain a large proportion of newly seen access points, the widget assumes that the user is at least moving at a moderate pace.

As a reference, the standard deviation of the magnitude of the acceleration vector, $\sqrt{a_x^2 + a_y^2 + a_z^2}$, is also plotted. It is apparent that there is correlation between high Accel STD values and detected movement, but high physical activity does not necessarily imply that a user is in transit between places.

5   Discussion

When people carry mobile phones through out the day, it enables a unique opportunity to capture life data from a wide range of sensors. Together these sensors provide an interesting source of information about activities, people, places and other entities. As such, the mobile phone serves as a proxy in terms of providing information about the context of the human user.

With mobile phones being ubiquitous, context frameworks like ours have interesting potential within several application areas. Continuous logging of sensor data allow detailed information about our lives (private, work and social context) to be made available. This could be used for instance in health applications for "self monitoring" with the purpose of self-reflection. Another area is information retrieval and information management, where the logs could allow context-based retrieval of information [8].

As evident from our initial studies the applications as envisioned here are within reach in term of technical feasibility, even though the results indicate the additional power consumption introduced hereby. However, the privacy implications of such applications raises a set of concerns. Who owns and who gets the right to the data captured is an issue that must be considered.

We plan to continue work on the Mobile Context Toolbox and to make it available as open source in order to allow others to utilize the framework for further field studies like the one presented here and to contribute to the further development of the Mobile Context Toolbox itself. Obvious extensions include additional adapters providing additional phone information, status, application events and data, and access to additional built-in sensors. Additional sets of context widgets can be developed utilizing information aggregation to infer more precise context information based on multiple sensors. Thereby, the Mobile Context Toolbox can become an even more useful tool in terms of lowering the barrier to the development of and experiments with context-aware mobile applications.

6   Related Work

In the last decade several context frameworks have been proposed, in order to faciliate the process of developing context-aware applications by partly hiding the level of complexity involved. Generic context frameworks include "the context toolkit" [12] and JCAF [13], where the intention is to help develop and deploy context-aware applications. More recently the developments of mobile phones have included multiple sensors, thus creating an opportunity to use mobile phones as a basis for not only obtaining but also processing multiple sensor data. Thus allowing mobile context-aware applications to be exploited. One recent example is the CenseMe [14] application which implements a system similar to Mobile Context Toolbox for obtaining multiple sensor data also from S60 mobile phones. However, the focus in CenseMe has been on fewer sensors (Bluetooth, accelerometer, audio, images, GPS) and classification of the data. A concern has also been the limitations of the mobile device in terms of the computational requirements in order to carry out classification of the sensor data. For instance in classification of audio to determine talking/not talking. Finally the CenseMe application has aimed to establish a social context by means of the output of the classifiers in order to provide input for an experimental social network, similar to the work done in IYOUIT [15]. In IYOUIT an application (also for the S60 platform) has been created which similarly utilize multiple built-in sensors to establish a context. This context can be fed into a social network, enabling users to automatically monitor context descriptions of their friends in the network, which has been a focus of IYOUIT. Earlier approaches include ContextPhone [16] which provide a programming platform for earlier versions of the S60 mobile platform, where only a few sensors were deployed. Thus this environment does not provide a set of features at the level of Mobile Context Toolbox and the related approaches mentioned above. Similar ContextPhone provides a framework on which context-aware mobile applications can be built, with ContextContacts [17] as one example. However, the ContextPhone framework is not open and extensible like the Mobile Context Toolbox.

7 Conclusions

We have presented the Mobile Context Toolbox as a framework for developing context-aware mobile applications on the S60 platform, along with results of initial experiments with applications built on top of the toolbox. Our main focus has been to create a tool for the collection of multiple sensor data from standard off-the-shelf smart phones in order to carry out field tests. The toolbox has been designed with an open and extensible layered architecture so that it can be extended and other context-aware mobile applications can be built on top of the framework. Our architecture subscribes to the model of context widgets allowing the framework to be extended with new ways of analyzing and aggregating contexts from multiple sensors. Using this approach, a proof-of-concept *Context Logger* application has enabled us to carry out a survey with 14 participants continuously using the application for 48 days per user on average. These initial experiments and the initial data analysis have provided insights into the future potential use of the Mobile Context Toolbox. This allows us to examine the feasibility for potential applications and has provided indications of the stability of the Mobile Context Toolbox for longer-lasting field tests under real-life-usage conditions. Further work could include approaches to optimize the use of resources when using multiple sensors.

Acknowledgments. The authors would like to thank the 14 participants which took part in the initial experiments with the Mobile Context Toolbox prototype and the *Context Logger* application. Also thanks to Forum Nokia for the equipment used for the experiments.

References

1. Scheible, J., Tuulos, V., Asproulis, P.: Mobile Python: Rapid Prototyping of Applications on the Mobile Platform. John Wiley & Sons, Chichester (2007)
2. LaMarca, A., Chawathe, Y., Consolvo, S., Hightower, J., Smith, I., Scott, J., Sohn, T., Howard, J., Hughes, J., Potter, F., et al.: Place lab: Device positioning using radio beacons in the wild. In: Gellersen, H.-W., Want, R., Schmidt, A. (eds.) PERVASIVE 2005. LNCS, vol. 3468, pp. 116–133. Springer, Heidelberg (2005)
3. Trevisani, E., Vitaletti, A.: Cell-ID location technique, limits and benefits: an experimental study. In: Sixth IEEE Workshop on Mobile Computing Systems and Applications, vol. 23, pp. 51–60 (2004)
4. Eagle, N., Pentland, A.: Reality mining: Sensing complex social systems. Personal and Ubiquitous Computing 10(4), 255–268 (2006)
5. Bluetooth: Specification of the Bluetooth system. Core, version 1.1 1 (2002)

6. Welbourne, E., Lester, J., LaMarca, A., Borriello, G.: Mobile context inference using low-cost sensors. In: Strang, T., Linnhoff-Popien, C. (eds.) LoCA 2005. LNCS, vol. 3479, pp. 254–263. Springer, Heidelberg (2005)

7. Clarkson, B., Pentland, A.: Unsupervised clustering of ambulatory audio and video, vol. 6, pp. 3037–3040 (1999)

8. Salber, D., Dey, A.K., Abowd, G.D.: The context toolkit: aiding the development of context-enabled applications. In: CHI 1999: Proceedings of the SIGCHI conference on Human factors in computing systems, pp. 434–441. ACM, New York (1999)

9. Nokia: Forum Nokia PyS60 extensions, http://wiki.opensource.nokia.com/

10. Dey, A.K., Abowd, G.D., Salber, D.: A Conceptual Framework and a Toolkit for Supporting the Rapid Prototyping of Context-Aware Applications. Human-Computer Interaction 16(2), 97–166 (2001)

11. Nokia: Nokia Energy Profiler, http://www.forum.nokia.com/

12. Salber, D., Dey, A.K., Abowd, G.D.: The context toolkit: aiding the development of context-enabled applications. In: Proceedings of the SIGCHI conference on Human factors in computing systems: the CHI is the limit, pp. 434–441. ACM Press, New York (1999)

13. Bardram, J.E.: The Java Context Awareness Framework (JCAF) a Service Infrastructure and Programming Framework for Context-Aware Applications. In: Gellersen, H.-W., Want, R., Schmidt, A. (eds.) PERVASIVE 2005. LNCS, vol. 3468, pp. 98–115. Springer, Heidelberg (2005)

14. Miluzzo, E., Lane, N., Fodor, K., Peterson, R., Lu, H., Musolesi, M., Eisenman, S., Zheng, X., Campbell, A.: Sensing meets mobile social networks: The design, implementation and evaluation of the CenceMe application. In: Proceedings of the 6th ACM conference on Embedded network sensor systems, pp. 337–350. ACM, New York (2008)

15. Boehm, S., Koolwaaij, J., Luther, M., Souville, B., Wagner, M., Wibbels, M.: Introducing IYOUIT. In: Sheth, A.P., Staab, S., Dean, M., Paolucci, M., Maynard, D., Finin, T., Thirunarayan, K. (eds.) ISWC 2008. LNCS, vol. 5318, pp. 804–817. Springer, Heidelberg (2008)

16. Raento, M., Oulasvirta, A., Petit, R., Toivonen, H.: ContextPhone: A prototyping platform for context-aware mobile applications. IEEE Pervasive Computing 4(2), 51–59 (2005)

17. Oulasvirta, A., Raento, M., Tiitta, S.: ContextContacts: re-designing SmartPhone's contact book to support mobile awareness and collaboration. In: Proceedings of the 7th international conference on Human computer interaction with mobile devices & services, pp. 167–174. ACM, New York (2005)

Statistic-Based Context Recognition in Smart Car

Jie Sun and Kejia He

School of Electronic and Information Engineering, Ningbo University of Technology,
Zhejiang, China
sunjie@nbut.cn, start_learn@163.com

Abstract. Smart cars are promising application domain for ubiquitous computing. Context recognition is important support for a smart car to avoid accidents proactively. Despite many techniques have been developed, we find a lack of complex situation recognition in the smart car environment. This paper presents a novel context recognition approach that is composed of two parts: offline statistic-based situation pattern training and online situation recognition. The training phase is done to learn the statistical relationship between simple context atoms and complex context situations and hence generate the pattern of every single situation. The online recognition phase will recognize the current situation according to its pattern in the running time of a smart car. The implementation of the software and prototype is given to provide the running environment for the approach. Performance evaluation shows that our approach is effective and applicable in a smart car.

Keywords: Smart car, Context-aware, Context recognition, Ubiquitous computting.

1 Introduction

A smart car aims at assisting its driver with easier driving, less workload and less chance of getting injured [1]. For this purpose, a smart car must be aware of the road environment, which means sensing and recognizing the context around the car and the driver.

There are many techniques developed in the area of pattern recognition, most of which have been utilized to the context recognition domain. However, the current approaches neglect the nature of context, especially in the smart car area. Without the analysis of context data in depth, the recognition of context can not be applicable in the specific area. This paper focuses on the analysis of context nature and hence proposes a novel recognition approach.

The remainder of the paper is organized as follows. Section 2 introduces the related work of context recognition. Section 3 analyzes the nature of context by a hierarchical context model, with the definition and classification of information in a smart car environment. The recognition approach is presented in Section 4. In Section 5, the implementation of smart car prototype is introduced. The performance evaluation is shown in Section 6 and the conclusions are given in Section 7.

P. Barnaghi et al. (Eds.): EuroSSC 2009, LNCS 5741, pp. 207–218, 2009.

2 Related Work

Context recognition includes raw data collection and preprocessing, feature extraction and selection, and recognition method.

Raw data from various sensors are first preprocessed after they are collected for particular purpose. Preprocessing typically includes noise removal, data calibration and reforming of data distributions [2].

The main objective for feature extraction and selection is to enable the best classification performance. Features extracted from sensor signals are called features [3], cues [4] or context atoms [5]. Extracting methods are classified into two groups: the time domain and frequency domain. Commonly used feature extraction methods in the time domain include the calculation of signal characteristics such as mean, root mean square, and standard deviation. Commonly used feature extraction methods in the frequency domain include coarse spectrum estimates, spectral centroid, spectral roll-off point and spectral flux.

Context recognition from several sources at an instant of time has similar aspects to sensor fusion. Clustering algorithm, Hidden Markov Model (HMM), Bayesian classifier and neural network are commonly used methods.

Data clustering is a widely used method in context recognition where the extracted features correspond to high level contexts. K-means clustering [6] and the Self-Organizing Map (SOM) [7] are two common clustering methods. TEA (Technology for Enabling Awareness) project applies Kohonen's Self-Organizing Maps (KSOM) to derive contexts from cues and its variants [8].

HMM has a long history in speech, face and activity recognition [9, 10]. Clarkson applies HMM for context recognition based on audio-visual information from a wearable camera and microphone. The results show that by using HMM models it is possible to generate context models with different time resolutions and obtain good recognition accuracies for various contexts [11]. Mark compares the performance between Bayesian, C4.5, HMM for recognition of posture, speech, location and activity [12]. The c4.5 decision trees seem to perform better in overall accuracy.

Bayesian classifier is used to classify different contexts from sensor data [13, 14]. Context recognition based on Naïve Bayesian classification gives a good performance, but a lot of background knowledge is required and over-specific background information may cause the loss of generality in recognition.

Neural networks are widely applied methods in the fields of pattern recognition and data analysis. Multilayer perceptron (MLP) classifier is used to separate different walking patterns of a user and orientation of a mobile device [15].

3 The Nature of Context

Context is any information that can be used to characterize the situation of an entity [16]. Before recognition, we must analyze the nature of context. As a kind of knowledge about the driving environment, context data can be separated into three layers according to the degree of abstraction and semantics: sensor layer, context atom layer and context situation layer, as shown in Figure 1. Sensor layer is the source of context data, context atom layer serves as an abstraction between the physical world and

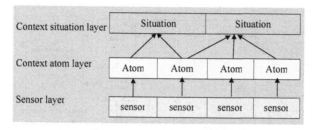

Fig. 1. The three-layer of context data

semantic world, and context situation layer provides description of complex facts with fusion of context atoms.

(1) Sensor data: we use S to denote the output set of sensor layer.

$$S = (S_{t,1}, S_{t,2}, ..., S_{t,n}), S_{t,i} = (V_t, t, q_i). \tag{1}$$

Where $S_{t,i}$ denotes the sensor output set of sensor i at time t, V_t is the value of sensor i at time t, and q_i is the degree of credibility of the value.

(2) Context atom: we use A to denote the atom set.

$$A = (A_{t,1}, A_{t,2}, ...A_{t,m}), A_{t,i} = (\Gamma_i, t, q). \tag{2}$$

Where $A_{t,i}$ denotes a semantic piece retrieved from sensor i at time t, called a context atom. Γ denotes an assertion retrieved from the sensor data with the assistance of ontology technology, which cannot be divided to more trivial ones.

(3) Context situation: we use C to denote the situation set.

$$C = (C_1, ..., C_s), C_i = (A_i, Ser_i, p_i), where \ A_i = (A_{t,1}, ..., A_{t,i}). \tag{3}$$

A context situation represents the current state of an entity. A_i denotes the set of atoms that constitute a situation. Ser_i denotes the sets of services that should be performed in this situation, which may be null. p_i is the priority of a situation. We define the priority of situations for safety higher than that for entertainment.

Context atoms layer provides the elementary conceptual data pieces and use ontology to provide the definition of attributes and classes. However, it is unable to represent complex knowledge, such as the potential danger of two-car collision. Thus a situation layer is built on the top of atom layer. The main purpose of situation layer is to fuses individual context atoms into meaningful context situations, and the recognition of context in this paper means the recognition of context situation.

4 Context Recognition

The recognition approach can be summarized as follows: a pattern-based inference engine is developed and is composed of two parts: offline statistic-based situation pattern training and online situation recognition, as shown in Figure 2. The training phase is done to learn the statistical relationship between context atoms and situations

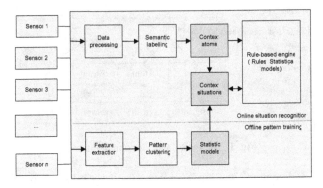

Fig. 2. The architecture of context recognition engine

and hence generate the pattern of every single situation. The online recognition phase will recognize the current situation according to its pattern in the running time of a smart car.

In order to facilitate saving, loading and visualization of models, an XML-based interface was developed. Model parameters that are pre-defined in the designing phase are exported to profile in a standard XML format, as shown in Figure 3, which can be loaded by the real-time classifiers.

The profile includes information including:
- id: the unique identity of a particular situation;
- action: the measure that will be taken during the situation

```xml
<?xml version="1.0" encoding="us-ascii"?>
<scxml version="1.0" xmlns="http://www.w3.org/2005/07/scxml">

  <state id="S1">
    <onentry>
      <<ccxml:playmusic name="'sweet home'"/>
    </onentry>
    <transition event="EyeDrifting">
      <target next="S21"/>
    </transition>
    <transition event="HeadTurn">
      <target next="S31"/>
    </transition>
    <transition event=" AlcoholDensity">
      <target next="S41"/>
    </transition>
    <transition event="BreathAbnomal">
      <target next="S51"/>
    </transition>
  </state>

  <state id="S5">
    <onentry>
      <send targettype="ccxml" event="ccxml:stopcar" namelist="can.brake"/>
      <ccxml:createcall dest="'tel:999'" connectionid="myEmergencyCall"/>
    </onentry>
    <transition event="HalfCure">
      <target next="S51" />
    </transition>
  </state>

</scxml>
```

Fig. 3. An example of XML-based context situation profile

- onentry: an optional property holding executable content to be run upon entering this state.
- onexit: an optional property holding executable content to be run when exiting this state.
- transition: defines an outgoing transition from this situation. May occur 0 or more times, including the target, i.e., the new situation for the current situation to switch to, and the event triggering the transition.

4.1 Context Situation Training

The situation training model is a grid of M*M nodes, with a vector of atom sets $A_k(t)$ and a weight vector $X_k(t)$ associated with each node k, where $A_k(t) = \{a_1^k(t), a_2^k(t), ..., a_n^k(t)\}$ and $a_j^k(t) = \{a_{j,1}^k, a_{j,2}^k, ..., a_{j,n(k,j,t)}^k\}$. $a_{j,i}^k$ is the ith value from the context source j at time t of node k. $X_k(t) = \{x_1^k(t), x_2^k(t), ..., x_n^k(t)\}$ and $x_j^k(t) = \{x_{j,1}^k, x_{j,2}^k, ..., x_{j,n(k,j,t)}^k\}$. Each $x_{j,i}^k \in [0,1]$. We denote the input training vector at time t as $\overline{A_k}(t) = \{\overline{a}_1(t), \overline{a}_2(t), ..., \overline{a}_n(t)\}$. The similarity function is defined as

$$G_k(t) = \frac{(\sum_{i=1}^{\overline{n}(t)} \sum_{j=1}^{n(k,t)} \overline{\delta}_{k,i}(t)\delta_{k,i}(t))^2}{n_{k,i}(t)\overline{n}(t)}, \delta_{k,i}(t) = \begin{cases} 1, a_j(t) \in a_j^k(t) \\ 0, a_j(t) \notin a_j^k(t) \end{cases} \tag{4}$$

$\overline{\delta}_{k,i}(t)$ is defined in the same way. A node with the highest similarity will be chosen: $v(t) = \arg \max_{1 \le k \le M \times M} G_k(t)$. The update algorithm of weight vector is described below:

For each node $k = 1, 2, ..., M*M$,

(a) If $a_{j,i}^k(t) \in \overline{A}(t)$, then $x_{j,i}^k(t) = x_{j,i}^k(t) + \alpha(t)h_m(dl)(1.0 - x_{j,i}^k(t))$;

(b) If $a_{j,i}^k(t) \notin \overline{A}(t)$, then $x_{j,i}^k(t) = x_{j,i}^k(t)(1.0 - x_{j,i}^k(t) \mid h_m(dl)$;

(c) If $a_{j,i}^k(t) \notin A_j^k(t)$ and $h_m(dl) > 0$, then $n(k,j,t) = n(k,j,t) + 1$, $a_{j,n(k,j,t)}^k(t) = \overline{a}_j(t)$, $x_{j,n(k,j,t)}^k(t) = \alpha(t)h_m(dl)$;

(d) If $x_j(t) < \beta(t)$, then $n(k,j,t) = n(k,j,t) - 1$.

where $h_m(i) = (1 - a \times b \times i^2)\exp(-a \times i^2)$ and dl is the Euclidean distance between the winner node and the node k being updated.

The training procedure orders the inputs by assigning map-units to each kind of input, and the resulting map will be topologically ordered, i.e. similar inputs activate neighboring units. After a few iterations, neurons start to organize themselves in a structured, topological way: different inputs activate different neurons. A cluster of approximate atom sets corresponds to a situation.

4.2 Context Situation Recognition

Context recognition is to assign an unknown set of context atoms to the correct context situation pattern according to its feature vector. The process can be denoted as:

$$A_{t_1,i_1} \otimes A_{t_2,i_2} \otimes ... \otimes A_{t_m,i_m} \rightarrow C_i, A_{t_k,i_k} \in A, C_i \in C. \tag{5}$$

In the current experiment, we define 14 situations in the scenario as shown in Figure 4, including five driver situations, five car situations and three transportation situations. Since they apply different features and have different target, three separate classifiers are developed. Whenever any input atom changes, the recognition engine performs the classification in real-time. It is convenient for developers to extend the number of situations, for the framework has been built successfully and the whole approach is extensive.

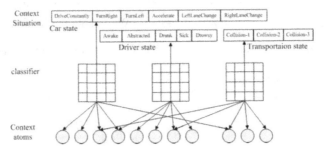

Fig. 4. Recognition classifier

(1) Transportation state classifier

Collision-1, -2, and -3 are risk assessments and mean the danger level. The transportation contexts are acquired by Crossbow sensor board, which is combined with a wireless module. It provides sensing capabilities include: ambient light, barometric pressure, magnetic field, photo-sensitive light, humidity and temperature. Ultrasound sensors are used to estimate the distance between two adjacent cars. In the current stage, we only apply the distance to assess the potential danger of collision.

(2) Car state classifier

Five analog signals are collected to determine the current behavior of the car, including: a) break pedal pressure, ranging from 0 to 50 kgf/cm^2; b) accelerator pedal pressure, ranging from 0 to 50 kgf/cm^2; c) engine speed, ranging from 0 to 8,000 rpm (Revolutions Per-minute); d) vehicle speed, ranging from 0 to 120 km/h; and e) steering wheel angel, ranging from -1800 degrees to -1800 degrees. They are sampled at 1.0 kHz and recorded in unsigned 16-bit format.

(3) Driver state classifier

Cameras, commonly used for natural and unobtrusive detection, are installed to track the movement of eyes and head of the driver. Real-time face detecting and eye tracking are achieved by fusion of ASM [17] and cascaded Adaboost [18]. Detection of eye blink behavior is implemented by the work in [19]. For image-based user recognition, we use Fisherface algorithm [20] to compare the detected face with the registered users' face images.

5   Implementation

We have developed a context-aware software platform for the smart car, shown in Figure 5. The presented platform includes four layers: network layer, broker layer, context infrastructure, and services layer.

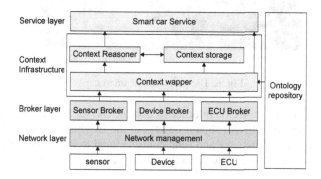

Fig. 5. The software platform for smart car

(1) Network layer

In order to collect context information, the smart car supports different communication approaches. A ZigBee wireless sensor network connects all mini-sensors. CAN bus is used to receive information from the engine and steering system. The WLAN 802.11a/b/g network supports the communication between digital devices. The CDMA 1xRTT network is responsible for wide-area communication.

(2) Broker layer

The sensor broker is responsible for discovery and registration of new sensors adding into the smart car. One broker manages one category of sensor. Sensors can transmit data via WLAN, serial port, Ethernet, and USB. The broker will assign a globally unique address or identity to a sensor, specify the updating frequency, and define the way for the sensor to transmit data and for the system to parse data. The device broker is responsible for discovering new devices and registering them for cooperation in the smart car. The ECU broker aims at managing processors and collecting specific contexts such as spare memories.

(3) Context infrastructure

The context infrastructure has been implemented on the basis of Context Toolkit [21] and consists of three parts: a) The context wrapper, which transforms sensor data into semantic context atoms; b) The context reasoner, which trains and recognizes context situations by aggregating various types of context atoms; c) The context storage, which is a repository for historical contexts and provides the advanced query services.

(4) Service layer

Smart cars intend to create safer, more efficient and more convenient driving environment for drivers, so specific services should be developed. In a smart car, most services, such as slowing down when the distance to the front adjacent car is less than the safety limit, need to transfer signal via CAN to control a certain actuator. Each

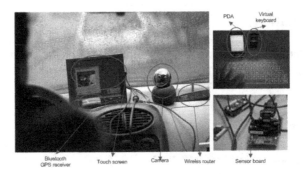

Fig. 6. The prototype of smart car

actuator is managed by an ECU. In order to execute the service, a message including the service API and parameters should be sent to the ECU that manages the actuator. The ECU will parse the message and send control signal to a relay, which will control the actuator to change its state. Some of the devices are shown in Figure 6.

6 Performance Evaluation

In order to assess the performance of the classification and real-time implementation, twenty volunteers, each for 0.5 hours, are invited to drive the smart car for 15 times. The road contains 12 surface street segments and three signalized intersections. Two performance metrics are evaluated: accuracy of the context recognition and efficiency of the recognition.

Experiment 1: Situations recognition

Figure 7 shows the clustering result for five driver situations. The clustering algorithm successfully mapped sensor readings into a two-dimensional grid in which areas of high activation correspond to these contexts.

The transitions between different situations can be simplified in Table 1. In the real-time recognition, each situation is associated with an intermediary state, called the critical situation.

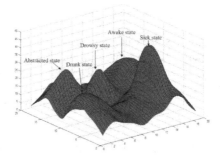

Fig. 7. The prototype of smart car

Table 1. The transition of driver context situations

Situation transition	Transition Atom set
Awake→Drowsy	EyeMovement=Drifting OR EyeLid=Close
Drowsy→Awake	EyeLid=Open AND EyeMovement= Concentrated
Awake→Abstracted	Gaze ≠ LookForward AND Face≠forward
Abstracted→Awake	Gaze = LookForward
Awake→Drunk	AlcoholDensity >= Medium
Drunk→Awake	null
Awake→Sick	Breath= Abnormal AND HeartBeating= Arrhythmia
Sick→Awake	Breath=Normal AND HeartBeating= Normal

Experiment 2: Accuracy of context situation recognition

We define 13 situations of the smart car prototype. The driver situation is the most complex one since it deals with face image processing. So we will use driver recognition as the worst-case evaluation.

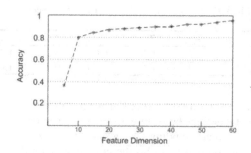

Fig. 8. Accuracy of Driver situation classifier

From Figure 8 we can see the feature dimension of context situations will impact the accuracy. Appropriate features will contribute to reducing the error probability. Naturally, the most useful features are those that distinguish one situation from another, especially for situations that are most frequently confused. An obvious way to reduce the error rate is to introduce new and independent features providing additional information. Although increasing the number of features will increase the computational cost of both the feature extraction and the classification, it is often reasonable to believe that the performance will improve.

The classification results indicated that the classifier can extract situations fairly well, even from continuous input, but also showed that some results are likely valid only in restricted scenarios. In real-world conditions, undefined situations and situation transitions will decrease the performance, and the overall recognition accuracy fell to 87 percent.

Table 2. The accuracy of car situation(%)

situation	Drive Constantly	Turn Left	Turn Right	LeftLane Change	RightLan- eChange	Accelerate	Decelerate
Accuracy	100.0	97.4	93.7	87.6	92.5	99.9	99.9

Experiment 3: Efficiency of the context situation recognition

We use the time consumption for the processing sequence of context sensing, processing, situation clustering, and service invoking to assess efficiency of context recognition. The response time equation is denoted as:

$$T = T_s + T_{wap} + T_{recg} + T_{parse} + T_{net}$$

where T_s is the delay time for conveying the data from the sensor to the context infrastructure, T_{wap} is the delay time for context atom management, including mapping sensor data into semantic atoms and publishing them to those subscribing the context, T_{recg} is the delay time to match the current context atoms into a situation pattern, T_{parse} is the delay time to parse the situation profile to find out the appropriate service of the situation, and T_{net} is the delay time for conveying the service message to a certain actuator.

Table 3 shows the response time performance. The delay appears close in each session, so the averages are listed for evaluation.

Table 3. Response time in the smart car (unit: second)

Person	T_s	T_{wap}	T_{recg}	T_{parse}	T_{net}	Total
One	0.1	0.2	0.8	0.08	0.2	1.4
Two	0.1	0.4	0.8	0.09	0.2	1.6

The data rate of the sensor network using ZigBee is 250 kbit/s in the 2.4 GHz band, with a 14-byte format including the head and the data. The data rate of CAN bus is 1Mbps, with an 8-byte format including the message identity in the first byte and the priority and length in the second byte. So the communication delay from the sensor network to the context infrastructure and the delay from the context infrastructure to the actuator are less than 1ms and can be neglected.

Context recognition is a computationally intensive task. However, it is still feasible for non-time-critical applications, so the efficiency (with delay of nearly 1.5 second) is acceptable. For time-critical applications such as collision avoidance systems and navigating systems, we need to improve the sensing technology and the analysis method of situation recognition.

7   Conclusion and Future Work

As a promising application domain of ubiquitous computing, smart cars draw more and more attentions. This paper proposes a novel context recognition approach in the smart car. Our contributions are three folds: 1) the nature of context from the viewpoint of knowledge fusion is analyzed; 2) a novel context recognition mechanism is developed; 3) a software platform is implemented.

Our future work includes applying more sophisticated sensing technologies to recognize the physiological and psychological status of the driver to enhance safe driving. More real-time inference techniques will be inserted into the risk assessment module for more reliable recognition.

Acknowledgments. I would like to express my sincere gratitude to Dr. Gang Pan of Zhejiang University who offered his invaluable advices in the face recognition part of this paper.

References

1. Moite, S.: How smart can a car be. In: Proceedings of the Intelligent Vehicles 1992 Symposium, pp. 277–279. IEEE Press, Los Alamitos (1992)
2. Pyle, D.: Data Preparation for Data Mining. Morgan Kaufmann, San Francisco (1999)
3. Clarkson, B., Mase, K., Pentland, A.: Recognizing user context via wearable sensors. In: The 4th Intl. Symposium on Wearable Computers, pp. 69–75 (2000)
4. Schmidt, A.: Ubiquitous computing – computing in context. Ph.D. Thesis, Lancaster University, UK (2002)
5. Sun, J., Wu, Z.H.: A comprehensive context model for next generation ubiquitous computing applications. In: 11th IEEE International Conference on Embedded and Real-Time Computing Systems and Applications, pp. 447–450 (2005)
6. Flanagan, J.A.: Clustering of Context Data Using K-Means with an Integrate and Fire Type Neuron Model. In: 5th Workshop on Self-Organizing Maps, Paris, France, pp. 17–24 (2005)
7. Schmidt, A., Aidoo, K.A., Takaluoma, A., Tuomela, U., Van Laerhoven, K., Van de Velde, W.: Advanced Interaction in Context. In: Gellersen, H.-W. (ed.) HUC 1999. LNCS, vol. 1707, pp. 89–101. Springer, Heidelberg (1999)
8. Van Laerhoven, K., Cakmakci, O.: What shall we teach our pants? In: The 4th IEEE International Symposium on Wearable Computers, pp. 77–83 (2000)
9. Sanchez, D., Tentori, M., Favela, J.: Hidden Markov Models for Activity Recognition in Ambient Intelligence Environments. In: Eighth Mexican International Conference on Current Trends in Computer Science, pp. 33–40 (2007)
10. van Kasteren, T., Noulas, A., Englebienne, G., Kröse, B.: Accurate activity recognition in a home setting. In: The 10th international conference on Ubiquitous computing, Korea, pp. 1–9 (2008)
11. Clarkson, B., Mase, K., Pentland, A.: Recognizing User Context via Wearable Sensors. In: The Fourth International Symposium on Wearable Computers, pp. 69–75 (2000)
12. Blum, M.: Real-time context recognition. Swiss Federal Institute of Technology Zurich, Master thesis (2005)
13. van Kasteren, T., Krose, B.: Bayesian activity recognition in residence for elders. In: The third IET International Conference on Intelligent Environments, pp. 209–212 (2007)
14. Muncaster, J., Ma, Y.: Activity Recognition using Dynamic Bayesian Networks with Automatic State Selection. In: IEEE Workshop on Motion and Video Computing (2007)
15. Jani, M.: Sensor-based context recognition for mobile applications, PHD thesis, University of Oulu, Finland (2003)
16. Abowd, G.D., Dey, A.K., Brown, P.J., Davies, N., Smith, M., Steggles, P.: Towards a Better Understanding of Context and Context-Awareness. In: Gellersen, H.-W. (ed.) HUC 1999. LNCS, vol. 1707, pp. 304–307. Springer, Heidelberg (1999)
17. Cootes, T.F., Edwards, G.J., Taylor, C.J.: Active Appearance Models. IEEE Transactions on Medical Imaging 23(6), 681–685 (2001)
18. Viola, P., Jones, M.J.: Robust Real-Time Face Detection. International Journal of Computer Vision 57(2), 137–154 (2004)

19. Pan, G., Sun, L., Wu, Z.H., Lao, S.H.: Eyeblink-based Anti-spoofing in Face Recognition from a Generic Webcamera. In: The 11th IEEE International Conference on Computer Vision, Rio de Janeiro, Brazil, October 14-20, pp. 1–8 (2007)
20. Pelhumeur, P., Kriegman, D.J.: Eigenfaces vs. Fisherfaces: Recognition using Class Specific Linear Projection. IEEE Trans. Pattern Analysis and Machine Intelligence 19(7), 711–720 (1997)
21. Daniel, S., Anind, K.D., Gregory, D.A.: The context toolkit: aiding the development of context-enabled applications. In: The SIGCHI conference on Human factors in computing systems, pp. 434–441 (1999)

Author Index